Developing Inclusive Teacher Education

Inclusion concerns the overcoming of barriers to learning and participation for all, regardless of ethnicity, gender, social background, sexual orientation, disability or attainment, and is now a central tenet of basic education policy globally. Increasingly, teachers need to be able to implement inclusion into their daily practice.

This book stems from its contributors' shared attitude towards education based on the values of equity, entitlement, community, participation and respect for diversity. It examines how teachers are prepared for inclusion in teacher education institutions as well as schools.

Using examples of practice from schools and teaching institutions in England, Scotland, Norway, New Zealand and the USA, the contributors use a valuable comparative approach to explore crucial questions, such as:

- To what extent does the curriculum of teacher education encourage the development of inclusion in schools?
- What preparation and support do teachers need to implement inclusion?
- What are the policy and cultural contexts for the development of inclusion?
- How are barriers to learning and participation overcome in teacher education?

This book provides an insightful analysis of how inclusion might be promoted in teacher education in the twenty-first century. Its international array of experienced contributors have put together a text that ranges from pedagogy to policy, making it a key reference for academics, students and researchers everywhere.

Professor Tony Booth is Professor of Inclusive and International Education at Canterbury Christ Church University College, UK. **Kari Nes** and **Marit Strømstad** are Assistant Professors of Education at Hedmark University College, Norway.

Developing Inclusive Teacher Education

Tony Booth, Kari Nes and Marit Strømstad

RoutledgeFalmer
Taylor & Francis Group

First published 2003 by RoutledgeFalmer
11 New Fetter Lane, London EC4P 4EE

Simultaneously published in the USA and Canada
by RoutledgeFalmer
29 West 35th Street, New York, NY 10001

RoutledgeFalmer is an imprint of the Taylor & Francis Group

Typeset in Times New Roman by Exe Valley Dataset Ltd, Exeter
Printed and bound in Great Britain by Antony Rowe Ltd,
Chippenham, Wiltshire

British Library Cataloguing in Publication Data
A catalogue record for this book is available from the British Library

Library of Congress Cataloging in Publication Data
Booth, Tony, 1944
    Developing inclusive teacher education / Tony Booth, Kari Nes, and
Marit Strømstad.
        p.cm.
    Includes bibliographical references and index.
    1. Inclusive education–Study and teaching (Higher)–Cross-cultural
studies. 2. Special education–Study and teaching (Higher)–Cross-
cultural studies. 3. Teachers–Training of–Cross-cultural studies. I. Nes,
Kari, 1946–II. Strømstad, Marit, 1945 III. Title.

LC1200.B66 2003
371.9'046'0711–dc21   2003045917

ISBN 0-415-30317-6 (hbk)
ISBN 0-415-30318-4 (pbk)

Contents

Acknowledgements   vii
List of contributors   ix

1   **Developing inclusive teacher education? Introducing the book**   **1**
     TONY BOOTH, KARI NES AND MARIT STRØMSTAD

2   **Using teacher development to foster inclusive classroom
     practices**   **15**
     MEL AINSCOW

3   **Views from the institution: overcoming barriers to
     inclusive teacher education?**   **33**
     TONY BOOTH

4   **The analysis of context: some thoughts on teacher
     education, culture, colonisation and inequality**   **59**
     KEITH BALLARD

5   **'Sometimes I two-times think . . .': competing
     interpretations of inclusion for language minority students**   **78**
     THOR OLA ENGEN

6   **Qualifying teachers for the school for all**   **97**
     PEDER HAUG

7   **Creating structures for inclusive development in teacher
     education**   **116**
     KARI NES AND MARIT STRØMSTAD

8   **Inclusion and exclusion in the university**   **130**
     JULIE ALLAN

9   **Understanding disability and transforming schools**   **146**
LINDA WARE

10   **Developing inclusive teacher education: drawing the
book together**   **166**
TONY BOOTH, KARI NES AND MARIT STRØMSTAD

Index   178

Acknowledgements

We would like to thank the Norwegian Research Council and Hedmark University College who funded the meeting in Norway which gave rise to this book. Many thanks also to Sharon Rustemier who collected basic information about teacher education in the different countries.

Contributors

Mel Ainscow, Professor of Education, Dean of the Research and Graduate School, School of Education, University of Manchester, England. <Mel.Ainscow@man.ac.auk>

Julie Allan, Professor of Education, Institute of Education, University of Stirling, Scotland. <j.e.allan@stir.ac.uk>

Keith Ballard, Professor and Dean, School of Education, University of Otago, PO Box 56, Dunedin, New Zealand. <keith.ballard@stonebow. otago.ac.nz>

Tony Booth, Professor of Inclusive and International Education, Canterbury Christ Church University College, Canterbury, England. <t.j.booth@ canterbury.ac.uk>

Thor Ola Engen, Professor of Education, Hedmark University College, Faculty of Teacher Education, 2318 Hamar, Norway. <Thor.Engen@ luh.hihm.no>

Peder Haug, Professor of Education, Volda University College, 6100 Volda, Norway, Hasleveien 21, 6100 Volda, Norway. <peder.haug@hivolda.no>

Kari Nes, Assistant Professor of Education, Hedmark University College, 2318 Hamar, Norway. <Kari.Nes@luh.hihm.no>

Marit Strømstad, Assistant Professor of Education, Hedmark University College, 2318 Hamar, Norway. <Marit.Stromstad@luh.hihm.no>

Linda Ware, Assistant Professor, Warner Graduate School of Education, University of Rochester, PO Box 270425 Rochester, NY 14627, USA <warel@troi.cc.rochester.edu>

Chapter 1

Developing inclusive teacher education?

Introduction

Tony Booth, Kari Nes and Marit Strømstad

Introduction

This book arose out of a meeting of the International Research Colloquium on Inclusive Education in Norway in 2000, involving people from five countries: England, New Zealand, Norway, Scotland and USA. The purpose of the meeting was to discuss the implications of inclusion for teacher education. The participants at that meeting produced draft papers, which following detailed critical discussion were developed as the chapters for this book (Nes *et al.* 2002). Previous meetings of the group produced a series of publications looking at a variety of other aspects of inclusion and exclusion in education (Allan 2003; Ballard 1999; Booth and Ainscow 1998; Clark *et al.* 1995). These previous books were focused, largely, on the activities of schools. It seemed that if we wished to examine the possiblities for the inclusive development of schools we should look more deeply at the possi-bilities for developing inclusion within and from our own institutions. The development of inclusion in schools depends in part on the way teachers are prepared for their work by teacher educators.

A view of inclusion

Inclusion, as an idea, is a feature of the documents regulating curricula and education systems of many countries, though the meaning that it is given differs from country to country and within different elements of the education systems. On our view, inclusion is about consciously putting into action values based on equity, entitlement, community, participation and respect for diversity. Increasing inclusion is always linked with reducing exclusion. It is concerned with the reduction of inequality, both economic and social, both in starting positions and in opportunities. While commonly inclusion is identified with a concern with disabled students or those categorised as having special educational needs, for us it is about reducing barriers to learning and participation for all learners. It is about reducing discrimination on the basis of gender, class, disability, sexual orientation, ethnicity and family background. If we focus on only one aspect of the identity of learners we cannot include them in education as whole people.

Inclusion does not just involve a focus on the barriers experienced by learners but is about the development of the detail of the cultures, policies and practices in education systems and educational institutions so that they are responsive to the diversity of learners and value them equally. It is about curricula and ways of organising learning. It is concerned with developing schools for both staff and students, with emphasising the conditions for learning as well as the outcomes of learning, and for reintegrating special needs education into mainstream education thinking. It views participation as involving active learner involvement and collaboration and acceptance of each student for himself or herself. This is a transformative view of inclusion. It is to be contrasted with an assimilationist or 'melting pot' view in which learners, irrespective of their backgrounds, interests, identities, gender, attainments or disabilities are meant to fit into a monocultural education system, with fixed curricula and approaches to teaching and learning.

Inclusion is about *the prevention* of barriers to learning and participation for all children, young people and adults. As part of this process, diversity is assumed, welcomed and viewed as a rich resource rather than seen as a problem. Given the variety and prevalence of exclusionary pressures within society, inclusion has to be seen as a process towards an unattainable goal. An inclusive school is one that is on the move rather than at a destination. Inclusion is about taking real practical steps rather than being caught in the glare of high ideals. But having a view of the destination makes it possible to take a step in the right direction.

It has become common to link the purposes of education with personal and national economic performances, but education is always interlinked with wider social policy. Most broadly, inclusion is related to a fundamental aim of education as contributing to the development of sustainable ways of life in sustainable communities and environments. It is about schools and communities acting in a mutually supportive relationship. This involves the recognition that education is broader than schooling and that schools should support the education within communities rather be seen as its only source.

Inclusion involves the idea of schools supporting all learners within a locality. Within Northern Europe this is the idea of 'the school for all' or in England it might be seen as the comprehensive community school, though generally such a term is confined in that country to secondary schools. Many countries share a trend towards increasing competition between schools coupled with encouragement to parental choice which detaches schools from particular localities and redirects their social purpose. As illustrated within the chapters of this book, this has gone much further in some countries, such as New Zealand and England, than others. This 'standards agenda' with its associated 'accountability culture' is a major barrier to inclusive development.

The importance of teacher education for inclusion

So how do teacher educators respond to the challenge of inclusion? To what extent are teacher education institutions themselves developed in an inclusive way? What values, knowledge and skills do teachers need to possess to implement inclusion? What part does teacher training play in qualifying teachers to develop inclusion in schools? How can teacher educators support this process for teachers already working in schools? The authors of the chapters in this book attempt to throw light on these questions. They explore what inclusion means to them and others within and beyond their institutions. In the final chapter we draw together these differing ideas.

The book views teacher education broadly. Just as education cannot be identified with schooling so teacher education is not only about what goes on in institutions. Teacher education institutions contribute to the broader educational experience of teachers. Most teacher education is informal and unplanned, as teachers learn through experience with and from colleagues, students and others, in settings that may be both literally and metaphorically far removed from lecture rooms or classrooms. Most formal teacher education too, is outside of the control of those paid to think of themselves as teacher educators, organised by teachers themselves as they inform each other about areas of practice that are of direct relevance within their particular communities. Learning is life-long, even for teachers, and that includes people who work within higher education as well as schools and pre-school settings.

Efforts to support inclusion in teacher education take place in a variety of ways. Institutions have developed *new structures* (departments, faculties etc.), *new courses* with changed curricula and new names, *new ways of organising teaching and learning* in order to remove barriers for certain groups of students. Higher education institutions also work directly with teachers and schools to support inclusive development. Experiences with these differing approaches are described in the book.

The 'official' structure and content of teacher education

We have gathered together some of the official basic information about the structure and content of teacher education in the five countries involved, to provide a context for the chapters that follow. At the end of this chapter is a list of internet sources for those who want to take a closer look. Readers should be aware that we are reporting here what is said in official documents. What actually happens in practice may be quite different and is documented and discussed throughout the book. We provide only a brief overview here.

We wanted to know about access to, and the duration of, undergraduate teacher education, where it takes place and the nature of in-service training.

The extent of national or other guidelines for teacher education and what they say about inclusion is another issue of great relevance.

Although we have made it clear that our view of inclusion does not focus on children categorised as 'in need of special education' or special provision, we have included information about special teacher education in the various countries. The separation of the education system in general, and teacher education in particular, into mainstream and special strands has been a feature of all the countries included here although some no longer have special *initial* teacher education, expecting all teachers to qualify first as mainstream teachers.

The approach to such specialisation affects the way inclusion is viewed within schools and institutions of higher education. It has made it difficult to discuss and resolve certain important issues, such as the over-representation of boys or, in some areas of some countries, of ethnic minority students amongst those categorised as in need of special education. We argue that the notion of special needs education can involve a simplistic view of the origins of educational difficulties as arising within learners themselves, and can thereby deflect attention from barriers to learning and participation, arising from discriminatory practices, curricula, teaching approaches, school organisation and culture and from national and local policies. It implies a dichotomy between a homogeneous normality and special learners. While in many systems there is a recognition that inclusion is about more than the giving of special support to categorised learners, these realisations tend to be grafted on to a special education view in which learners who experience difficulties are expected to be assimilated within an unchanged mainstream. It is not part of our view to ignore the support that some students require to participate in the mainstream, but we think they are best served by also attempting to make schools responsive to all aspects of learner and teacher diversity.

The countries are presented in alphabetical order. Only those aspects that deviate from the first, England, are specifically described for each of the other nations.

England

Students generally qualify as teachers through one of three routes, a three- or four-year education degree for primary teachers, another degree followed usually by a one-year teacher qualification for primary or secondary teachers, or training on the job in schools in collaboration with a institution of higher education or local education authority. This last route is relatively rare. There are also some two-year conversion courses aimed at providing teachers in shortage subjects, who have studied a subject for a first degree other than the one they wish to teach. Applicants for a teacher education course all have to have reached a minimum standard in English and Maths and in Science for primary teachers. They are medically assessed for 'fitness to teach' and their criminal background is checked.

Before qualification all teachers have to pass additional tests in literacy, numeracy and ICT skills. New professional standards or 'outcome statements' came into force in September 2002 (DfES/TTA 2002). They are in addition to the detailed requirements of the national curriculum for schools, which is the key document for teacher education for both primary and secondary schools (DfEE QCA 1999). The number of hours devoted to any area of the teacher education curriculum is not centrally specified. However, the amount of school practice during the studies is centrally decided, for example 32 weeks in a four-year programme. The national standards with the accompanying *Handbook for the Award of Qualified Teacher Status* contain several formulations related to inclusion, including attitudes to social, ethnic or religious background, attainment, gender and disability. A couple of examples are given here and these are also examined in Chapter 3.

- Standard 1.1 'They (teachers) have high expectations of all pupils; respect their social, cultural, linguistic, religious and ethnic backgrounds; and are committed to raising their educational achievement.' *The Handbook of Guidance says: 'All children and young people are entitled to an education that develops their potential and widens their opportunities. Teachers are expected to have a professional commitment to raising the educational achievement of* all *their pupils, whatever their background or current level of attainment. . . .'* (p. 3)
- Standard 2.4 'They understand how pupils' learning can be affected by their physical, intellectual, linguistic, social, cultural and emotional development.' *The Handbook of Guidance says: 'Trainees need to have sufficient understanding of some of these factors to take account of and respond to individual pupils' needs, to plan lessons sensitively, and to teach in an inclusive way that recognises pupils have different motivations to learn and that pupils have different needs at different times.'* (p. 21)

An inclusion statement within the National Curriculum views inclusion as the creation of 'learning environments . . . which respond to pupils' diverse needs' . . . and 'provide opportunities for all pupils to achieve, including boys and girls, pupils with special educational needs, pupils with disabilities, pupils from all social and cultural backgrounds, pupils of different ethnic groups including travellers, refugees and asylum seekers, and those from diverse linguistic backgrounds'. It requires all teachers to plan their teaching with due regard to three principles: 'setting suitable learning challenges', 'responding to pupils' diverse learning needs', and 'overcoming potential barriers to learning and assessment for individuals and groups of pupils' (DfEE/QCA 1999: 31). It gives detailed examples of what these might mean in practice.

Basic knowledge about 'special educational needs' is meant to be part of all initial teacher education in England. Students are expected to know about the 'Special Educational Needs Code of Practice' and be able to identify pupils with special educational needs. Once they are qualified teachers they may take courses in various areas of special education. The courses have to conform to the specialist standards of the Teacher Training Agency, one of the Quangos (Quasi-autonomous non-governmental organisations) involved in the control of education. The 'National Standards for special educational needs specialist teachers' refer to an intention of increasing the proportion of pupils categorised as 'having special educational needs' in mainstream provisions. Special teachers as well as other teachers must also have 'due regard' to the principles for inclusion set out by the Qualifications and Curriculum Authority (QCA) quoted above.

When it comes to in-service training, newly qualified teachers have an induction period of three terms supported by an advice and guidance programme. *All* teachers have to engage in 'continuing professional development', including a minimum of five days school-based in-service education for all teaching staff. While there are considerable variations between schools in the way these days are organised the content is often determined by the need to respond to government requirements within an increasingly centralised system.

New Zealand

In New Zealand there is a three-year course for primary education. Teacher education is offered by universities, polytechnics and private establishments. The programmes must be approved by the New Zealand Teachers Council. There is no national teacher education curriculum, but 'Satisfactory Teacher Dimensions' explain minimum levels. Further specification is done by the colleges and can vary considerably. Increasing the quality of Māori education is specifically mentioned. In early childhood education there is a compulsory unit about inclusion, but not in other courses. Many of the Teacher Education Unit Standards concerned with Teaching in the New Zealand National Qualifications Framework call for teachers of all subjects to evaluate their own teaching in terms of inclusiveness, defined as including 'gender inclusiveness, cultural appropriateness and special needs'. The standards also require teachers to identify and address 'barriers to learning' and maintain 'an inclusive learning environment'. One unit standard is called 'Relate knowledge of cultural and linguistic diversity to teaching'. Another calls for effectiveness of teaching and learning experiences for all to be assessed in terms of 'considerations such as success for Māori students, gender inclusiveness, cultural appropriateness, success for students with special needs'.

A growing number of courses in special education are nationally recognised. A system of learning and behaviour resource teachers support classroom teachers, specifically in the fields of literacy, moderate vision and hearing impairments. Established standards for these teachers are geared to 'the promotion of an inclusive education system'. A professional course is provided by the ministry to all newly appointed resource teachers. The programme includes a specific focus on Mäori students who have special needs. Full registration of teaching practitioners takes place after an advice and guidance programme for at least two years after entering teaching profession. In order to practise teachers have to have a certificate which has to be renewed every three years.

Norway

Four-year studies (or more) for primary and lower secondary teachers are offered mainly at state university colleges, but also at the universities and at private colleges. To enter teacher education students must show a police statement verifying that they have not committed crimes against children. There is a national curriculum for all kinds of teacher education. There are no national standards or tests for teachers. The principle of 'adapted education for all' is a compulsory overall approach, and should inform the teaching of all subjects. The notion of inclusion is also part of the curriculum. Equality issues concerning gender, ethnicity, language, social class and 'special needs' are specified:

> Since the compulsory school includes all children and adolescents, general teachers must be able to adapt teaching material and methods to pupils with different backgrounds and interests. For example, they must be able to understand how the social and ethnic backgrounds of their pupils affect their ability to understand and learn. Thus the education must provide an understanding of teaching methods and specialist subjects, as well as develop teaching skills. The students must learn how to adapt teaching materials and teaching methods to the different presuppositions of their students.
>
> (National Curriculum, p. 21)

A course in special education is offered as an option in many colleges in addition to the special education content for all student teachers. Once they are trained, teachers may qualify additionally in special education at different levels. A view of inclusion is generally integrated into the courses of special needs education though this tends to focus on disabled children or children otherwise categorised as having special educational needs. The University of Oslo offers special needs education degrees up to Ph.D.

There is no induction period for new teachers. In-service training or staff development programmes are part of all teachers' work.

Scotland

Applicants to teacher education are medically assessed for teacher fitness. There is a four-year course (B.Ed) for primary school and this is extended to 4.5 years for certain subjects in secondary schools. These studies are offered in the five universities. There is a 'national standard' for teacher education (SEED 2000). In all primary teacher education the three major elements are: professional studies, curricular studies and school experience (30 weeks) (SOED 1998). Inclusion has been given a much higher profile within Scottish official policy with the publication of *Count Us In. Achieving Inclusion in Scottish Schools* (SEED 2002). This report adopts a broad view of inclusion as concerned with the achievement and well-being of all learners. The notion of inclusion is not mentioned in national standards, but concepts such as anti-discriminatory practices and equal opportunities, especially for pupils with disabilities, are part of expected teacher competence. The standards state that 'the programme of initial teacher education will enable students to value and demonstrate a commitment to social justice and inclusion' (benchmark 3.1). Among other things teachers should 'demonstrate that they value and promote fairness and justice and adopt anti-discriminatory practices in respect of gender, sexual orientation, race, disability, age, religion and culture' (benchmark 3.1).

In primary teacher education special educational needs is an optional topic. Once qualified, teachers may qualify further in special educational needs (Certificate, Diploma or Master degree). There is also in-service support for staff working with children with special needs, as required by the Scottish Executive Education Department (SEED).

There is an induction period of one year (from August 2002) for newly qualified teachers (replacing the earlier two-year period of probation and assessment). All teachers are supposed to take part in 'continuing professional development'.

United States of America

The traditional route for teacher education is four years in college, but may be five. Students are accepted in teacher education usually at the end of their second year in college. Studies are offered mainly at teacher education colleges. There is neither a national curriculum nor national standards for teacher education; the standards vary between states, though advisory national standards are being developed, but the suggested prescriptions are so far not compulsory. There is a new national reporting system on the quality of teacher preparation (Title II, Higher Education Act).

Most programmes pay attention to diversity in ethnic, linguistic, religious and socio-economic respects. The topics may or may not be compulsory. Less attention is paid to disability. There has recently been a call for more special education content in the general education curriculum (AACTE 2002), which is seen as necessary since most children with disabilities are expected to be educated in the regular classroom. On the other hand, traditional special teachers may have little knowledge of the curriculum in school since special teachers do not necessarily have to have a general teacher education certificate.

In most states there is no induction programme for newly qualified teachers, but some states do have organised support. Other forms of in-service training and teacher support programmes vary considerably between states. In Oregon for example, teachers are originally licensed for three years. This licence may be renewed for six years. After that teachers must prove advanced proficiency in order to qualify for further licensing every five years, demonstrating continuing professional development (Ferguson 2000).

President Bush's educational reforms *No Child Left Behind* and *Meeting the High Quality Teachers Challenge* are widely debated. The challenge is that by the end of school year 2005–6, every classroom in America has a teacher who is 'highly qualified'. The importance of subject specific knowledge and teachers' responsibility for raising levels is emphasised in the reforms.

A summary

To sum up, teacher education for primary education in the five countries explored, mainly involves four years of study, sometimes more (New Zealand and some courses in England have three years). Most countries also have a one-year qualification for students who have a degree or the equivalent in other subjects. In Scotland teacher education is offered at the universities, in USA mainly at teacher education colleges; in the remaining three countries in both kinds of institutions, as well as in polytechnics (New Zealand) or other agencies (England, New Zealand). The main requirements for access to teacher education are the same as for universities, but some countries have additional selection processes. England has the most extensive entrance procedures, including an interview and an assessment of physical and mental fitness to teach, as well as a criminal background check. As far as we know, England is also the only of these countries testing new entrants to the teaching profession in literacy, numeracy and ICT skills.

Only Norway has a National Curriculum for Teacher Education, but all the other countries, except for USA, have some kind of national standards for teacher education. In USA many states have their own standards. Issues relating to inclusion, like a concern that opportunities should be equal, irrespective of gender, ethnicity, class and disability, are formally present curricula or standards for teachers in all the countries.

In England, New Zealand and Norway, knowledge about 'special educational needs' is statutory for all students in primary teacher education. In USA this varies from state to state. Most countries emphasise the commitment to inclusion in their prescriptions for special teachers and special teacher education. All countries offer further studies in special education for registered teachers. In the USA you may also qualify to become a special teacher without a general teacher certificate.

An important element of in-service education is advice and guidance programmes for newly qualified teachers. Taking part in such an induction programme, for a year or more, is prescribed for all new teachers in England, Scotland and New Zealand but not in Norway and most American states. But 'continuing professional development' is increasingly becoming an integral part of *all* teachers' work in most of the countries. However, there are large variations in the amount, organisation and contents of professional development. Responsibility for this activity is typically shared between central and local authorities, colleges, universities and other agencies.

What the book is about

The book then is concerned with initial, post-qualification and in-service education, broadly interpreted to mean work in which teachers in institutions of higher education support teacher and school development. It is about the current nature of higher education institutions, and schools and how they can be changed to become more inclusive. It asks what student teachers actually learn about inclusion, regardless of what is said in official documents and how teacher education can be improved. Some chapters look across a range of issues while some focus on particular groups of learners such as disabled students or those from ethnic minorities. This is not because inclusion is seen to be restricted to certain groups in these latter chapters, but because, as articulated by Haug, the way teachers have been educated to deal with vulnerable groups may 'give(s) a clue to how they are prepared to meet and teach the complete heterogeneity of pupils and therefore the inclusive school'.

The representation of a diversity of staff and students within teacher education is addressed, as is the extent to which institutions, schools and teachers can provide models of inclusive development. The book asks questions like: How are barriers to learning and participation overcome in teacher education? What is access like for students or staff with a physical impairment, or for students or staff with a minority language as their first language? Is diversity celebrated? Do different categories of staff and students treat each other with respect? What do institutional policies reveal about inclusionary or exclusionary practices? Who get the jobs as lecturers? Who get admitted as students? Who is regarded as 'fit to teach' (see Nes 2000)? The development of cultures, policies and practices within teacher education are set within the context of national policies and ideologies underlying, for example, an accountability culture or managerialism within institutions.

The book provides a diversity of approaches to the issues raised. The methods used include deconstruction of texts, historical, political and conceptual analyses, qualitative descriptive studies and empirical evaluation studies as well as a synthesis of existing literature.

The contents of chapters

In Chapter 2 Mel Ainscow argues that teacher development has to at be the heart of initiatives for developing inclusive practices in schools. Using examples from his own research in English schools, he describes forms of teacher development that can help to move practice forward. He concludes that such approaches have to be school-based and set within organisational arrangements that will provide appropriate support for teacher reflection and experimentation.

Tony Booth, in Chapter 3, discusses the way inclusion is supported and opposed within national policies in England. He argues that the national approach to the development of public institutions, including schools, colleges and universities, with its strong emphasis on standards and account-ability, tends to produce managerialist institutions of higher education which act as a barrier to inclusion. He presents the views of colleagues about the meaning and implications of inclusion for his own institution. He considers some ideas about how barriers to inclusive development of teacher education institutions may be countered.

In Chapter 4, Keith Ballard refers particularly to the discrimination within education towards the Māori indigenous population in New Zealand. Student teachers, he argues, must engage with how a dominating theory, ideology or culture may create social and educational environments that disadvantage some people, not only ethnic minorities or disabled persons, but any group or individual. It is therefore important that racism and sexism and other forms of discrimination are discussed as part of teacher education. Ballard suggests that the present libertarian ideology of individualism in the country provides a particular barrier to the development of inclusion.

Thor Ola Engen argues in Chapter 5 that inclusion in Norway has been understood in at least two ways, emerging from two separate discourses on equity. One equity tradition is linked to the mainstream school, the other is connected to the situation of minority groups. The historical and political roots of the two discourses are explored. In the light of this the author shows how teachers' understanding of 'integration' differs. Engen is particularly concerned about the Sami and immigrant children of Norway and the importance for student teachers of acquiring an understanding of how bilingual children learn.

In Chapter 6, with a focus on special needs education, Peder Haug discusses the extent to which teacher education qualifies new teachers to working with all pupils in the compulsory school. He presents and discusses a study of Norwegian teacher education which focuses on how teachers are prepared for implementing inclusive ideas. The results from this study suggest that there are considerable limitations in the competence of new teachers for meeting the heterogeneity of the learner population and developing the school for all.

Kari Nes and Marit Strømstad discuss, in Chapter 7, their approach to inclusion in schools and how this relates to the view in Norwegian legislation. After exploring the inclusiveness of teacher education in their own institution, they outline how inclusion is taught formally in pre-service and postgraduate education. Finally, they describe and discuss how staff from the institution have been involved in creating more inclusive schools through a school development project, which functioned as in-service training for the participating teachers. The authors argue that though policies in many ways are inclusive, the cultures and practices of teacher education are less inclusive.

In Chapter 8 Julie Allan looks into implications of the regulations for 'teacher fitness' by deconstructing two important documents which dictate teacher education practice within Scotland. These are the 'Code of practice for students with disabilities' and the 'Medical Examination Standards for admission to courses of initial teacher education and training . . . and for admission to the Register of Teachers'. The documents govern entry into teacher education and the teaching profession. Exclusionary pressures are revealed. The chapter then shifts to teacher education practice and explores exclusion experienced by newly qualified teachers in Scotland.

Linda Ware (Chapter 9) examines school reform through an inclusion initiative in the United States: Understanding Disability and Transforming Schools. This project was initiated by a large suburban school district that funded her to develop a school-based partnership with the school of education at her university. She asks how inclusion might affect students, educators, curricula and pedagogies in a school of education. The question is explored through close examination of the workings of privilege, entitlement and exclusion embedded in the university.

In the final chapter (10), after summing up the writers' view on inclusion, we ask to what extent teacher education is inclusive. We discuss how the barriers to an inclusive teacher education can be reduced, how teacher education can develop, and how teachers can be enabled to meet the challenge of inclusion in their daily work. We consider what can be learnt from the differences between countries in the attempts to develop inclusive teacher education.

References

Allan, J. (ed.) (2003) *Inclusion, Participation and Democracy: What is the Purpose?*, The Netherlands: Kluwer Academic Publishers, in press.

American Association of Colleges for Teacher Education (2002) *Preparing Teachers to Work With Students With Disabilities: Possibilities and Challenges for Special and General Teacher Education,* White Paper, AACTE.

Ballard, K. (ed.) (1999) *Inclusive Education. International Voices on Disability and Justice*, London: Falmer Press.

Booth, T. and Ainscow, M. (eds) (1998) *From Them to Us: An International Study of Inclusion in Education,* London: Routledge.

Clark, C., Dyson, A. and Millward, A. (eds) (1995) *Towards Inclusive Schools,* London: Fulton.

Ferguson, D.L. (2000) 'Reforming initial and ongoing professional development; trends and examples', in Ainscow, M. and Mittler, P. *Including the Excluded*, Proceedings of the 5th International Special Education Conference, University of Manchester.

DfEE/QCA (1999) *The National Curriculum.* Handbook for Primary Teachers in England, London: DfEE.

Department for Education and Skills and Teacher Training Agency (2002) *Qualifying to Teach: Professional Standards for Qualified Teacher Status and Requirements for Initial Teacher Training*, London: DfES/TTA.

Nes, K., Engen, T.O. and Strømstad, M. (eds) (2002) *Unitary School – Inclusive School*, report no. 9, Hamar: Hedmark University College.

Nes, K. (2000) 'The inclusive school and teacher education: about curricula and cultures in initial teacher education', in Ainscow, M and Mittler, P. *Including the Excluded.* Proceedings of the 5th International Special Education Conference, University of Manchester.

Scottish Executive Education Department (2000) *Quality Assurance in Initial Teacher Education in Scotland*, Edinburgh: SEED.

Scottish Executive Education Department (2002) *Count Us In. Achieving Inclusion in Scottish Schools*, Edinburgh: SEED.

Scottish Office Education Department (1998) *Guidelines for Initial Teacher Education Courses*, Edinburgh: SOED.

Scottish Office Education Deparment (2000a) *Standards for Initial Teacher Education in Scotland*, Edinburgh: SOED.

Scottish Office Education Department (2000b) *The Standards in Scotland's Schools etc. Act,* Edinburgh: SOED.

Teacher education – Internet sources

England
Dept for Education and Skills – www.dfes.gov.uk
Eurydice – www.eurydice.org/
National Curriculum – www.nc.uk.net
Qualifications and Curriculum Authority – www.qca.org.uk
Teacher Training Agency – www.canteach.gov.uk

New Zealand
Association of Colleges of Education in New Zealand – www.acenz.ac.nz
Education New Zealand – www.nzeil.co.nz
Ministry of Education – www.minedu.govt.nz – also www.tki.org
Ministry of Education, Group Special Education – www.ses.org.nz
New Zealand Qualifications Authority – www.nzqa.govt.nz

New Zealand Teachers Council – www.trb.govt.nz
Teach NZ – www.teachnz.govt.nz

Norway
Eurydice – www.eurydice.org/
General Plan and Regulations for General Teacher Education – www.nnr.no/html/publ/rammeplaner/vedtatt/grunn/laerer/alu-eng.pdf
Norwegian Embassy in London – www.dep.no

Scotland
Euridice – www.eurydice.org/
General Teaching Council for Scotland – www.gtcs.org.uk
Learning and Teaching Scotland – www.ltscotland.com
Quality Assurance Agency for Higher Education – www.qaa.ac.uk
Scottish Executive – www.scotland.gov.uk

USA
American Association of Colleges of Teacher Education – www.aacte.org
American Federation of Teachers – www.aft.org
Education World – www.educationworld.com
ERIC, The Educational Resources Information Center – www.ericsp.org
National Association of State Directors of Teacher Education and Certification – www.nasdtec.org
National Board for Professional Teaching Standards – www.nbpts.org
National Commission on Teaching and America's Future – www.nctaf.org
State reports on teacher education – www.title2.org
US Dept of Education www.ed.gov

Chapter 2

Using teacher development to foster inclusive classroom practices

Mel Ainscow

Introduction

In this chapter I argue that teacher development has to be at the heart of initiatives for developing inclusive practices in schools. Using examples from my own research, I describe forms of teacher development that can help to move practice forward. This leads me to conclude that such approaches have to be school-based, set within organisational arrangements that will provide appropriate support for teacher reflection and experimentation.

Inclusion is arguably the major issue facing education systems throughout the world. In the economically poorer countries of the South, the issue is most urgently focused on providing schools and teachers for the 113 million or so children who have no access to any form of basic education. Meanwhile, in the wealthier parts of the world the concern is with those children and young people who make little or no progress within existing arrangements and, in some cases, drop out because they see no value in what schools provide. In England, for example, whilst the Government boasts about apparent improvements in national test and examination results, many pupils still feel marginalised, others are excluded because of their behaviour, and, of course, a significant minority are separated into special education provision. Meanwhile, following the publication of national examination results in the summer of 2002, it was widely reported that some 30,000 youngsters had just left school without any qualifications at all.

My own approach defines inclusion as the process of addressing barriers to the presence, participation and achievement of pupils in local neighbourhood schools. Like Keith Ballard (1997), I see this as part of the wider struggle to overcome exclusive discourse and practices, and against the ideology that asserts that we are each completely separate and independent. This means that the agenda of inclusive education has to be concerned with overcoming barriers that may be experienced by any pupils, recognising, of course, that within any context, certain groups are likely to be particularly vulnerable.

All of this moves the issue of inclusion to the centre of discussions about the improvement of education (Ainscow 1997). Rather than being a somewhat marginal theme concerned with how a relatively small group of pupils might be placed in mainstream schools, it lays the foundations for an approach that is intended to lead to the transformation of the system itself. Of course, none of this is easy, not least in that it requires the active support of everybody involved in the business of schooling, some of whom may be reluctant to address the challenge.

Collaborative inquiry

Over many years my own research has involved a search for forms of inquiry that can help to throw further light on how progress can be made in the development of inclusive practices (e.g. Ainscow and Tweddle 1988; Ainscow 1991, 1994 and 1999). In particular, I have attempted to develop an approach to research that has the flexibility to deal with the uniqueness of particular educational occurrences and contexts; that allows social organisations, such as schools and classrooms to be understood from the perspectives of different participants, not least children themselves; and that encourages stakeholders to investigate their own situations and practices with a view to bringing about improvements (e.g. Ainscow *et al.* 1995, 1998; Ainscow 1998). It has involved the development of a form of action research, an approach to inquiry that in its original form sought to use the experimental approach of social science with programmes of social action in response to social problems (Lewin 1946). More recently, action research has come to refer to a process of inquiry undertaken by practitioners in their own workplaces. Here the aim is to improve practice and understanding through a combination of systematic reflection and strategic innovation (Kemmis and McTaggart 1982).

Action research is sometimes dismissed as not being 'proper' research by researchers working within more traditional research paradigms. Others, whilst acknowledging it as a worthwhile activity for practitioners, are anxious that claims for the validity of findings should not be made beyond the particular contexts in which the investigation is carried out (e.g. Hammersley 1992). Proponents of action research, on the other hand, have responded to these criticisms by rejecting the conceptions of rigour imposed by traditional social science, and by mounting their own counter-criticism of the methododology and assumptions about knowledge upon which these conceptions of rigour are dependent (e.g. Winter 1989). They claim, for example, that the notions of rigour to which both positivist and inter-pretative researchers aspire are oppressive, restrictive and prescriptive, designed to perpetuate the hierarchical divisions between the producers and users of research (Iano 1986).

In devising a suitable methodology I have been aware of others who have attempted to follow a similar path. For example, Poplin and Weeres (1992) report a study called 'Voices From the Inside', carried out by students, teachers, administrators and parents in four schools. Here the aim was ' to create strategies that allowed everyone at the school site to speak and ensured that everyone be heard'. Thus the research allowed all participants to be both the researchers and, at the same time, the subjects of the research. Since the study began with the assumption that academics had already 'misnamed the problems of schooling', the roles of outsiders had to be re-thought so that those on the inside could come to know and articulate the problems they experience. The use of this process was reported to have led to many changes in the schools, although it was also found to be extremely time-consuming.

In developing my own approach I have been keen to pursue a similar, participatory orientation, along the lines of what has been defined as 'colla-borative inquiry' (Reason and Rowan 1980; Reason 1988). The use of such approaches emphasises the value of group processes and the use of varied methods of recording. Here my own thinking has been influenced by experience of using collaborative inquiry methods in English schools (e.g. Ainscow *et al.* 1994, 1995, 1998), and approaches developed for use in countries of the South, such as 'participatory rural appraisal' (PRA), as developed by Chambers (1992) and refined by Stubbs (1995) and Ainscow (1999) for use in educational contexts.

From these earlier experiences I have found it useful to take account of four principles as I seek to involve colleagues in the research process. These are that it should: be of direct help to people in the contexts involved; demonstrate rigour and trustworthiness such that the findings are worthy of wider attention; contribute to the development of policies and practices elsewhere; and inform the thinking of the 'outsider' research team. As a result of earlier experiences of using this orientation I have become clearer about both the advantages and, of course, the difficulties involved in carrying out such a study.

In terms of advantages, from the point of view of the research contexts, there was strong evidence that those involved often found the process to be both informative and stimulating. Specifically they found that the need to engage with multiple interpretations of events forced them to think much more deeply about their own perceptions. Furthermore, exploring ways of valuing points of view that they might more usually ignore, or even oppose, also seemed to stimulate them to consider previously ignored possibilities for the development of thinking and practice. At the same time they found the process to be affirming, giving them an opportunity to celebrate many achievements in their working contexts.

Turning to difficulties, these earlier experiences highlight some of the problems that can occur when practitioners take on the task of carrying out what might be referred to as insider research. We found, for example, that despite a commitment to reporting a wide range of opinions, some accounts revealed little evidence of alternative voices, thus giving the impression of what seemed to be a most unlikely level of consensus. Sometimes there was very little evidence presented from children and parents, gaps that seem particularly regrettable when I read the findings of the Poplin and Weeres study, reported earlier. Finally there remain some concerns about confidentiality. Specifically, as the accounts are read by those within a particular context can we be sure that the views of certain individuals will remain anonymous?

Overall, then, the methodology described here can be characterised as essentially a social process. It requires a group of stakeholders within a particular context to engage in a search for a common agenda to guide their enquiries and, at much the same time, a series of struggles to establish ways of working that enable them to collect and find meaning in different types of information. They also have to find ways of reporting their conclusions. All of this has to be carried out in a way that will be of direct benefit to those in the contexts under consideration. In so doing the members of the group are exposed to manifestations of one another's perspectives and assumptions. At its best all of this provides wonderful opportunities for developing new understandings. However, such possibilities can only be utilised if potential social, cultural, linguistic and micro-political barriers are overcome.

It seems to me that such an orientation helps to overcome the traditional gap between research and practice. As Robinson (1998) argues, it has generally been assumed that this gap has resulted from inadequate dissemination strategies. The implication is that educational research *does* speak to issues of practice, if only the right people would listen. She suggests an alternative explanation, pointing out that research findings may well continue to be ignored, regardless of how well they are communicated, because they bypass the ways in which practitioners formulate the problems they face and the constraints within which they have to work. As I have noted, participatory research is fraught with difficulties. On the other hand, the potential benefits are enormous, not least in that the understandings gained can have an immediate impact on the development of thinking and practice

Developing inclusive practices

In recent years my colleagues and I have been involved in a series of such collaborative research activities in relation to the development of more inclusive practices in schools (e.g. Ainscow *et al.* 1994, 2001; Hopkins *et al.* 1994; Ainscow 1999, 2002). In essence this work seeks to address the question, how do we create educational contexts that 'reach out to all learners'? It points towards certain ingredients that seem to be helpful to those in schools wishing to formulate strategies for moving practice forward. These are as follows:

- *Starting with existing practices and knowledge.* Our research suggests that most schools know more than they use. Thus development has to make better use of existing expertise and creativity. Increasingly, therefore, I have found it necessary to collaborate with teachers as they are developing ways of analysing their own practices through mutual observation and discussion. Here the particular focus is on the details of classroom interventions and how these can be adjusted in order to foster a more responsive engagement between teachers and learners.

- *Seeing differences as opportunities for learning.* Adjusting existing arrangements seems to require a process of improvisation as teachers respond to feedback provided by members of the class. For the experienced teacher this involves the application of tacit knowledge gained from years of 'learning through doing'. Pupils who do not fit into existing arrangements can be seen as offering 'surprises' that invite further improvisation. This implies a more positive view of difference, one that is difficult to encourage where teachers feel unsupported or threatened.

- *Scrutinising barriers to participation.* In examining existing ways of working, it is also necessary to consider whether aspects of these practices are, themselves, acting as barriers to participation. Once again there is a need to engage with the details of classroom interaction. Our research illustrates how some pupils receive subtle 'messages' from their teachers that suggest that they are not valued as learners. Development processes have to incorporate ways of determining the barriers experienced by some learners and addressing these in a supportive way. The views of the pupils themselves are a promising source of evidence for stimulating discussion.

- *Making use of available resources to support learning.* At the heart of the processes described is an emphasis on making better use of resources, particularly human resources, in order to foster more welcoming and supportive classrooms. The possibilities are massive, involving ways of working that make more effective use of human energy through greater cooperation between teachers, support staff, parents and, of course, the pupils themselves. There is strong evidence that better use of child-to-child cooperation can contribute to the development of a more inclusive classroom in ways that improve learning conditions for all members of a class.

- *Developing a language of practice.* Encouraging teachers to experiment in order to develop more inclusive practices is by no means easy, particularly in contexts where there are poor arrangements for mutual support. The traditional school organisation within which teachers rarely have opportunities to observe one another's practice represents a particular barrier to progress. It makes it difficult for teachers to develop a common language of practice that enables them to share ideas and reflect upon their own styles of working. Progress in developing more responsive practices seems to be associated with opportunities for teachers to spend time in one another's classrooms. We have also found that discussion of video recordings of lessons is a powerful strategy for encouraging reflection and experimentation.

- *Creating conditions that encourage risk-taking.* Unlike most other professions, teachers have to carry out their work in front of an audience. In asking colleagues to experiment with their practices we are, therefore, inviting them to take risks. The approaches I am proposing require a working atmosphere that provides support for such risk-taking. This is why the management of change is so central in creating the conditions for the growth of more inclusive practices. In this respect, improved collaboration within a school community seems to be a necessary ingredient.

These six ingredients are overlapping and inter-connected in a number of ways. Perhaps more than anything they are linked by the idea that attempts to 'reach out to all learners' within a school have to include the adults as well as the pupils. Our research indicates that schools that make progress in this respect do so by developing conditions within which every member of the school community, not least the teachers themselves, are encouraged to be learners.

In what follows, I use examples from a collaborative inquiry project in order to illustrate the nature of the process and the types of outcomes that are generated. As I have suggested, such studies do not set out to develop understandings that can tell practitioners what to do. Rather they provide frameworks and accounts that practitioners can use to reflect on their own contexts and their own ways of working in order to formulate relevant ways of moving their practices forward. These particular examples also illustrate the nature of teacher development processes that can help to foster inclusive practices within a school.

Improving teaching

The examples arise from a recent initiative, known as the 'Improving Teaching' project, carried out with groups of teachers in eight schools in Lewisham, a local education authority in south London (Ainscow and Brown 1999).

Example 1

As part of the project, I watched a reading lesson in a primary school. It was taught by Janice, the deputy headteacher. Also present was one of her colleagues, a recently qualified teacher named Felicia. The lesson involved 27 year-four pupils (aged 8–9 years). During the initial phase the children were sitting on a carpet in a circle, each holding their reading book. In her introduction Janice discussed the idea of the 'main characters' in a story. She used questions to draw out the children's existing knowledge, such as, 'What do we call the person who writes a book?' Then they were asked to work in pairs talking about the main characters in their own books. Janice moved round the circle of children indicating whom each child should partner. She then explained that eventually each person would be required to summarise what their partner had said. One boy, Gary, was to work with her.

After a few moments of this activity it became evident that quite a few members of the class remained uncertain as to what was required. Consequently, Janice stopped the class and gave further clarification of the task. The children then talked in their pairs for about five minutes.

Eventually the class members were asked to finish talking to their partner and then each person took it in turn to report to the class. After listening to each child's summary Janice wrote certain words on a flip chart. Occassionally she questioned them to clarify their responses, for example 'Would you do the same thing as [main character]? . . . Why not?' Many of the questions seemed to be aimed at making connections with children's day-to-day experiences, deepening their thinking and, at the same time, extending their vocabulary, for example 'Getting expelled – what does that mean?' Despite the fact that this phase of the lesson took some time and involved a lot of listening, the children remained engaged. Indeed, towards the end of the process Janice congratulated all the children on their concentration. She then asked them to read the words she had listed choral fashion.

The class were told that they now had to return to their tables and carry out a writing task about what would happen if one of their main characters visited the school. As they moved to their places one child, clearly feeling very involved in what had been discussed, asked if this was really going to happen!

The children were seated at five tables, apparently grouped on the basis of their reading attainment. As they began work Janice distributed various worksheets. Then she moved to certain tables helping individuals to get started. After a while she stopped the class and asked them to listen to one boy reading his text aloud so that they could all help him to determine where the full stops should be located.

After the lesson the three of us reflected on various things that had happened. We talked, for example, about the care Janice seemed to take with language and her use of questioning to probe the children's own understandings. We also discussed her use of paired discussion. Apparently the children are familiar with this approach since it had been used in previous lessons. Certainly we were all impressed by their concentration and their ability to express themselves. I mentioned the way she had chosen to work with Gary. Apparently this had been by chance, although she had steered him to the front of the class so as to 'keep a close eye on him'. It seems that Gary can be disruptive sometimes. We talked about different tactics for keeping an eye on potentially difficult pupils.

Perhaps the most interesting aspect of our discussion, however, concerned ways of catering for differences within the class. I expressed my worry that sometimes so-called 'differentiation' strategies of the type that are currently fashionable can set limits on our expectation of certain children in such a way as to lower their performance. Janice explained how an experience early on in her career had made her aware of this danger. She noted, 'All children have things in them to surprise us . . . all can surprise us'. Felicia and I recalled different ways in which this lesson had allowed opportunities for 'surprises' whilst, at the same time, offering individuals varied degrees of support in order that they could participate. We recalled, for example, the way in which some children were encouraged to respond by the use of carefully judged questions. We also noted how Janice had quietly offered different levels of support once the children began the writing task. So, for example, she immediately moved to give further oral instructions to those she assumed would need them. She also gave additional written prompt sheets to some children but in a way that did not draw attention to their need for further support (in fact, I had not noticed her doing this). In these ways all the children took part in a common lesson, within which they shared a similar learning agenda, but in a way that attempted to respond to their particular needs.

I think we all three felt that our discussions had helped us to reflect in detail on aspects of our own thinking and practice. In this sense the experience demonstrated the value of having an opportunity to observe practice and then participate in detailed discussions of the shared experience. For me, too, it was yet another example, amongst many, of how much expertise is available within schools that can form the basis of a more inclusive pedagogy. Indeed, my experience over the years leads me to believe that in most schools the expertise needed in order to teach all the pupils effectively is usually available amongst the teaching staff. The problem is that most schools know more than they use. Thus the task of moving things forward becomes one of finding ways of making better use of existing knowledge and skills, including the often dormant skill of working together in order to invent new possibilities for overcoming barriers to participation and learning (Ainscow 1999; Hart 1996).

Example 2

A current area of practice in the English education system that, in my experience, can sometimes lead to barriers to the participation of some learners, arises from the presence of teaching assistants (i.e. unqualified adults who work alongside teachers to support the learning of pupils categorised as having special educational needs). Here it is important to stress that the idea of having extra adults around who can help facilitate the participation of pupils is an excellent one. The problem is that many schools have yet to work out how to make such a strategy work effectively.

For example, some colleagues and I described the impact of the work of a team of assistants on student participation in one secondary school (Booth *et al*. 1998). In art, for example, two students with 'statements' completed the tasks of the lesson even though they were both absent! In fact, the classroom assistant did the work for them. Meanwhile there was another group of students in the same lesson who had no support and spent most of the lesson talking. Presumably the assistant had been told to concentrate her efforts solely on the 'targeted' students.

In general our impression was that whilst those students seen as having special needs were following broadly the same activities as their classmates, the constant presence of a 'helper' meant that often the challenges posed by these activities were significantly reduced. For example, the assistant might hold the paper for a student with a physical impairment, write the words for a student experiencing learning difficulties, and so on. In these ways it seemed likely that at some point the continual availability of adult support would cease to ensure participation in the lesson, whilst at the same time effectively trivialising the activity. To take a specific example, Carol, a student with Down's Syndrome, was observed in a series of lessons. Given the level of support she received 'she' always completed the set tasks, although it seemed apparent that some of these held little meaning for her. Having said that, in many other ways she presented as a full participant in the classroom.

The constant presence of an assistant may well, of course, be socially reassuring for a student and we also saw examples of how this can facilitate interactions between students. On the other hand, however, we saw many instances where an assistant's actions acted as a barrier between students and their classmates. This was particularly the case where assistants elected to group supported students together. This tended to encourage these students to talk to and seek help from the assistant rather than their classmates or, indeed, the teacher. As a result, it was evident in some classes that the teacher spent little time interacting with those students seen as having special needs and would more often address their remarks to the assistant. Thus the presence of an assistant, acting as an intermediary in communication and supporter in carrying out the required tasks, means that the teacher may, in effect, carry less responsibility for some members of the class than might otherwise be the case. Consequently, the lesson can continue in the usual way knowing that the implications for these students will be dealt with by the assistant. This being the case it can be argued that the existence of support may eliminate the possibility that the demands of these individuals could stimulate a consideration of how practice might be changed in an attempt to facilitate their participation.

The way forward, therefore, has to be with the development within a school of a policy for working with assistants that does not fall into these traps, as suggested by Balshaw (1999). Once again here an analysis of existing practice can often provide examples that can be used to encourage further developments. Another example from the Lewisham project illustrates some possibilities.

I watched a year-two lesson where a teacher and an assistant worked well together. At the start of the lesson the children were all sitting on a carpet at one side of the classroom. The teacher engaged with the whole class, asking them to suggest what they would do when they were 99 years old. Lots of interesting ideas were generated, such as, 'I would eat gallons of ice cream and jelly' and 'I will live at Disneyland'. During this time the assistant was sitting at the back of the group, occasionally joining in with discussions. Eventually the children moved to their tables where they were to sit in groups working on individual writing tasks. As they started work the teacher went over and began talking intensively with one group, who, she felt, needed more detailed discussion about what they were going to write. Meanwhile the assistant moved around the other five groups, encouraging individuals, providing help where necessary and keeping an overall eye on the class. After about ten minutes the two colleagues exchanged a quick nod. A moment later they swapped roles, with the teacher moving to work with the class as a whole and the assistant giving further attention to the group that was seen as needing more assistance. All of this was carried out in a relaxed and fluent way, suggesting that the two partners had established prior agreements as to how each of their contributions would be made in such a way as to offer maximum support to all members of the class.

Example 3

In one of the secondary schools in the Lewisham project (an all-girls school) I had discussions with Pam, who is Head of Humanities, and Rosie, who is a member of the English Department. They explained how the shared experience of watching video recordings of their lessons had stimulated them to reflect on aspects of their practice. Both talked about the way that looking at themselves 'through the eyes of a colleague' had made them more aware of things they do as they teach. Pam noted the way she walks around holding her hands behind her back, whilst Rosie observed that she tends to keep saying 'right'.

One of Pam's recordings was of a lesson with a 'top set', year nine (13–14 years old) geography class (children within year groups were grouped by attainment for different subjects). The class were seated, some girls in rows but with two sets of tables pointing towards the centre of the room. Rosie mentioned that seeing Pam's room arrangement was leading her to think about the set-up in her own classroom and its impact on student participation. Pam had been working on the development of 'teaching through questions' in her lessons (e.g. 'Why does it rain?'), using questions to encourage the students to think more deeply about the content and to link the ideas to their day-to-day experiences. Having read a play, the students were set a series of writing tasks. As they worked Pam moved around the room, appearing to think aloud, posing more and more questions. Her style at this point struck me as being relaxed and conversational. It was noticeable that students were not put on the spot to answer and Pam suggested that she was trying to avoid an atmosphere of having to find the correct answer. Rather she wanted the girls to feel free to think creatively. They were asked to write about the sun and Pam wrote on the blackboard, 'What does the sun do?'

Pam explained that she had worked in a similar way with the lower sets, although placing less emphasis on writing. She noted that some of the most interesting responses had come from girls in the middle set. It struck me that this relates to a research article I had read recently in which the author explains how students who are seen as being less able may give unusual responses, but that sometimes teachers may reject these because they are seen as being 'incorrect'. Perhaps a way to raise expectations is to learn how to use questioning more effectively and to value diversity of responses.

We discussed the forms of lesson preparation necessary for this way of working. Pam felt that you had to 'know your stuff'. Certainly a deep understanding of the content would seem to be important in order to form-ulate probing questions, both before and during the lesson, and to use student responses to further stimulate their thinking. Timing also seems to be important and Pam felt that this came with experience.

Rosie is in her second year of teaching and her video showed her working with a potentially difficult, 'lower set' year eleven (15–16 years old) English class. She worked on 'figures of speech' using a mnemonics technique. During the early part of the lesson this clearly worked well and the girls appeared, in the main, to be engaged in what was rather an abstract set of ideas. It was interesting for me to see the different ways in which the girls responded, given that many of them had lost confidence in themselves as learners. Some girls were clearly reluctant to be seen failing and they used different ploys to ensure that they did not take any risks in front of their peers. This seemed to be one of the advantages of Rosie's approach in that, as in Pam's lesson, nobody was put on the spot.

Mid-way through the lesson Rosie felt that she was losing the interest of some students. She explained how she decided to try something that she had been thinking about but had not done before. This involved a singing/chanting approach to the various figures of speech, with everybody finger-snapping the rhythm. The impact of this was very striking. The more confident girls clearly enjoyed all of this, joining in very enthusiastically. Even more impressive, however, was the way in which the fun of the activity appeared to give confidence to certain girls who had previously seemed reluctant to participate.

Our discussion of this lesson became inter-linked with the earlier example. In particular we reflected on ways of drawing out the learning potential of students who have lost confidence and/or interest and, as a result, become marginalised within school. It occurred to us that in order to reach these students, teachers had to be prepared to 'take risks' in trying out ways of working that they had not previously used. Of course, this was exactly what Rosie had done here.

For me all of this confirmed the value of having time and opportunity to discuss practice in detail. However, this would be difficult without the shared experience that facilitates the creation of a detailed language of technique and the supportive relationship that Pam and Rosie clearly have.

A framework for improving teaching

An important feature of the project in Lewisham were the meetings at which the groups of teachers from each of the participating schools came together to share their experiences and ideas, in oral, video and written forms. It struck me that at such gatherings the stories of colleagues from other schools had the potential to 'make the familiar unfamiliar' in ways that can stimulate yet further reflection and experimentation. In other words, the stories would sometimes create 'interruptions' to existing thinking that stimulated those involved to reconsider their ideas and to identify overlooked possibilities for moving their practice forward.

Towards the end of the project, at such a meeting, the whole group carried out a detailed scrutiny of their work in order to develop materials that could be disseminated across the LEA. This led us to formulate a tentative framework for considering how more inclusive classroom practices might be developed. Specifically, the framework provides a means by which teachers can help one another to identify areas that need attention in order to move practice forward. It focuses attention on the following interconnected dimensions that seem to be associated with the development of more inclusive ways of working:

Dimension 1: Teaching techniques

Use of questions. Work in the project schools suggests that skilled use of questioning during lessons helps to encourage the active participation of class members. Issues to consider include: the formulation of appropriate questions for particular individuals; use of supportive prompts, as and when necessary; and allowing time for students to formulate their responses. Decisions about these matters have to be taken many times during a session and require rapid evaluation of what might be appropriate, based on a knowledge of individual children and observations of their responses during lessons.

Formative assessment. The monitoring of the responses of individuals within the class in order to make these instant decisions seems to be an important means of adapting overall lesson plans to the needs of individual class members. Our research suggests that this involves a process of improvisation, carried out at a largely intuitive level, as the teacher observes the reactions of the students and attempts to take account of the feedback from the class as the lesson proceeds.

Planning-in-action. Monitoring of student responses informs the many decisions that teachers have to make during their lessons, not least about the pace and direction of activities. Certainly, a lively pace that maintains the children's concentration seems to be important. It is also necessary to know when to move on to a new activity and how to encourage a degree of 'uncertainty' such that individuals are involved in thinking about their own responses as they anticipate those of other members of the class.

Dimension 2: Support for learning

Child-to-child. Using the potential of students as a resource to one another seems to be a powerful strategy for supporting the learning of all class members. A striking feature of lessons that encourage participation is the way in which students are asked to 'think aloud', sometimes with the class as a whole, as a result of the teacher's sensitive questioning, or with their classmates in well-managed group situations.

Adults working together. Team work is particularly important where more than one adult is working in the same classroom. Effective practice, whether it involves support teachers or teaching assistants, seems to be associated with a shared commitment to make activities successful and planning that ensures that each adult understands the overall aims and their roles during the lesson.

Preparation for participation. Additional support provided outside of lessons can prepare students for participation, as well as reinforcing learning that has taken place. Some students may need such over-learning in order that they can be helped to keep up with their peers. This can be encouraged by close home-school partnerships.

Dimension 3: Arrangements for developing practice

The scrutiny of existing practice. The experience of the project indicates that, often, the practices that exist within a school provide a sound basis for development. Analysis of these practices through systematic observation, focusing, in particular, on detailed and often unarticulated strategies, enables teachers to recognise factors that can be adjusted in order to overcome barriers to participation.

The development of a detailed language of practice. Without the development of an appropriate pedagogical language, teachers, particularly experienced teachers, find it difficult to define what they currently do and to consider how their practices might change. Consequently, it is necessary to create opportunities that encourage the generation of a language that describes the adjustments involved in inclusive practice.

The use of partnerships that encourage experimentation and reflection. There was strong evidence that teacher partnerships that included planned opportunities to observe classroom practice and carry out peer coaching can be a powerful stimulus for such professional development. Within some project schools, teachers also found it helpful to see students as 'partners' by inviting them to comment on current teaching arrangements and how these might be developed.

These dimensions are intended to be used as the basis of an initial discussion of arrangements for fostering more inclusive ways of teaching which use existing practices as starting points for development. With this in mind, staff might be asked to relate their work to the three dimensions, focusing on issues such as:

- Do we have regular discussions about the details of our teaching techniques?
- How can we give more attention to such discussions?
- Are there resources for supporting learning that we might use more effectively?
- How can we work together to make better use of these resources?
- Do we provide opportunities for all colleagues to observe classroom practice?
- Have we developed a common language that enables us to share ideas about teaching and learning?

Culture and leadership

Accounts such as this one throw further light on what is meant by inclusion in education. It involves the creation of a school culture that encourages a preoccupation with the development of ways of working that attempt to reduce barriers to learner participation. In this sense, it can be seen as a significant contribution to overall school improvement through the use of powerful forms of teacher development.

Of course, none of this is easy. Deep changes are needed if we are to transform schools that were designed to serve a minority of the population in such a way that they can achieve excellence for all children and young people. Inevitably, therefore, effective leadership will be required, particularly at the school level.

There is considerable evidence that norms of teaching are socially negotiated within the everyday context of schooling. It seems that the culture of the workplace impacts upon how teachers see their work and, indeed, their pupils. However, the concept of culture is rather difficult to define. Schein (1985) suggests that it is about the deeper levels of basic assumptions and beliefs that are shared by members of an organisation, operating unconsciously to define an organisation's view of itself and its environment. It manifests itself in norms that suggest to people what they should do and how. In a similar way, Hargreaves (1995) argues that school cultures can be seen as having a reality-defining function, enabling those within an institution to make sense of themselves, their actions and their environment. A current reality-defining function of culture, he suggests, is often a problem-solving function inherited from the past. In this way today's cultural form created to solve an emergent problem often becomes tomorrow's taken-for-granted recipe for dealing with matters shorn of their novelty. Hargreaves concludes that by examining the reality-defining aspects of a culture it should be possible to gain an understanding of the routines the organisation has developed in response to the tasks it faces.

Our own research suggests that when schools are successful in moving their practice forward this tends to have a more general impact upon how teachers perceive themselves and their work (Ainscow 1999). In this way the school begins to take on some of the features of what Senge (1989) calls a learning organisation, i.e. 'an organisation that is continually expanding its capacity to create its future'. Or, to borrow a useful phrase from Susan Rosenholtz (1989), it becomes 'a moving school': one that is continually seeking to develop and refine its responses to the challenges it meets.

It seems that as schools move in such directions the cultural changes that occur can also impact upon the ways in which teachers perceive pupils in their classes whose progress is a matter of concern. As the overall climate in a school improves, such children are gradually seen in a more positive light. Rather than simply presenting problems that have to be overcome or, possibly, referred elsewhere for separate attention, such pupils may be perceived as providing feedback on existing classroom arrangements. Indeed they may be seen as sources of understanding as to how these arrangements might be improved in ways that would benefit all pupils.

It is important to recognise, of course, that all of this implies profound changes in many schools. Traditional school cultures, supported by rigid organisational arrangements, teacher isolation and high levels of specialism amongst staff who are geared to predetermined tasks, are often in trouble when faced with unexpected circumstances. On the other hand, the presence of children who are not suited to the existing 'menu' of the school provides some encouragement to explore a more collegiate culture within which teachers are supported in experimenting with new teaching responses. In this way problem-solving activities may gradually become the reality-defining, taken-for-granted functions that are the culture of a more inclusive school.

Our observations of schools that move successfully towards more inclusive ways of working also reveal a shift in thinking about leadership. This shift involves an emphasis on what has been called 'transformational' approaches, which are intended to distribute and empower, rather than 'transactional' approaches, which sustain traditional concepts of hierarchy and control.

Typically this requires the head teacher and other senior staff to foster an overall vision of the school that encourages a recognition that individuality is something to be respected and, indeed, celebrated. Such a vision is usually created through an emphasis on group processes that are also used to facilitate a problem-solving climate. All of this helps to create a context within which leadership functions can be spread throughout the staff group. This means accepting that leadership is a function to which many staff contribute, rather than a set of responsibilities vested in a small number of individuals. It also seems to involve approaches to working with colleagues that make use of teachers' existing knowledge of how learning can be encouraged derived from their work with pupils.

For this to happen we need 'educative leaders' (Ainscow and Southworth 1996). Such leaders recognise that school growth hinges on the capacity of colleagues to develop. Moreover they understand that professional development is about both individuals and collegiality; it is to do with each teacher increasing his or her confidence and competence, and the staff increasing their capacity to work together as a team. Educative leadership has been shown to be a key element in creating more collaborative school cultures because leaders are instrumental in establishing certain beliefs upon which such cultures are founded (Nias *et al.* 1989). This means that individuals have to be valued and, because they are inseparable from the groups of which they are a part, so too should groups. It also seems that the most effective way of promoting these values are through ways of working that encourage openness and a sense of mutual security. These beliefs, it now seems, are also central to the establishment and sustenance of schools that are seeking to become more inclusive.

Educational change is not easy, nor straightforward. It involves a complex weave of individual and micro-political strands that take on idiosyncratic forms within each school context. Consequently it involves much negotiation, arbitration and coalition-building, as well as sensitivity to colleagues' professional views and personal feelings. It is about changing attitudes and actions; beliefs and behaviour.

It follows that providing leadership in schools that are attempting to become more inclusive is not for the faint-hearted. Nor is it comfortable for any other colleagues in these schools. Teachers in such a school have to be able to accept and deal with questions being asked of their beliefs, ideas, plans and teaching practices. In such a context inter-professional challenge becomes common. Therefore, those who provide leadership must model not only a willingness to participate in discussions and debates, but also a readiness to answer questions and challenges from staff members. Furthermore, they need to enable staff to feel sufficiently confident about their practice to cope with the challenges they meet.

References

Ainscow, M. (ed.) (1991) *Effective Schools for All*, London: Fulton.

Ainscow, M. (1994) *Special Needs in the Classroom: A Teacher Education Guide*, London: Jessica Kingsley/UNESCO.

Ainscow, M. (1997) 'Towards inclusive schooling', *British Journal of Special Education* 24, 3–6.

Ainscow, M. (1998) 'Would it work in theory? Arguments for practitioner research and theorising in the special needs field', in Clark, C., Dyson, A. and Millward, A. (eds) *Theorising Special Education*, London: Routledge.

Ainscow, M. (1999) *Understanding the Development of Inclusive Schools*, London: Falmer.

Ainscow, M. (2002) 'Using research to encourage the development of inclusive practices', Farrell, P. and Ainscow, M. (eds) *Making Special Education Inclusive*, London: Fulton.

Ainscow, M., Barrs, D. and Martin. J. (1998) 'Taking school improvement into the classroom', paper presented at the International Conference on School Effectiveness and Improvement, Manchester, January 1998.

Ainscow, M., Booth, T. and Dyson, A. (2001) 'Understanding and developing inclusive practices in schools', paper presented at the American Educational Research Association Conference, Seattle, USA, April.

Ainscow, M. and Brown, D. (1999) (eds) *Guidance on Improving Teaching*, London: Lewisham LEA.

Ainscow, M., Hargreaves, D.H. and Hopkins, D. (1995) 'Mapping the process of change in schools: the development of six new research techniques', *Evaluation and Research in Education* 9(2), 75–89.

Ainscow, M., Hopkins, D., Southworth, G. and West, M. (1994) *Creating the Conditions for School Improvement*, London: Fulton.

Ainscow, M. and Southworth, G. (1996) 'School improvement: a study of the roles of leaders and external consultants', *School Effectiveness and School Improvement* 7(3), 229–51.

Ainscow, M. and Tweddle, D.A. (1988) *Encouraging Classroom Success*, London: Fulton.

Ballard, K. (1997) 'Researching disability and inclusive education: participation, construction and interpretation', *International Journal of Inclusive Education* 1(3), 243–56.

Balshaw, M. (1999) *Help in the Classroom*, London: Fulton.

Booth, T., Ainscow, M. and Dyson, A. (1998) 'Inclusion and exclusion in a competitive system', in Booth, T. and Ainscow, M. (eds) *From Them to Us: An International Study of Inclusion in Education*, London: Routledge.

Chambers, R. (1992) *Rural Appraisal: Rapid, Relaxed and Participatory*, Brighton: Institute of Development Studies.

Hammersley, M. (1992) *What's Wrong With Ethnography?*, London: Routledge.

Hargreaves, D.H. (1995) 'School culture, school effectiveness and school improvement', *School Effectiveness and School Improvement* 6(1), 23–46.

Hart, S. (1996) *Beyond Special Needs: Enhancing Children's Learning Through Innovative Thinking*, Paul Chapman.

Hopkins, D., Ainscow, M. and West, M. (1994) *School Improvement in an Era of Change,* London: Cassell.

Iano, R.P. (1986). 'The study and development of teaching: with implications for the advancement of special education', *Remedial and Special Education* 7(5), 50–61.

Kemmis, S. and McTaggart, R. (1982) *The Action Research Planner*, Victoria: Deakin University Press.

Lewin, K. (1946) 'Action research and minority problems', *Journal of Social Issues* 2, 34–6.

Nias, J., Southworth, G. and Yeomans, R. (1989) *Staff Relations in the Primary School*, London: Cassell.

Poplin, M. and Weeres, J. (1992) *Voices from the Inside: A Report on Schooling from Inside the Classroom*, Claremont, CA: Institute for Education in Transformation.

Reason, P. (1988) *Human Inquiry in Action: Developments in New Paradigm Research*, London: Sage.

Reason, P. and Rowan, J. (1981) *Human Inquiry: A Sourcebook for New Pardigm Research*, Chichester: Wiley.

Robinson, V.M.J. (1998) 'Methodology and the research-practice gap', *Educational Researcher* 27, 17–26.

Rosenholtz, S. (1989) *Teachers' Workplace: The Social Organisation of Schools*, New York: Longman.

Schein, E. (1985) *Organisational Culture and Leadership*, San Francisco: Jossey-Bass.

Senge, P.M. (1989) *The Fifth Discipline: The Art and Practice of the Learning Organisation*, London: Century.

Stubbs, S. (1995) 'The Lesotho National Integrated Education Programme: a case study of implementation', M.Ed. Thesis, University of Cambridge.

Winter, R. (1989) *Learning from Experience: Principles and Practice in Action Research*, London: Falmer.

Chapter 3

Views from the institution

Overcoming barriers to inclusive teacher education?

Tony Booth

Introduction

In this chapter I will discuss some of the barriers to the development of inclusive teacher education in England and how they might be reduced. I will consider the way inclusion is supported and opposed within national policies. I will argue that the national approach to the development of public institutions, including schools, colleges and universities, with its strong emphasis on standards and accountability has particular implications for teacher education institutions. I then analyse what inclusion means for colleagues in my institution, the barriers to inclusion that they encounter and the progress towards inclusion that they perceive. I will offer some suggestions for how barriers to inclusive development may be countered. I ground my analysis of the implications of inclusion for teacher education with extracts from interviews and a discussion with colleagues about its themes.

Policies on inclusion and exclusion: the England context

There have been an expanding number of policies overtly about inclusion and exclusion in England, particularly since the advent of the government of 1997, which creates an appearance that inclusion has strong government support. At the same time general education policies run counter to inclusion in their emphasis on competition between schools and selection by them. They adopt an approach to the raising of standards which stresses simple measurable attainments and so concentrates on outcomes rather than the conditions, including the social conditions, for learning. I provide only a brief account of such policies here (see Booth 2000, 2003a).

Overtly support inclusion

Inclusion policies can be divided into several strands. Some appear to identify inclusion with special needs education (DfEE 1998, 2001a), others are focused on increasing the participation of particular groups: disabled students, the 'gifted and/or talented', ethnic minority students. There is also a strand under the heading of 'social inclusion and social exclusion' related in many teachers' minds to issues of behaviour but also concerned with truancy, children and young people in the care of the State, and girls who become pregnant while in full-time education (DfEE 1999a, 1999b). A substrand within social inclusion policies is concerned more broadly with community stresses brought about by poverty and lack of housing and recreational space (SEU 1998, 2000a, 2000b, 2001).

There are a number of documents directly concerned with overcoming forms of discrimination such as racism or disablism, homophobia and other forms of bullying (CRE 2002; DfEE 2000; Disability Rights Commission 2002; Home Office 2000; Ofsted 2002a; Warwick and Douglas 2001). A particular concern to overcome 'institutional racism' followed the publication of an inquiry into the police handling of the racist murder of a black teenager (Macpherson 1999). However, a distinct strand of policy is more concerned with the responsiveness of schools to diversity than with particular groups of students. For example, guidance to government inspectors asks them to 'judge whether the school promotes respect and understanding of diverse cultures, languages and ethnic groups' (Ofsted 2000: 23). In addition the government has sponsored other documents concerned with the valuing of diversity, such as the Commission for Racial Equality's 'Learning for All' (CRE 2000) and the Index for Inclusion (Booth and Ainscow 2002). The latter document is recommended to schools in statutory guidance (DfES 2001b).

Key documents for teacher education

The view of inclusion within the compulsory National Curriculum is similarly broad. Teachers are required to 'promote equal opportunities and enable pupils to challenge discrimination and stereotyping', to contribute to 'understanding of the spiritual, moral, social and cultural heritages of Britain's diverse society' and to 'secure' pupils' 'commitment to sustainable development at a personal, local, national and global level' (DfEE/QCA 1999: 11). There is a specific inclusion statement within the curriculum, as described in Chapter 1. The National Curriculum documents themselves, and their associated numeracy and literacy strategies, contain the core knowledge that students are expected to acquire. Aspects of the National Curriculum are regarded by some as discriminatory (see for example Blackledge 1998). The encouragement within the literacy and numeracy strategies for teachers to group by attainment, in line with continuous government pressure for more attainment grouping between classes in primary and secondary schools, works against more inclusive solutions to teaching a diversity of students.

The Teacher Training Agency has produced a set of standards that all student teachers have to reach. In the draft version of the standards sent out for consultation there had been a strong emphasis on inclusion, stressing the statutory nature of the inclusion principles in the National Curriculum (standard 2.5) and with standard 3.4 being on 'class management on inclusion' (DfEE/TTA 2001). Yet in the revised version of the standards the emphasis on inclusion is dropped. Attention is drawn to the Special Educational Needs Code of Practice (DfEE 2001a) but not to the National Curriculum Inclusion Statement. There is no reference to inclusion in the standards themselves but only to social inclusion in the context of behaviour management within the foreword to the document by the Secretary of State for Education (DfES/TTA 2002: 1) It seems that a concern with issues of difficult behaviour in schools has led to a de-emphasis on broader issues of inclusion. There is not even a mention of the Code of Practice for Schools on Disability (Disability Rights Commission 2002), raising the thought that those who drafted the standards may not know about it. These twists make it more difficult to persuade people to adopt a broad view of inclusion as a matter of principle.

Policy as rhetoric?

The sheer numbers of initiatives and the different principles on which they are based make it difficult for staff in schools and colleges to become familiar with them all, let alone put them into practice. If they have serious intent, policies have to be linked to clear implementation strategies. Yet how can so many disparate policies be integrated into practice? They are undermined, too, when members of the government make populist speeches which contradict their own legislation. Thus when a former Secretary of State for Education raises fears of schools being 'swamped' with asylum seekers (Travis 2002), despite the statutory requirement that teachers should be prepared to teach these children, or when the prime minister urges a tough response towards students found to be disruptive in schools, and their families, despite the detailed statutory guidance on ways to defuse and prevent disruption, this blurs the messages of policy. It gives an impression that despite the detail and depth of many policy documents, they may be as concerned with conveying the right image for some voters as with changing practice in a particular direction.

Covertly opposing inclusion?

The Index for Inclusion is built on the idea of the 'school for all', which supports education for all children and young people within its local communities. Within England this idea is carried by the notion of 'comprehensive community education'. However, such an idea is not supported within government policies, and this undermines the development of an inclusive system. Members of the government talk of the need to move away from the one-size-fits-all comprehensive (for example, Morris 2002). Schools are expected to compete with each other and popular schools are able to select the most desirable students. In this process middle-class and relatively wealthy families are further advantaged (see Hutton 2002). At secondary level the emphasis is on creating a diversity of schools rather than the responsiveness of schools to the diversity of students in their locality. A third of all schools are attached to a particular faith and the government and religious organisations are recommending the building of more of them (Archbishops' Council 2000; Booth 2003b; DfES 2002). In addition a variety of other forms of selection are encouraged at secondary level. There are highly selective grammar schools, specialist schools which can select up to 10% of their students by 'aptitude' for a particular curriculum area, and there are also beacon schools, training schools and city academies. There is a hierarchy of school value, with what have been called by an adviser to the prime minister, 'bog-standard comprehensives' near the bottom and perhaps special schools at the very bottom (see Edwards and Tomlinson 2002). Of course, these tiers are only for public education: the private sector continues to offer a privileged education to about 8% of students.

The standards agenda

Inclusion is also restricted by the 'standards agenda', the principal ideological framework for the educational system. It concentrates on the outcomes, rather than on the conditions for learning including the quality of relationships in schools. Work in many schools is dominated by a continuous fear of inspection and an obsession with meeting centrally set targets so that the balance of the curriculum is disrupted and education can become an incessant process of preparing for the tests and being tested. The standards agenda ignores the significance of values in education and the importance of building community and relationships in favour of a view that the sole criterion for the adoption of a proposed educational change should be that it 'works'. These reforms embrace a technicist ideology which reduces education to a technology and teachers to operatives in a system designed by others.

Managerialism in higher education

The standards agenda and its associated accountability culture have had as much effect on higher education institutions as schools. Teacher education institutions are subject to regular inspection from both the Office for Standards in Education (Ofsted) and the Teacher Training Agency. All institutions of higher education compete for research funds in the Research Assessment Exercise which takes place every four years. In her 2002 Reith

Lectures, Onora O'Neill referred to the detailed control over professional life that is now experienced:

> The new accountability takes the form of detailed control. An unending stream of new legislation and regulation, memoranda and instructions, guidance and advice floods into public sector organisations . . . Central planning may have failed in the Soviet Union but it is alive and well in Britain today. The new accountability aims at ever more perfect control of institutional and professional life.
>
> (Onora O'Neill, Lecture 3: 2)

In its replacement of important with easily measurable targets the accountability culture 'is widely experienced not just as changing but . . . as distorting the proper aims of professional practice and indeed as damaging professional pride and integrity' (Lecture 3: 4). She points to the paradox of encouraging trust through an audit culture which constantly demonstrates mistrust.

The view of institutional management and relationships which serve the accountability culture has come to be called managerialism. Managerialist institutions emphasise hierarchies, 'line-management' and vertical communication, rather than collegiality, self-management and democratic or even horizontal communication. The managerialist ideology can lead to a culture of compliance and deference, a concern to implement the requirements from those closer to the centres of power. It acts as an exclusionary pressure, discouraging people from an active part in the decisions about their own working lives, from making explicit links between what they do and the values that they hold, from collaborative ways of working and from discovering and drawing on the skills and knowledge that lie behind the official job designations of colleagues. It results in an infantilisation of those with little power, who are expected to behave as if they are children in an authoritarian family.

The metaphor of line-management has connotations of puppetry although the identity of the puppeteer may be unclear. For, generally, the managers in such institutions are implementers of agendas set further up a hierarchy rather than creative leaders of communities attempting to define an agenda based on shared commitments. Managerialist institutions replace the strength of rational argument with power, and the outcome of an argument is then determined by the relative power of the participants. However this power does not reside within individual managers, it is not authoritative power, based on greater experience and knowledge, but referred power from a point higher up the chain. Managerialist power can be characterised as poodle-power, since apparently strong leaders may be slavishly carrying out the bidding of others. Leadership within such institutions encourages, and is itself, a form of followership.

Inclusion in the institution

In order to increase my understanding of how staff in a teacher education institution might think about the implications of inclusion for practice within it, I tape-recorded a discussion with a group of ten staff (including myself) and then did follow-up interviews with three of those unable to join the initial discussion, to expand the range of experience and perspectives represented. I set out to invite people with differing views, though these could not be seen as entirely representative of the faculty. It would be interesting to carry out a detailed survey of staff opinion drawing on the issues raised.

Participants in the discussion articulated a connection between the competitive culture in schools and the college:

> Inclusion in schools is trying to sit with raising standards, jumping through hoops and I think inclusion in Christ Church [our college] would have a similar problem. It is imposed on a framework which has been traditionally hierarchically competitive.

Teacher education institutions are under almost incessant pressure from inspection of one course or another. Colleagues stressed the effect that this has on their room to think about developing inclusion, one arguing that 'my life is totally dominated by Ofsted'. His plea referred to the key issue identified by Onora O'Neill: 'Why can't they trust us more?'

The meaning of inclusion/exclusion in the institution

Colleagues gave a wide variety of meanings to inclusion. Some colleagues wanted to escape from the rhetorical force of inclusion and substitute an alternative term: 'I would much prefer to conceptualise it as embracing diversity or meeting the needs of diversity.' A couple were reaching for connections with other concepts, one asking 'what sort of relationship is there between equal opportunities and inclusion?' and another coming back to it: 'that link between inclusion and equal opportunities, I can't quite articulate the connection, I can't articulate clearly where that link is.' But the link can be misleading. If inclusion means that everyone is to be included within the same narrow range of opportunities then this can ignore the inequity in starting positions and the diversity of aspirations and achievements that have to be valued if citizens are to be *equally* valued. As an ideology, equality of opportunity has the effect of obscuring inequalities. Nevertheless, given the present structured inequalities in society, one of the main means to gain status and power within society is to achieve according to the dominant criteria, and schools have to try to ensure that some groups are not disadvantaged in such achievements. This involves a critical, reflective and strategic approach to inclusion which in starting from current arrangements can look like an assimilationist view.

Once the discussion was underway, the variety of views expressed may have been reduced, by the influence of preceding speakers. This may have been greater than for some other groups since several colleagues remarked that this was the first detailed discussion about inclusion in which they had been involved. This is itself a comment on the reality behind a rhetoric that inclusion is a dominating influence on current practice. Though I should also report that colleagues and I have found that those professionally involved in conveying ideas about inclusion, hold perspectives which are extremely resistant to moderation even after detailed discussion (Booth and Ainscow 1998). In that book we set out a large number of dimensions along which perspectives on inclusion were found to differ (ibid.: 234). The pressure on time within academic institutions which leads to a paradoxical difficulty in engaging in academic debate can lead people to take short cuts in their thinking, according to one member of the group:

> A lot of people think they know what inclusion is all about, and they don't. I'm not trying to be disrespectful, but I think people have got carried away on the buzz word, 'Inclusion, oh yes, I know all about that!'

Although none of the participants in the discussion or interviews saw inclusion as purely about 'special needs education' some suggested that others did.

> I don't think there is a shared view. One view is about equality for everyone and for others it's something to do with special needs, still, and to do with integration of children with disabilities.

> There's a view of some that support is required to those who need it [so that they can] do the same thing with additional support and there are others who think here are alternative ways of doing things.

However, many of the views expressed created an uncontroversial jigsaw of ideas, piecing together the implications of inclusion for a complex institution.

Inclusions big and small

Colleagues tended to pitch into the discussion at different levels. Some focused on political dimensions of inclusion, 'it's about social justice', and others on its implications for children and their families: 'inclusion means an increased opportunity to be involved and to have increased choice', 'it's about making allowances':

so for instance with certain children, they don't all want to get changed together, they want to get changed in privacy and the school has to make allowances.

Some participants made a strong link between inclusion and values, one arguing that 'a genuine sense of shared values' was necessary before inclusion could be taken forward in the institution. And another linked it to the consequences of regarding some people as having greater value than others:

> When we start attaching difference in background or attainment to a difference in human worth, that's where you get trouble. Three thousand dead at ground zero [the site of the 11 September 2001 massacre in New York] is huge, but fifty thousand dying in Somalia is not so newsworthy. I don't know how we develop in our students a commitment to human dignity for all.

Education itself was seen to embody inclusion by one member of the discussion group: 'I think everything we do is about inclusion because it's about education.' She may have been alluding to education as socialisation, as induction into society, but she was also expressing a basic commitment that education is about equity: 'It's for everyone.' Another felt somewhat overwhelmed by the idea of inclusion, or perhaps education, as embodying a social and political philosophy:

> If we are looking at inclusion as a social justice, a social rights issue, then that's huge isn't it? I have trouble with it because it's so big, it's almost as if you need to entirely restructure society . . . .

Most colleagues agreed that inclusion might be about big issues but was also about the minutiae of day-to-day engagement in schools and within the institution.

Inclusion and exclusion

A strong link was made between inclusion and exclusion: '[When] . . . you talk about inclusion you are obviously thinking about exclusion and vice versa'; 'I think I only really understand the term 'inclusive' because I know what it is to be excluded.' Some colleagues focused on particular groups, though they might see this as their starting point for their thinking rather than setting its parameters:

> I have gone from special needs outwards . . . because that's where I started.

> I come to inclusion with a particular concern: Why, when black children

come into education at the age of five and are doing well do they come out with the worst qualifications at sixteen? Why does that happen?

I have had an obsession with the specific issue of [disciplinary] exclusion from school and have tried to locate it within structures, cultures and policies that operate at national level.

For one colleague, his starting point was the disparities in wealth and power in the world. Inclusion was about bringing global concerns into our locality:

Inclusion for me is about making global connections. I'm very interested in the developing world and the fact that they are excluded from decisions about their own development and from the economic prosperity of the rich world.

Representation, access and participation

Within teacher education institutions, inclusion is concerned with issues of representation: who attends the institution as students, who is employed as staff, how children, young people, and adults of differing backgrounds and cultures, genders, attainments, ethnicities, sexual orientations, disabilities are portrayed in courses and in the fabric of buildings. It is about access to the institution, both physical and psychological, and the way the participation of a diversity of staff and students is encouraged or discouraged. It is not just about representing a local diversity but ensuring that a rounded education is fostered through attention to global issues.

In terms of diversity amongst staff and students, some argue that a college situated in Kent should reflect the local rather than the national situation. In the discussion there was a familiar exchange: 'Kent is 98% white anyway' – 'but the college is a national and international institution.' It has an intake of about 1% of non-white students, whereas this might be expected to be about 7% on national figures or perhaps higher, given its proximity to areas with high numbers of ethnic minorities in London. One participant identified a vicious circle within the institution:

How can Christ Church help people to gain multicultural experience or work with disabled students? You can bring it to Christ Church, but the college won't help you get it.

A desire for change is certainly expressed by management at the college. This may need a consideration of how religious and cultural diversity is supported within the cultures of the college. In both my present and previous employments I have been struck by the lack of images of children, young people and education, let alone diversity in education within the faculty buildings. Nevertheless there are the beginnings of change:

> After I'd been here for just a few months, when I'd talked to students, all I'd see was a sea of white faces and I'm not used to that . . . Now I see a more diverse range of students that I'm working with and that's only going to add to the richness of what I'm doing, and that richness is for all students and all colleagues.

Representation should not be a matter of counting off the groups given a mention but needs to attend to diversity in difference, and the challenging of stereotypes.

The government has urged higher education institutions to increase the proportion of students that they serve, from the low base compared to other economically rich countries. It is difficult to see that this 'widening participation' is going to involve a massive increase in higher education places and is likely to be accomplished through a range of outreach courses. Thus the composition of the student population may change to a much greater extent than the nature of the intake of students into the central campus.

An inclusive pedagogy?

Attention to representation and support for participation within courses are aspects of an inclusive pedagogy. It is also about the way courses are taught, how students are valued and how they are actively involved in their own learning. A colleague who was educated as a teacher in the same college thirty years previously suggested that a dramatic change in approach had occurred.

> When I was trained there were definite subjects which I felt excluded from: I was in the remedial maths group . . . and I remember only one science lesson in which I understood absolutely nothing and no attempt was made to help me understand. Nobody in music gave me the impression that music was for me, music was for people who had grades . . . Now I know from reading a student's work how inclusive the curriculum is for them, how every effort is made for them to feel that the subject is not just *for* them, but also exciting for them.

However, colleagues acknowledged that government pressures and a concern to make sure the curriculum is covered can lead to more didactic teaching than some would wish.

Inclusion and standards

One colleague mentioned the possibility that entry requirements for courses could be made more flexible so that people without conventional qualifications might meet the necessary requirements even for masters-level courses. However, there was some concern in the discussion that inclusion and particularly the government's drive to 'widen participation' could lead to a lack of concern with excellence.

> This is the first inclusion debate I've ever had and it seems to me that inclusion is linked with dumbing down . . . At the end of the day there are standards . . . .

Colleagues wanted to both convey the sense that everyone should have a go in music or languages, for example, and also to encourage a view that some performances were better than others. They did not wish to think that by holding such views they were being 'exclusive'. A further participant thought that colleagues who were concerned that inclusion meant disregarding high achievement misunderstood it, seeing it as a ' tyranny of sameness' rather than 'the appreciation of diversity, the acceptance of difference'. On my view, an inclusive approach to education implies that we value students equally irrespective of their attainments and also avoid placing limits on what we expect students to achieve, an idea well portrayed in the work of Susan Hart and her colleagues: 'Learning without limits' (Dixon *et al.* 2003).

Working with the schools

What colleaugues saw as the implications of inclusion for their work with schools reflected their differing points of contact with them. Some saw it as affecting the nature of an institutional relationship and others as about how students were prepared to develop the schools in which they would teach.

Inclusive partnerships?

Those schools perceived by the national inspectorate as being in difficulties are not allowed to support teacher education students on school practice. A colleague was particularly concerned about how this affected the prospects of fast-track students recruited into teacher education with financial inducements and with the expectation of fast advancement:

> [It is important] for fast-track students to have experience of schools in difficulties if they are going off to be leaders in the profession. We have tried to respond, in our connections with one school in special measures,

by having a project without breaking the rules by having students on placement, we did some work with music and art students working in ways that broke down groupings in the schools.

The same colleague was concerned at the way mentors, school teachers appointed to support teachers on teaching practice, were selected and deselected:

> We have been having serious discussions about how you do that so that people who have problems can work with others on developing themselves rather than us just saying we are going to cut you out of this.

Prepare to meet thy school

Most colleagues saw inclusion as affecting the way students are prepared to work in schools, and felt this was problematic for a variety of reasons. There might be deep-seated prejudices in staff as well as students:

> I have concerns about cultural prejudices surrounding notions of inclusion, how much our own personal values our own personal beliefs get in the way.

> The students are coming in, their attitudes to race and gender are set . . . They have all these life experiences of being selected or not being selected, being excluded from all sorts of things, then we bring them into college and we try to send them out again to be inclusive. It just sounds like we are forgetting about the enormity of the whole process.

Others found that students were increasingly open to change. They saw students arriving with 'pretty stereotyped views about other cultures' and then 'very quickly they change their views about this left, right and centre'. The attitudes of students were contrasted with the views of 'those already out there' who 'feel that it's a good idea but you can't do it in practice' because they are 'constrained by their targets and doing things that are imposed upon you'. This potential clash with the cultures and practices of schools was widely recognised:

> I've had some really interesting debates with our students about inclusion where they take on a lot, then you send them out to schools and they come back quite demoralised because what they believe is not being replicated in the institutions in which they are being placed, and they really don't know the way forward.

In previous discussions with colleagues about representation several had reported that students encountered racism in some of the schools and that this posed a particular problem for ethnic minority students. As one colleague in the present group remarked:

> Over the years that I have been here there have been some quite serious issues involving racism. There have also been [times] when students from ethnic minorities have felt excluded in one way or another from what is going on.

It was suggested previously that there should be a recording of all racist, sexist, and disablist incidents encountered by students in schools and that a clear code should be negotiated with partner schools for school practice. It was argued, too, that alternative arrangements might be developed for supporting the school practice of students where students might be grouped together and there was an expectation that mentors in schools, tutors and students would jointly discuss inclusion issues such as problems of racism and the different achievements of boys and girls.

Engaging with selection

The local education authority around the college is one of the few areas in the country to have retained a selective system of secondary education. In their last year of primary school, at the age of 11, children sit a public examination assessing the levels of their attainments and presumed general ability. The highest scoring 25% are offered a place at a grammar school and the remainder, in this simple division, go to what used to be called secondary modern schools but now, given the devalued status of this title, have a variety of other names. The last year in many of the primary schools is dominated by preparation for these examinations which the students take in addition to the government required Standard Tests for 11-year-olds. Many secondary students in the college are keen to work within the grammar schools. The existence of this widespread selective system, then, has a major effect on the way inclusion is conceived by the students and by staff, even though the encouragement of schools in other areas to specialise and select students has brought them closer to the Kent model: 'Most of our students have been through the selective education system to get here, and because this is such a local college they don't question it.'

Many staff within the faculty favour the comprehensive system, yet they are caught up in servicing a selective one. Some have joined the college after teaching in local schools and know of the difficulty of changing attitudes amongst parents as one ex-primary head teacher remarked:

> All my head teacher colleagues argued against the 11+ to their parents and the response was that we do want privilege for our children if we can get it, and that is why it's continually voted in by the parents in the county because there is a greater amount of privilege.

> If you are in that position, and you see other people with privilege, you do want it.

An aspiration for privilege makes people more accepting of inequality. However, there has been relatively little discussion about selection within the faculty. When I joined the college it felt as if this, a major area of academic discussion and debate elsewhere, was a taboo subject. This muting of a critical voice in one area can prevent the examination of the excluding implications of others.

The effects of the Anglican, Christian foundation of the college is another area where debate is generally avoided. One colleague felt that the location of the college in Canterbury was perceived by people in London as both 'exclusively middle class' and as 'a long way from anywhere'. The Christian title also contributed to *a perception* that the college was selective.

> I think the label but not the mission statement of a Church college obviously has an impact because it's Christian. If you read the mission statement it's very catholic with a small c because it's about respecting all cultures and backgrounds, nevertheless the label to other people who don't know the mission is a bit of a barrier . . . .

When they join the college all staff are asked at interview whether they would be happy to work within a Christian foundation college. However this cannot mean that they can be held to support arguments for the continuation of such arrangements. There are parallel arguments to be made about the excluding effects of faith schools and higher education institutions. I am not in favour of faith schools. I share this view with many others including several head teachers of faith schools. In the present circumstances the principle of equity means that we should give equal encouragement to all faiths to establish their own schools. However, this can result in increasing division in society as we have learnt from Northern Ireland where almost all schools are denominational. The reports on ethnic tension in Oldham, Bradford and Burnley pointed to the way faith schools contributed to ethnic divisions and hence tensions in these areas (Home Office 2001a and b). In order to begin to dismantle faith schools there would have to be a severing of the relationship between the Anglican Church and the state (see Booth 2003b).

There are strong arguments, too, for suggesting that denominational institutions of higher education, apart from those that prepare people for religious vocations, are unnecessary or even counterproductive, in serving a multi-ethnic, religiously diverse society and preparing teachers to teach in one. I do not know how widely such a view is held in my college.

Identifying and overcoming barriers

To overcome barriers to inclusion in the institution there has to be a concerted and consistent attempt to develop the institution in an inclusive way. Those of us who advocate the inclusive development of schools have a special responsibility to reflect on the nature of the institutions in which we work. If we are to make suggestions about the inclusive development of schools then we should attempt to change our own institutions and experience the possibilities and barriers in doing so. A teacher education institution that invites students to develop inclusion in schools might be expected to try to create inclusive values, approaches to teaching and learning, relationships with staff and students and an inclusive process for its own development: 'we really need a genuine sense of mission, a genuine sense of shared values.'

In discussing barriers and the way they may be overcome, colleagues returned to the effects of external pressures which may be greater within an institution that is aspiring to university status:

> We live in fear of Ofsted. We live in fear of HEFC [Higher Education Funding Council]. We are also aspiring to university status. We are going down a traditional conservative route and we're scared of taking risks and perhaps we need to.

I had found myself tempted to edit out any reference to the aspiration to university status within this chapter. It emphasises the hierarchical nature of higher education institutions in England. Ours is a university college, at the bottom of the status ladder behind the ex-polytechnics, the new, the old and the ancient universities. I have no doubt of the gifts and talents of the staff and students at my college, but the faint sense of shame is there nevertheless. One interviewee argued that our status as a college meant that we were not in a position to encourage inclusion in schools:

> We don't encourage inclusion in the schools. No: Training is what we're best at. In other words doing what we're told. I don't think we're yet in the league of being policy shapers. Except for one or two individuals. Essentially what we do is fill in bidding forms that have externally imposed criteria and we demonstrate how we meet those.

I know too that staff in education departments within old and new universities have sometimes suffered from a sense of inferiority as they compete with departments based in pure research, populated with staff with more traditional academic careers, moving from undergraduate to postgraduate to university teaching. I may be in a minority in having such feelings. This is something else for the survey. But at least it provides me with a vantage point, if I am willing to occupy it, for contemplating the myriad of status differences in primary, secondary, further and higher education institutions which are all part of the complexity of understanding inclusion in education.

An inclusive approach to institutional development?

However, people within institutions of higher education are not used to producing development plans in a participatory way or ones which shape the future of the development of the institution over several years. In my own institution, it was felt that 'inclusion in terms of faculty management would have a huge impact' and would mean 'much more sharing of expertise and a reduction of workload because we would work more effectively'. There were also risks for individuals, 'exposing yourself to other people':

> In the competitive culture we are in at the moment, people may wish to limit the extent to which they get involved with others in case it reveals as many weaknesses as strengths.

There was a feeling from some that ' we work in pockets, in small teams and we don't work collaboratively'; 'development in the faculty is piecemeal, and departmentally led, compartmentalised, a lot of duplication of effort'; 'there are brick walls between departments.' It was suggested that there was a particular attempt to make new staff welcome but few collaborative structures thereafter: 'I think more and more effort is made for the induction of new staff, after that it comes down to your own forcefulness.'

There were contrasting views about whether the faculty was developing an inclusive way of working. It was argued by one colleague that 'generally development is not proceeding in an inclusive way' and by another more emphatically:

> The faculty has not made an attempt to develop itself in an inclusive way. None whatsoever. You would have to see that inclusion has some benefits. In this college, having had a long history of a particular way of functioning, at all layers there's a collusion about a particular style that works.

But the very compartmentalisation of the faculty can mean that the developments seen by some are missed by others:

> I think that lots of things have happened. Three years ago when we did something about inclusion, you should have seen the faces of some of the students and now you get them talking about this . . . It seems to me that there has been a concerted effort from most staff, that almost

everyone in this college is going in the same direction and we are changing a lot. I just feel very positive about the things that we are doing. We're nibbling away.

However, some staff were very cautious about suggesting in public that anything might be done differently, as the following exchange illustrates:

I think the way forward is that one or two people have to stand up and be counted . . . and everyone else will stand back and watch.

I think encouraging people to make individual and somewhat private responses is currently more empowering. There's no culture in this faculty of standing up and speaking your mind.

Shouldn't people be able to stand up and say, well, actually I disagree with you?

We need to nurture that possibility, right now we are not at that point.

From opposition to inclusion, to compliance and then ownership?

A managerialist ideology creates a busy-ness within institutions constantly struggling to meet the perceived demands on their time and avoid the stigma of failure. It was suggested within the discussion group that those colleagues in the faculty who appear to be opposed to inclusion may see it as requiring additional tasks within an already crammed schedule, echoing the sense of overload of teachers working in schools: 'they are bowed down with other things like raising the SATS level by 2 or 3%.' Within the institution one participant suggested that 'it's all about doing and not thinking' for both staff and students.

But if there are more demands on staff than they can hope to meet, how do they ration their reactions? To what extent do colleagues feel, for example, that they should comply with the inclusion requirements within the national curriculum and elsewhere? For one, who worked for the organisation that formulated the National Curriculum inclusion statement, her support was clear: 'I worked for the QCA [Qualifications and Curriculum Authority] and I was indoctrinated about inclusion when I was there.' But as I argued earlier, there is an ambivalent message within the new standards for the award of qualified teacher status, about how seriously this guidance should be taken. And in order to take this and other guidance seriously colleagues need to be familiar with it.

In my experience many colleagues and students are familiar with the inclusion guidance in the national curriculum, though it is unclear how far this stretches to other inclusion documents. But other colleagues have a different experience to mine, finding that many colleagues have limited knowledge of the inclusion documents. They argued that 'teacher training is very subject-oriented . . . so you wouldn't read the pages on inclusion':

> I work with groups on the documentation around inclusion and its consistency, I have never met a year-four [student] who has actually looked at the national curriculum guidance on inclusion and knows anything about it. I don't think many colleagues have a clue about it.

This participant felt that because other colleagues were unfamiliar with the national curriculum which views inclusion as involving a response of the whole school, they concentrated on issues of access 'rather than participation and engagement'. Another interviewee formulated this as meeting the minimum standards, as 'compliance' with institutional requirements rather than 'ownership' of the principles of inclusion:

> I've got someone who is visually impaired so off he toddled to the student support service, and he was given a programme that reads out what is typed on the computer. Not problem solved. Back covered. What we haven't got is alternative ways of meeting the criteria. For example, instead of writing an essay, presenting an artefact and talking about it could be a way of demonstrating criticality and reference to other sources of knowledge and so on . . . We go as far as portfolios but that's still written.

A wish to go beyond compliance was echoed by others:

> This word compliance . . . worries me immensely, because . . . we are in danger of going down the accountability route. It seems much more important that we are professionally inclusive . . . Otherwise, I think we are just covering our backs.

Compliance with government inclusion policies, in a situation where there are more policies than can possibly be implemented, can be seen as a step towards ownership of the ideas. Compliance with inclusion policy may involve giving less attention to other policies with an excluding effect.

When more within the faculty have taken ownership of inclusion then the faculty might have more of a voice on important educational issues. Strong emotions were expressed about the announcement of a former Secretary of State for Education, David Blunkett, that children seeking asylum who are housed in detention centres would be educated within these centres rather than attending local schools:

> I was furious. I couldn't believe that this government is pushing through segregated schools in detention centres. This is just a slap in our faces.

Now the students are reading that. What's going to be done about it? There's nothing on the e-mail. We are going to have segregated schooling based on race and ethnicity. We've totally depoliticised our environment.

However, many colleagues within the faculty and college are working hard to extend the diversity of students and support their participation. Conferences on inclusion issues are arranged for students and staff and there are regular events concerned with diversity and participation. For example, for inclusion week to mark the twentieth anniversary of the Centre for Studies on Inclusive Education, in November 2002, the department hosted an exhibition of photographs about refugees nationally and globally by Carlos Reyes-Manzo, entitled Journeys and Dreams, and instigated a debate with Oxfam about bringing a global dimension into teacher education.

Inclusion, special educational needs and the paradigm wars

Colleagues pointed out that there was a division between 'special needs education' and 'equality and diversity' approaches to inclusion in the institution as there was in schools and argued that this was hardly surprising given a similar division in government policies. One might have thought that agreement would be easy to reach between these positions given a common concern with those subject to exclusionary pressures. However, close observers of education institutions in England, and in other countries, will know that there exists what can be described as a paradigm war, between these perspectives. In part this is a clash between assimilationist and transformative perspectives on inclusion. It is about broad and narrow political issues, educational philosophies and approaches to teaching and learning and of disputes arising from personal, institutional and disciplinary allegiances and territories. As a colleague commented:

> Coming from a particular discipline you may find that your discipline is threatened. And your career may be rooted in a particular discipline, if you're an educational psychologist or whatever. You don't want to lose it. You have to ask what would be the risk of being much more open-minded?

In general, advocates of these different views put forward parallel justifications for their positions. Those concerned that the 'special educational needs' of people should be identified and supported argue that others concerned with 'participation for all' may deny and overlook such 'needs'. Those who take a broader view argue that the categorisation process and a narrow view of support can contribute to the ignoring of the real interests and identities of disabled people. That insufficient attention is paid to the education of disabled children within teacher education might be seen as common ground. Robertson for example, regards 'children with special educational needs' as 'the subject of almost eloquent neglect' within initial teacher education (Robertson 1999). Garner, however, sees an interest in inclusion as an irrelevance to resolving what he calls the Initial Teacher Education 'debacle' in its denial of 'responsibility for SEN' which 'represents an insult both to children and young people who have learning difficulties and to those who work with them' (Garner 2000: 114). I am concerned that we pay attention to all forms of exclusion within teacher education and that we create structures and cultures which support changes in the detail of practice so that exclusion is minimised.

In seeing her starting position as moving outwards from 'special educational needs', a colleague argued that there was scope for different views being productively explored, once we reflected on them:

> In academic circles you are actually trying to develop debates and arguments and maybe people commit themselves to one side of the argument for the purposes of writing. Maybe they think I'm not actually sure about some of this . . . Instead of discussing the models we have a competition between the models. There could be a better way of conducting this debate.

Researching with the institution

The Research Assessment Exercise has exerted a dominating pressure on higher education institutions, with status and large amounts of money and consequent jobs depending on its outcome. It has exerted a pressure on institutions to put forward for the assessment only those staff who publish in high-status journals, despite the fact that its own criteria emphasise the importance of research that is accessible to practitioners. Within my faculty a potential conflict is brewing about whether support for research should be channelled to 'the many or the few'. There remains a division between those who see their jobs as primarily to do with teaching and others whose main focus is research and who are seen to have higher status: 'There's an element of elitism. There are those that train and those that research'. Although in theory everyone belongs to a research group many people in the faculty find that their timetables are full with teaching obligations or 'do not have the confidence to get more involved'.

In my view, inclusion within the institution involves the development of an inclusive approach to research, so that all students and staff can see themselves as researchers as well as teachers and learners, or, indeed, the subjects of research. In my work with colleagues and students at the Open University we attempted to maintain the relationship between knowledge derived through research and the experience and practice of educators. Our definition of research was adapted from that of Stenhouse (1981), as 'systematic and self-critical inquiry made public' and relied heavily on basic techniques of observation, interviewing and critical analysis. We argued that the central methods for an inclusive approach to research should be those that can be applied within the boundaries of our own lives and those of our students and of teachers and students in schools.

Collaborative action-oriented research within our own institutions can help to develop the institution in inclusive ways, draw on the knowledge and experience of colleagues and support them to integrate research into lives dominated by teaching. Yet there are few reports of such attempts to develop institutions of higher education (see Campbell 2000; Skelton 2002). In doing such research, we have to resolve the discomfort that we or others may feel when we delve beneath the surface of our workplaces to uncover the barriers to learning and participation within them. A concern with image management may mean that some people do not want an alternative picture of the institution to emerge even if it is linked to making improvements. This may have been behind what I saw as the most significant, though incidental, finding of a doctoral study looking at the role of school cultures in inclusive school development. Kristine Black-Hawkins made a detailed study of one school, spending six months working as a teaching assistant within classrooms. The head teacher was pleased that she had given something back to the school by working voluntarily, but rejected an offer to see her detailed analysis of classroom practice and teacher and student relationships (Black-Hawkins 2002).

There are any number of projects that can reflect on institutional development. Two examples of projects within my institution illustrate the potential of such research.

A patchwork project: diversity as a resource for learning

For some years I have had the idea of developing a project on 'using diversity as a resource for learning' and I have decided to combine this interest with an attempt to create a college-wide project as a stimulus to reflection on teaching and learning. The project is intended to explore the variety of ways in which difference can be drawn upon as a resource for teaching and learning and to contribute to the development of teaching approaches that are responsive to a greater diversity of students. It may help departments to draw more fully on the diversity of staff and their varied expertise and to gain greater benefit from the visits of colleagues and students from outside England. It may also help to consider ways of conducting research that are accessible and encourage wide participation.

It is called a patchwork project because it will be built up from contributions across the college, drawing on the different experiences of staff and students. Contributions may be invited from people connected with the college, such as colleagues in other institutions, teachers and students in hospitals and schools, or even family members of all ages. It can help to develop opportunities for an exchange of ideas locally, nationally and internationally. The wider the participation across and beyond the college the greater will be the resource for the project, which is to be open to everyone at the college through a website. A patch consists of a sheet of A4 paper on which is set down an experience when differences in knowledge, experience, skills or personal qualities of teachers and/or students have been used as a resource for teaching and learning. This might involve complementary skills in teachers, peer tutoring amongst students or the unexpected contribution from a student who has unforeseen expertise in a particular area. It might reflect differences in local knowledge, or in age and maturity, religion, ethnicity, home country or gender.

Men into primary education

Two colleagues, one in the same institution as myself and one who has moved on to a different university, have jointly explored the experiences of the small numbers of men preparing to teach young children, in order to uncover barriers to recruitment and retention (Lewis and Weston 2002). They are concerned about the lack of male teachers in primary schools and the effects this has on school children (see also Balchin 2002; Burn 2002; Wadsworth 2002). While the number of men choosing to work with young children has traditionally been low, recruitment of men into primary teacher education courses had fallen to 13% by 1998. Lewis and Weston noted that although numbers within the institutions started out very low this was compounded by a disproportionate drop-out rate. Detailed interviews with the men revealed that they found it difficult to be in such a minority on courses, and in staff rooms, and all of them experienced comments on their sexuality. On a teaching practice, one student was given initial instructions by a deputy head teacher: 'Her first instructions to me were all negative. Stay away from the toilets, don't touch the children in any way'. Another commented 'When I tell people I want to be a teacher . . . they either call me a paedophile or gay' (Lewis and Weston 2002: 8).

Lewis and Weston recognise that men are considerably advantaged within primary education when it comes to promotion. This may contribute to some negativity within mainly female staff rooms. Nevertheless ways have to be found to avoid both negative and positive discrimination meted out to men within primary education. It would be interesting to explore this aspect of inclusion internationally. Within my own experience in primary schools in Norway, I have been struck by the lack of the kind of taboos about physical contact between male teachers or male visitors and children now ubiquitous in England. After visiting a classroom and reading a story to a group of children I was unable to leave until I had given a hug to each child in the queue that formed in my path.

A cross-faculty structure

Despite the obstacles to the development of inclusion perceived by some colleagues and reported in this chapter, there is, at the time of writing, a plan to put in place a cross-faculty structure to support the development of inclusion across the faculty, with representation from all departments.

Structures to support the development of inclusion are required at three levels. At the highest level one needs an inclusive set of principles which underpin the workings of the institution. Second one needs anti-discrimination policies which give the possibility of redress when the principles are breached, and third, one requires advocacy structures to raise concerns, to work on the progressive removal of barriers to participation and to mobilise resources to support participation for all. Within my institution a cross-faculty structure would occupy this third position.

It is intended that the group will address issues of representation, discrimination and participation, both within the faculty and in relationships with schools, and attempt to integrate research on inclusion with teaching in the faculty. It will combine a broad view of inclusion concerned with 'equality and diversity' while recognising the starting point of some in a concern with students they see as 'having special educational needs'. It will put on research/teaching days for staff and students across the faculty, integrated into courses so that others are freed from teaching commitments and to assist the permeation of inclusion across all courses. It will encourage cross-faculty research particularly on aspects of institutional development, and in collaboration with other institutions. It will provide a bridge with the research group on diversity and participation.

Concluding remarks

In this chapter, I have analysed the policy and institutional contexts which constrain and help teacher educators to develop inclusive cultures, policies and practices within their own institutions and in schools, particularly through their work with students. I have looked at the way colleagues within my own institution understand inclusion, the barriers to inclusion that they identify and some of the ways in which such barriers might be addressed. They expressed a variety of views, some complementary to, and others in conflict with, each other. They provided a very good basis for beginning a more structured representation of what inclusion might mean for the development of a complex institution of higher education like my own.

In many ways the picture of barriers within my institution echo earlier accounts such as those in the chapters of Iram Siraj-Blatchford (1993). The barriers to inclusion within teacher education remain formidable. Inclusion within the institutions is in conflict with the accountability culture and managerialism. Inclusion involves communication across a multiplicity of cultures, identities and ways of thinking. It requires that we replace a discourse fuelled by power with rational argument and explicit discussion of values, so that the development of the institution can be based on principled action. Nevertheless, many within institutions, including within my own, struggle to put in place different ways of working together, proper representation of diversity within staff, students and courses and new teachers prepared to relate actions to principles.

References

Archbishops' Council (2000) *Church Schools Review Group*, chaired by Lord Dearing, London, Archbishops' Council.

Balchin, T. (2002) 'Male teachers in primary education', *Forum* 44(1), 28–33.

Black-Hawkins, K. (2002) 'Cultures of Inclusion and Exclusion', Ph.D. thesis, University of Kent.

Blackledge, A. (1998) 'The institutionalisation of inequality: the initial teacher training national curriculum for primary English as cultural hegemony', *Educational Review* 50(1), 55–64.

Booth, T. (2000) 'Inclusion and exclusion policy in England: who controls the agenda?' in Armstrong, F., Armstrong D. and Barton L. (eds) *Inclusive Education; Policy, Contexts and Comparative Perspectives*, London: Fulton.

Booth, T. (2003a) 'Inclusion and exclusion in the city: concepts and contexts', in Potts, P. (ed.) *Inclusion in the City*, London: Routledge.

Booth, T. (2003b) 'Embracing the faith, including the community?', in Potts, P. (ed.) *Inclusion in the City*, London: Routledge.

Booth, T. and Ainscow, M. (1998) *From Them to Us: An International Study of Inclusion in Education*, London: Routledge.

Booth, T. and Ainscow, M. (2002) *The Index for Inclusion* (2nd edition), Bristol: Centre for Studies on Inclusive Education.

Burn, E. (2002) 'Do boys need male primary teachers as positive role models?', *Forum* 44(1), 34–40.

Campbell, A. (2000) 'Cultural diversity: practising what we preach in higher education', *Teaching in Higher Education* 5(3), 373–80.

Commission for Racial Equality (2000), *Learning for All*, London: CRE.

Commission for Racial Equality (2002) *Preparing a Race Equality Policy for Schools*, London: CRC.

Department for Education and Employment (1998) *Meeting Special Educational Needs: A Programme of Action*, London: DfEE.

Department for Education and Employment (1999a) *Excellence in Cities*, London: DfEE.

Department for Education and Employment (1999b) *Social Inclusion: Pupil Support*, London: DfEE.

Department for Education and Employment (2000) *Bullying: Don't Suffer in Silence*, London: DfEE.

Department for Education and Skills (2001a) *Special Educational Needs Code of Practice*, London: DfES.

Department for Education and Skills (2001b) *Inclusive Schooling: Children with Special Educational Needs*, London: DfES.

Department for Education and Skills (2002) *The Education Act*, London: The Stationery Office.

Department for Education and Employment/Qualifications and Curriculum Authority (1999) *The National Curriculum: Handbook for Primary Teachers in England*, London: DfEE/QCA.

Department for Education and Skills and Teaching Training Agency (2002) *Qualifying to Teach: Professional Standards for Qualified Teacher Status and Requirements for Initial Training*, London: DfES/TTA

Disability Rights Commission, (2002) *Disability Discrimination Act 1995 Part 4: Code of Practice for Schools*, London: DRC.

Dixon, A., Drummond, M.J., Hart, S. and McIntyre, D. (2003) *Learning Without Limits*, Milton Keynes: Open University Press.

Edwards, T. and Tomlinson, S. (2002) *Selection Isn't Working*, London: Catalyst.

Garner, P. (2000) 'Pretzel only policy? Inclusion and the real world of initial teacher education', *British Journal of Special Education* 27(3), 111–16.

Home Office (2000) *Race Relations (Amendment) Ac*t, London: The Home Office.

Home Office (2001a) *Building Cohesive Communities, A Report of the Ministerial Group on Public Order and Community Cohesion*, London: The Stationery Office.

Home Office (2001b) *Community Cohesion, A Report of the Independent Review Team*, Chaired by Ted Cantle, London: The Home Office.

Hutton, W. (2002) 'The class war destroying our schools', *Observer*, 26 May 2002.

Lewis, P. and Weston, C. (2002) 'Creating Boyzones, Conference of the British Education Research Association', University of Exeter.

Macpherson, W. (1999) *The Stephen Lawrence Inquiry*, London: HMSO.

Morris, E. (2002) 'Why comprehensives must change', *Observer*, 23 June 2002.

Office for Standards in Education (2000) *Evaluating Educational Inclusion*, London: Ofsted.

Office for Standards in Education (2002a) *Achievement of Black Caribbean Pupils: Three Successful Primary Schools*, London: Ofsted.

Office for Standards in Education (2002b) *Achievement of Black Caribbean Pupils, Good Practice in Secondary Schools*, London: Ofsted.

O'Neill, O. (2002) *A Question of Trust,* Reith Lectures, BBC Radio 4, www.bbc.co.uk/radio4/reith2002/ lecture3_text.shtml

Robertson, C. (1999) 'Initial teacher education and inclusive schooling', *Support for Learning* 14(4), 169–73.

Siraj-Blatchford, I. (ed.) (1993) *Race, Gender and the Education of Teachers*, Buckingham: Open University Press.

Skelton, A. (2002) 'Towards inclusive learning environments in higher education? Reflections on a professional development course for university lecturers', *Teaching in Higher Education* 7(2), 193–214.

Social Exclusion Unit (1998) *Bringing Britain Together a National Strategy for Neighbourhood Renewal*, London: The Stationery Office.

Social Exclusion Unit (2000a) *Minority Ethnic Issues in Social Exclusion and Neighbourhood Renewal*, London: Cabinet Office.

Social Exclusion Unit (2000b) *National Strategy for Neighbourhood Renewal: Policy Action Team Report Summaries: A Compendium*, London: The Stationery Office.

Social Exclusion Unit (2001) *Preventing Social Exclusion*, London: The Stationery Office.

Stenhouse, L. (1981) 'What counts as research?', *British Journal of Educational Studies* 29(2), 103–14.

Teacher Training Agency (2001) *Handbook to Accompany the Standards for the Award of Qualified Teacher Status and Requirements for the Provision of Initial Teacher Training*, London: TTA.

Travis, A. (2002) 'Blunkett deeper in "swamp" row', *Guardian*, 26 Apri 2002.

Wadsworth, J. (2002) 'The issues facing men working in early childhood education', *Forum* 44(1), 41–4.

Warwick, I. and Douglas, N. (2001) *Safe For All: A Best Practice Guide to Prevent Homophobic Bullying in Secondary Schools*, London: Citizenship 21.

Chapter 4

The analysis of context

Some thoughts on teacher education, culture, colonisation and inequality

Keith Ballard

Introduction

Inclusive education is concerned with issues of social justice. This means that graduates entering the teaching profession should understand how they might create classrooms and schools that address issues of respect, fairness and equity. As part of this endeavour they will need to understand the historical, sociocultural and ideological contexts that create discriminatory and oppressive practices in education. The isolation and rejection of disabled students is but one area of injustice. Others include gender discrimination, poverty and racism.

In this chapter I am interested in how a dominating theory, ideology or culture may create social and educational environments that disadvantage some people. Skrtic (1995: 235) uses the term 'metatheory' to refer to an overarching system of beliefs that names the world in particular ways and that therefore informs and shapes individual and institutional practices. This is similar to the way in which a paradigm, ideology or culture directs us in how to see our world and what sense to make of it. In this regard I have a particular interest in events in my own country, New Zealand, since 1984. From that time, New Zealand has adopted a New Right libertarian ideology of individualism that has shaped our economic, education and social policies. In this chapter I suggest that this is not a context that is supportive of inclusion.

Booth and Ainscow (1998) have suggested that inclusion should involve working against all forms of exclusion in schools and in wider social contexts beyond the classroom and school. It would seem difficult to envisage inclusive schools within a society that pursues policies and practices that exclude some of its citizens from social rights and participation. I am interested in policies and practices that exclude people through their effect on economic and community life in my society. I am also interested in examining inclusion in the context of teacher education which might acknowledge that teachers have a central role in educating children and young people into citizenship. If this is done in a way that is thoughtfully critical of the society in which they live, then teachers might play a role in communicating ideas that question the origins of exclusion and support relationships that are respectful of difference and diversity.

For teacher educators this is not an easy task. We will need to be explicit with our students in examining the assumptions and ideological positions on which our analysis of social issues is grounded. Our values, and theirs, will need to be identified and discussed in this critical context. Discomfort and uncertainty may need to be acknowledged together with an awareness that history teaches us that our best-intentioned insights and beliefs may be shown, in time, to be false or problematic for social justice.

A social context

Since 1984, New Zealand has adopted a New Right libertarian ideology of individualism that has shaped our policies and practices. After 16 years of this radical social experiment, the data shows a society increasingly divided between rich and poor (Waldegrave 1998). Labour Prime Minister Helen Clark has described New Zealand as a 'low-income country' which after 'decades of . . . getting poorer' now had 'difficulty in building its social infrastructure' (interviewed by Campbell 2001: 17). Since 1984, Labour Party politicians have implemented market economic policies when in power (1984–90, 1999–2002), but even they now show concern for what they refer to as 'closing the gaps' between those with substantial resources and those without (Te Puni Kōkiri 2000).

If we are to close the gaps I think we need to look carefully at how the gaps were created in the first place. The majority of New Zealand politicians and voters have supported ideas that, when enacted, have been shown from evidence across countries and cultures (a natural experiment in Bronfenbrenner's, 1979, terms) to result in inequity, injustice and social division (Galbraith 1992; Saul 1997).

That is not to say that all was well in New Zealand before 1984. It clearly was not, for the indigenous Māori in particular. But what seems evident now is that we are dominated by an individualistic ideology that evidence suggests will not promote equity and social justice and does create conditions of inequality and injustice. For example, the market model 'reforms' of education means that each of our primary and secondary schools now operates as an individual education 'provider' required to meet the wishes of its local parent Board of Trustee 'managers'. In such education markets schools compete for students and evidence suggests in New Zealand (Codd 1999; Tapp 1998; Thrupp 1998), as elsewhere (Barton 1997; Smyth 1993), that minority and equity issues may not be a priority where student intake is based on a school's reputation for academic performance.

In this chapter I present an analysis of some minority and equity issues that I suggest represent a social context for teachers and teaching and, therefore, for teacher education. In this analysis I use the term 'culture' to refer to 'particular groups of people and certain aspects of those people . . . [including] . . . notions of collective knowledge, attitudes, values and ways of thinking and acting' (Baxter 1998: 64). A culture shares a common language, meanings and understandings that construct how the world is and how it is to be known.

I use the term colonisation to refer to processes that replace the ideas, meanings, language and ways of being of one group of people by those of another group of people. These processes subjugate the colonised psychologically, socially and materially. The political effect is discrimination (Bhabha 1994) and 'where inequality and injustice disproportionately affect particular racial or ethnic groups' such oppression may be identified as racism (Malin 1999: 2). Linda Tuhiwai Smith (1999) says that 'colonialism is but one expression of imperialism' (p. 21). Imperialism involves economic expansion supported by strategies that name, define and control how we should know the world and what it is that is important to know.

In New Zealand, Mäori are a colonised indigenous people living with, and often resisting, imposed ideas and institutions (Bishop and Glynn 1999). I suggest that Mäori and Pakeha (New Zealanders of European descent) also experience a new, although related, wave of economic imperialism in which New Right ideas reshape our society and redefine our selves and our relationships with one another. One result is increasing inequality in New Zealand and in this context I use Merridy Malin's definition of the term 'social justice' to refer to 'equity of access to society's resources . . . self determination and the right to be treated with dignity and respect' (Malin 1999: 2).

A culture of commerce

Economist Brian Easton describes contemporary New Zealand as a commercialised society. He defines commercialisation as using 'the model of private business enterprise to organise economic (and even non-economic) activity' (Easton 1997: 14). The 1984–90 Labour Party government, in a radical move away from its former left-wing social democratic tradition, adopted the New Right ideology of Reagan and Thatcher and introduced 'reforms' grounded in an 'extreme version' of the Friedman and Von Hayek rationalist economic theories promoted by the Chicago School of Economics (Easton 1997: 93). The Labour government's reforms, pursued subsequently by National Party (traditionally conservative) governments, have meant that state activities have either been fully privatised or have been 'corporatised' and required to be run as if they were a business. For example, public hospitals became commercially operated Crown Health Enterprises with business goals and user charges (ibid.: 162). Schools became parent-operated educational enterprises (some state schools have commercial sponsors – Jesson 1999: 56) while universities and other tertiary institutions were 'recast as delivering private benefits to fee-paying students, in order to justify reduced government funding and force institutions to respond to market demand' (Kelsey 1997: 4).

The introduction of a market model for state education in New Zealand has been described as 'one of the most radical experiments in education policy . . . [in] the OECD' (Boston 2000: 11). Each school in New Zealand operates as an independent educational 'shop', competing for students. Reviewing a study on the effects of 16 years of the 'self-managing' school, Jonathon Boston (2000) wrote that:

> The combined impact of decentralised management and competition for students has been to intensify educational inequalities; the gap between high and low performing schools has widened; the degree of ethnic polarisation has sharpened; and schools have become more segregated socioeconomically.
>
> (2000: 11)

This system, says Boston, is harmful to minorities and to those least advantaged in society.

The commercial market model is evident in teacher education in New Zealand. Until the early 1990s, there were six institutions (two universities and four colleges of education with links to a university) offering preservice teacher education. New policies that encouraged competition for students made funding available to polytechnics and private agencies to offer teacher training. By 1992, more than 100 programmes of preservice teacher education were being offered by over 20 agencies (Alcorn 1999) and by 2002 there were 32 institutions offering teaching degrees and diplomas (Teachers Council 2002). For a total population of 3.4 million, this is clearly problematic. In 1996, preservice teacher education for primary teachers was reduced from four years to three years. This happened when a three-year programme was introduced by one major institution. The Ministry of Education saw cost savings in shorter programmes and offered three-year graduates the same salary as graduates of four-year programmes. Others then reduced their programmes in order to remain competitive, fearing that students would prefer a shorter, and therefore cheaper (all tertiary students pay tuition fees), course of study.

The 'free market' commercialisation of New Zealand has not just involved public sector reform. Import licensing has been abolished and tariffs reduced to the extent that all car manufacturers and many clothing factories have closed down with significant job losses (all motor vehicles are now imported, most being used vehicles from Japan). A single-minded commitment to a rigid ideology saw, between 1985 and the mid 1990s, unemployment at 'unprecedented levels . . . overseas debt quadrupled . . . and spending on research and development [fall] to half the OECD average' (Kelsey 1997: 9). The two state-owned television channels are both commercial and are required to operate as private businesses returning a profit to the government. The 1984–90 Labour government removed restrictions on overseas ownership of the media and most, including all of the major newspapers, are now owned offshore (ibid.: 112). Kelsey notes the cultural implications of this which, alongside the removal of quotas for local content, has meant that television in New Zealand is dominated by American 'soap operas, sit-coms and talk shows which [bear] little resemblance to the diversity of New Zealand life' (ibid.: 113).

A context of poverty

Waldegrave *et al.* (1995) use a poverty threshold of '60% of median, equivalent, household, disposable income' to show that, following the first period of economic and social 'reforms' under the Labour government of 1984–90, and further reductions in welfare support by a National Party government in 1991, in 1993 18.5% of all New Zealand households fell below the poverty threshold. This meant that 32.6% of all New Zealand children lived in poor households, and 72.6% of single-parent families lived below the poverty line. While 14.2% of Pakeha experienced poverty, 39.3% of Mäori and 51.1% of Pacific Island households lived below the poverty line. In this context, assistance from food banks operated by charities has been required by increasing numbers of people, and in the Auckland area alone the number of food banks increased from 16 in 1989 to 130 in 1994 (Waldegrave 1998). A significant number of those using food banks – up to 28% on the North Shore of Auckland city – are waged, indicating a working poor in a low-wage economy (New Zealand Council of Christian Social Services 1999).

A recent study of low-income New Zealand households (Waldegrave *et al.* 1999) emphasised the experience of overcrowded and poor housing, difficulty in affording health care, and not being able to afford essential food items (60% of respondents). The study concluded that 'social cohesion is being seriously undermined by classic expressions of poverty and an inability of poor New Zealanders to participate equitably in their own society' (p. 48). This reflects what Cantillon (1998) terms 'new poverty', which refers to the 'multi-dimensional character of disadvantage' with social, political and community isolation alongside economic deprivation (p. 130). Waldegrave and his colleagues (1999) note in their report that poverty was experienced 'disproportionately . . . among Mäori, Pacific Island people, women and children' (p. 47). From this data, the loss of social cohesion includes the increasing exclusion of Mäori and other minorities from mainstream economic and social activities.

Mäori and colonisation

The indigenous Mäori comprise 15% of the New Zealand total population. Between 1977 and 1997, the proportion of Mäori leaving school with no qualification decreased from 68.5% to 37.7% while the numbers leaving the final years of high school with Sixth or Seventh Form Certificate qualification almost trebled, from 14.4% to 40.2% (Te Puni Kökiri 1998: 11). Nevertheless, the disparities between Mäori and non-Mäori educational attainment had remained constant since 1992. As at 1997, Mäori were still three times more likely than non-Mäori to leave school without qualifications (ibid.: Figure 2, p. 11). Those Mäori who remained at school were less likely to sit national high school examinations, with 64% of Mäori students taking the Fifth Form School Certificate qualification (year 11 of schooling, age 15 years) compared to 92.3% non-Mäori. The greatest disparities were for qualifications that enabled tertiary study. In 1997, 37.9% of Mäori compared with 74.4% of non-Mäori sat Sixth Form Certificate (year 12 of schooling) while 24.1% of Mäori sat University Entrance and Bursary level exams (year 13 of schooling, age 17 years) compared with 58.3% non-Mäori (ibid.: Table 5, p. 11).

The Ministry of Education (1998) 'Annual Report on Mäori Education' found that less successful primary schooling and more repeating of classes meant that Mäori senior high school students were often older and ill-prepared for exams. Few Mäori reached the senior forms, often leaving school in the fourth form while, if they did progress, they were less likely to sit exams and more likely to achieve lower grades (Davies and Nicholl 1994). While Mäori are 15% of the population, they comprised 7.7% of all university graduates in 1996 (Te Puni Kökiri 1998: Figure 5 and Table 7, p. 12).

The economic restructuring of the 1980s impacted most heavily on those in less-skilled, labour-intensive industries, with the loss of over 100,000 jobs mainly in manufacturing, forestry and public works (Te Puni Kökiri 2000: 21). This led to dramatic increases in Mäori unemployment, which rose from 13.5% in 1988 to 27.3% in 1992 (Te Puni Kökiri 1998). The effect on non-Mäori unemployment levels was more gradual and stayed within a 5% range. In 1992 Mäori unemployment was three times the level of non-Mäori. Mäori are more vulnerable because of the young, low-skilled work force and their lower educational attainment. In 1992, 47.9% of Mäori teenagers available to take part in the labour force were unemployed, compared to 19.1% of non-Mäori. While unemployment fell between 1992 and 1997, Mäori youth were still twice as likely as non-Mäori youth to be unemployed (ibid.: Figure 9, p. 15). In 1999, Mäori unemployment at 19% remained at three times the non-Mäori rate with the Mäori youth rate (15–19 years of age) at 32%, twice that for non-Mäori (Te Puni Kökiri 1999).

This data suggests a mainstream economic, education, and social order that is not inclusive of Mäori. Mäori have created early childhood centres (Te

Kohanga Reo – Mäori language nests), Mäori language primary and secondary schools (Kura Kaupapa Mäori) and Mäori universities (Whare Wananga). Nevertheless, the majority of Mäori children and young people (more than 90% – Te Puni Kökiri 2001: Fact Sheets 14 and 16) attend regular state schools where the majority of their teachers are Pakeha (in 1998, 8% of teachers were Mäori, Te Puni Kökiri 2000: 20). The evidence suggests that, like minorities elsewhere, Mäori may be marginalised in classroom contexts that predominantly see their differences as deficiencies and that often involve the systematic devaluing of their cultural identity (Bishop and Glynn 1999; Weisman 1998; Wyatt-Smith and Dooley 1997). Weisman (1998) suggests that such educational systems involve pressure to assimilate into the majority culture, a process that 'instills an uncritical acceptance [of the dominant] social and political order' (Weisman 1998: 71). This does not foster achievement. Sylvia and White (1997) report that by eighth grade 40% of American minority students are 'at least one grade level below their expected performance' (p. 293). This is a failure of teaching and presents a challenge to teacher educators. Also, in the New Zealand context the evidence suggests that to recruit Mäori into teaching and to ensure that all teachers work to understand and address Mäori educational aspirations, we should strive to ensure that teachers from our programmes do not identify cultural differences as deficiencies – a position that privileges the dominant culture and that Wyatt-Smith and Dooley (1997) identify as racist. This means that the student teacher needs to consider evidence that the publicly funded state school system is failing to successfully teach many Mäori children, and must examine their responsibilities as teachers in this context.

Pakeha and colonisation

In 1769 the English voyager James Cook is recorded as taking 'formal possession' of areas of the North and South Islands of a country that Dutch explorer Abel Tasman had visited in 1642 and named 'New Zealand' (Wards 1968: 1). To be able to possess and to name a country and its people represents a significant power. This issue of power and dominance has had continuing implications for Mäori and for their education.

Bishop and Glynn (1999) note that visitors in the mid 1800s recorded Mäori having created extensive farming, with New Zealand's first Attorney-General Sir William Swainson describing in 1857 commercial enterprises on a large scale with, in one instance, a tribe operating 9,000 acres in cultivation of crops together with '200 head of cattle, 5,000 pigs, four water mills and 96 ploughs. They were also the owners of 43 small coastal vessels, averaging 20 tons each and upwards of 900 canoes' (from Temm 1990: 21, cited by Bishop and Glynn 1999: 31).

On 6 February 1840 the British Government signed a treaty with 213 Mäori chiefs at Waitangi. The Treaty of Waitangi gave Mäori 'exclusive and undisturbed possession of their lands and estates, forests, fisheries and other properties' (Article 2, text in English, Orange 1989: 31). Yet within a short while Mäori were being deceived and cheated and vast areas of their land were taken by government agents and by settlers. Where Mäori resisted incursions, this was seen as an excuse to imprison their leaders – including those articulating and organising passive resistance on a significant scale (Scott 1975) – and confiscate the land.

The effects were devastating. In the region that I live in, for example, the records show the 1840s as 'a time of prosperity and promise for Ngai Tahu [the local tribe], based on their traditional resource, the land' (Evison 1987: 16). By the 1880s, with the land mostly taken from them, Ngai Tahu people were impoverished. In 1891 Alexander Mackay, a government agent appointed to investigate Mäori land issues, reported to parliament that 'some of the younger men remarked that it would be better for them all to die as there appeared to be no future for them' (cited in Evison 1987: 60). I note that more than a century later, 1997 data showed that the suicide rate for Mäori youths aged 15–24 years was two and a half times greater than the rate for non-Mäori (56 per 100,000 and 22 per 100,000 respectively, Te Puni Kökiri 2000: 42).

Mäori have sustained themselves as a minority in the dominant European culture. Nevertheless, Mäori have had to struggle to have their language recognised in a resistant school system and have, in recent years, suffered extreme hardship as a New Right agenda created unemployment and reduced welfare support. In education, as many communities have become poorer, the schools in these communities have become poorer and Mäori in particular have been disadvantaged. Data indicate that about '42% of Mäori enrolments compared to 14% of non Mäori enrolments' are in schools in the poorest communities (Te Puni Kökiri 2001).

In 1991, a National (conservative) government legislated to allow state secondary schools to administer their own enrolment schemes. No longer did a school have to accept children from its local community 'zone'. Open competition was encouraged with the claim that it would give parents more 'choice'. Harker's (2000) analysis of Ministry of Education data shows that in the period 1995–98 schools in higher socioeconomic areas grew in student numbers, mostly increasing the intake of Pakeha and Asian students. Schools in poorer areas declined in numbers and included a greater proportion of Mäori and Pacific Island students. Harker suggests the development of a 'dual track' state education system with 'one set of schools for the (mostly Pakeha) middle classes and . . . another set for the (mostly Polynesian and Mäori) poorer classes' (p. 7).

Martin Thrupp (1998) has reported on a series of seven case studies of New Zealand schools in which, irrespective of their size or the socioeconomic background of their community, almost all of the teachers and principals interviewed saw themselves in competition with other schools.

Thrupp noted that, in different socioeconomic areas, competition was based on different factors. Schools in higher socioeconomic communities saw themselves competing for top students, while for schools in lower socioeconomic areas the concern was to stop 'white flight', the move of European children away from the school, which further concentrated Mäori and Pacific Island children in those schools. In this regard Thrupp reported on 'the perceived mandate markets gave to racism and the breaking down of the social fabric of communities' (p. 14). One principal in this study said that before the 1984–90 Labour government's 'Tomorrow's Schools' (Department of Education 1988) reforms, the local primary school had been a feature of our communities and had been a New Zealand 'cultural icon':

> Because that's . . . your family area. That's what *we* recognised as kids . . . and I think that's gone now, and I think the *consequences* are all in terms of dislocation, of people feeling ill at ease where they live, of not liking their community, of not relating.
>
> (p.14; emphasis in original)

Teachers are clearly affected by the social, political and cultural contexts within which they work. Many have felt harmed by changes in their schools and society. The principal referred to above, in Thrupp's study, said that the market model of education was 'destabilising . . . communities. . . . That's terrifying in a way. And I think, for a Labour government to have introduced that, and legitimise that, I think is absolutely appalling, just terrible' (p. 14).

Teachers may be seen as having a role in resisting and overcoming policy and practices they see as harmful to children and to education. One way to do this is to devise ways by which teachers, teacher educators and student teachers may analyse policies and practices for their effects on equity and justice.

Contexts with alternatives

Along with a number of educational (Codd 1999; Thrupp 1998), legal (Kelsey 1993, 1997) and economic (Easton 1997) researchers, I believe that New Zealand has, since 1984, experienced a sustained and highly successful attack on egalitarian values and on policies that might have developed to support a more inclusive society. This has involved changes to the values, practices and language asserted by the dominant power and political groupings to the extent that a new 'culture' of New Right individualism and commercialism is now predominant throughout media and institutional discourse. Many of the students who come into our teacher education programmes are likely to have been socialised into this culture (Mathews 1999) and may have little experience of opposition to the Thatcherian notion that 'there is no alternative'. Will they be inclusive or exclusive in their teaching practices? We may give them theoretical tools of analysis that will help them to see injustice and understand its institutional and structural origins. But if *we* are not supportive of diversity in our institutional (for example, only 6% of New Zealand secondary teachers in 1998 identified as Māori, Te Puni Kōkiri 2001: Fact Sheet 16) and personal practices, our education of student teachers will model neither our stated values and goals nor the praxis we may teach about.

Inclusionist ideology, says Ellen Brantlinger (1997), is 'optimistic about school reform and individual transmutability' (p. 449), focusing on 'ideas for eliminating oppression from social structures' (p. 448). In her analysis, Brantlinger urges that we attend to the power for naming and controlling things that the dominant ideology takes to itself.

In this context I suggest that teacher education should include a focus on issues of oppression, and specifically should address racism, sexism, gay and lesbian issues, and the ideological origins of poverty. What follows are some ideas for introducing student teachers to ways of thinking about the social contexts of teaching and education. The emphasis is on poverty, racism and the role of language in creating and sustaining ideas and values that shape our actions. I draw on the work of others in this area. My thoughts are offered as a contribution to ongoing conversations and actions in and across our various countries and institutions.

A culture of contentment

In the media of the dominant New Right Pakeha culture in New Zealand, there is rarely information or critical analysis about poverty. Nevertheless, our economic and social policies since 1984 have benefited a few and harmed many. Waldegrave (1998) cites a report of the Joseph Rowntree Foundation in Britain that notes that 'income inequality has been growing more rapidly in the UK than in other countries except New Zealand' (Barclay 1995: 14, cited in Waldegrave 1998: 3). Blaiklock (1999) reports that since 1982 the wealthiest 10% in New Zealand have increased their disposable incomes by a third or more, while the poorest decile has experienced a significant decline. O'Dea (2000: 2) says that New Zealand now has 'one of the highest levels of inequality in the OECD'. If we will watch the emergence of increasing inequality, and people in our own communities becoming unemployed and growing poorer, how shall we speak of equity and justice? I think that we do not and, increasingly, will not.

In his analysis of such a context, American economist John Kenneth Galbraith (1992) identifies what he terms a 'culture of contentment' within societies where an economically affluent group supports policies that impoverish a significant proportion of their fellow citizens who become a dispossessed underclass. This situation is explained by the dominant group as natural and inevitable. Wealth and poverty are seen as the outcome of individual effort or lack of effort. Once the poor are held to be accountable for their fate, the wealthy can remain content that a correct moral order is in place. To use taxation to assist the poor is determined to be in error because this is said to reduce the will of the poor to strive to be successful. This simplistic and crude model of human motivation and behaviour ignores alternative models of the causes and effects of poverty. This includes the analysis of 'cultural capital' in which dominant groups design education and other social institutions according to their own cultural wishes and values.

Economist Brian Easton (1997) argues that the New Zealand Treasury is dominated by 'Chicago school extremists' (p. 88) committed to a minimum of taxation and welfare provision. This is a position close to that referred to by Galbraith. Reflecting this ideology in the popular media is a discourse focusing on 'welfare dependency' as a strategy for blaming the poor for their poverty. The slogan 'politically correct' is also used as part of a discourse that is designed to prevent discussion of poverty and racial issues. A language of individualism, populism and simplistic dualism dominates debate and prevents the articulation of alternative positions.

The challenge, therefore, is to introduce students in teacher education to a literature that offers a critical analysis of the New Right project, including important work by New Zealanders such as Jane Kelsey (1993, 1997), who has written about the privatisation of power in this country as the state retreats from a wide area of responsibilities, and Bruce Jesson (1999), who records 'a definite erosion of a sense of community and the spread of an acquisitive individualism' (p. 37). We should discuss the banality and the power of the inevitable comment that when we do this we are being 'politically correct', a slogan meant to suppress dissent from a dominant view. And we should include a focus on the role of language in cultural imperialism.

Culture and language

Gerald Grace (1988) has shown how Treasury advice to the 1984–90 Labour government promoted a new way of thinking about education. This was to be derived from an 'industrial production function' analysis of education, an accounting assessment of 'inputs' and 'outputs' (Grace 1988: 6–7). Treasury set out to ensure that its market analysis became the new model of educational thought and practice. A key strategy was the constant use of the language of libertarian market ideology, with teachers and schools identified as providers, and children, students and parents framed as customers in an educational marketplace.

The cultural, social, emotional, moral and interpersonal complexities of education were thus rendered into a model in which education was a commodity – like food, books, shoes or any other – to be purchased. Treasury and its New Right supporters were successful in commodifying education in New Zealand because this market approach and its language have come to dominate economic, social and political discussion. Qualifications are referred to as 'a form of currency in society' (Barker 1995: 15) and students are 'consumers of services' (p. 20).

The notion of teaching as a commercial relationship of providers and consumers dehumanises the complex nature of student–teacher relationships. The pervasive use of a commercial language in New Zealand is also evident in the area of research. The Foundation for Research, Science and Technology is the major government research funding agency. The foundation has told 'science providers' (which means researchers) that it is 'outcome-oriented', that its funding is through a 'negotiated portfolio purchasing system', and that it has as its goal to 'grow the innovation system' using four organisational units focused on policy, portfolio management, investment operations and corporate development (Thompson 2000). Described in such terms, research becomes just another corporate commodity to be purchased and sold. If that is all a teacher knows as they begin their first year in a classroom, then they will teach the ideas of commerce and commodification to the children entrusted to them, maintaining this new culture and its values through communication in its particular language. The challenge for teacher education is to ensure that student teachers have experience in the critical analysis of dominant discourses and the theoretical knowledge to examine the implications these discourses have for policy and practice.

Challenging racism and other forms of oppression

Education students in New Zealand are likely to be familiar with disparity between Pakeha and Māori school achievement. They may also be influenced by the dominant use of deficit theory to explain this. Their teacher education programmes should require them to look at historical evidence about what has happened to Māori and also to attend to contemporary literature that examines the impact of colonisation on people. For example, the Waitangi Tribunal, established by the government to consider Māori rights and concerns under the Treaty, has said, 'judging by the systems own standards Māori children are not being successfully taught. . .' (cited in Bishop and Glynn 1999, p. 27).

Students could be referred to literature on other indigenous people where there is evidence for similar effects from the colonisation of their language and ways of life (for example, Australian research by Malin (1999) and Wyatt-Smith and Dooley (1997). They might examine New Zealand evidence such as that by Mason Durie (1997) who has shown how imperialist processes such as the Native Land Acts (1862 and 1865),

largely did away with customary land titles, freeing up land for sale . . .
undermining the social links between families and within tribes . . . [so
that] Mäori identity and wellbeing were rendered vulnerable . . .

(Ibid.: 33)

As Linda Tuhiwai Smith (1999) records, the European colonisers 'cut a
devastating swath, and left a permanent wound on the societies and
communities . . . claimed under imperialism' (p. 21).

If your identity is denied, you are wounded by those who take to
themselves the power to name you. Perhaps a language of wounding, harm
and identity may help some student teachers engage with (identify with)
issues of difference and exclusion of which they may be a part. For example,
Nancy Higgins (2001) has described the educational experiences of some
blind people in New Zealand. One of the participants in her study, Stuart,
talked about living in a residential school for the blind, a setting he described
as 'an alien environment' where children 'were forced into believing that
[their] blindness was the only thing that mattered'. This was not the identity
that Stuart had for himself. He reported that he reacted with rebellion,
damaging things and bullying others – comments that may cause a student
teacher to consider the possible contextual origins of aberrant child
behaviours. He said that some of the things he did were 'cruel' but he did
them because 'I wanted to demonstrate . . . that I had no time whatsoever for
the system that they were operating under' (p. 229).

In a study of young lesbians in New Zealand high schools (Vincent and
Ballard 1997), we reported how they came to view themselves negatively in
the context of a dominant homophobic environment. There was evidence in
this account of harm that some of these young people inflicted on
themselves. Jane said:

Basically I came home from school and I was either in my room doing
homework or mutilating myself. I tattooed myself . . . [had] 7 holes in
my ear ... or I was mutilating myself in sport. It was the same thing, the
emotional anguish and pain I felt. I had to take it out on my body . . .

(Ibid.: 154)

We believed that the young people in this study were like those described in
American research by Kissen (1991) who talked of young gays and lesbians
as victims of violence, 'the deep psychological violence of having to deny
who they were in order to protect themselves' (p. 7, cited in Vincent and
Ballard 1997: 158).

Student teachers may read about what is happening to oppressed
minorities and may themselves share such experiences. However, in the New
Zealand context, accounts by Mäori of their experiences under colonisation
seem often to have been suppressed, or action is taken to deny the account

(Consedine and Consedine 2001). The relative invisibility of a Mäori account maintains a context in which the colonisation of Mäori by Pakeha can be seen as a relatively benign and even natural and inevitable event. As the Pakeha version of history remains dominant, Mäori may believe the myths reported about them. Bishop and Glynn (1999) suggest that this creates a 'deeper psychological problem' in which Mäori identity is 'being defined and shaped by non Mäori' (p. 28). This means that I need to interrogate my own role in commenting on Mäori in this paper. I must consider the danger of presenting people as 'other' and the problem of the writer (and reader) as voyeur of minority experiences of which they may not be part.

Such concerns are evident in Merridy Malin's (1999) account of her work in anti-racism in preservice teacher education. The experiences she reports of majority-culture Australian students as they deny, resist and are uncomfortable with work on racism and anti-racism, parallels what we have seen in work in New Zealand. This includes the need to support both majority and minority students through difficult personal, and sometimes transformative, learning experiences of prejudice and identity. Also, attention needs to be given to educating staff and to the possibility of harmful experiences occurring to Mäori and other minority group staff if they present material that students view as unwelcome and reject from a dominant cultural or ideological position.

Adrienne Alton-Lee and her colleagues have modelled ways in which research may be used in teacher education and teacher professional development to critically examine concepts and actions in teaching (Alton-Lee et al. 2000). Using case studies, they focus on striving to make explicit the assumptions and theoretical positions behind teacher actions and behind the reader's interpretations and expectations of those actions. This leads to examination of, for example, ethnocentrism, racism and deficit discourses in the area of disability. Alternatives to oppressive thinking and related actions can then be considered (Alton-Lee et al. 2000). The focus on discussing 'teacher actions' is seen as causing teachers to consider the effects of their actions and to propose alternatives (ibid.: 2000). As Rizvi (1992) suggests, racism may not be overcome by logic but by examining and changing everyday behaviour.

Malin (1999) defines racism as a 'pervasive force permeating . . . people's attitudes . . . the workings of our institutions and the ideological and cultural fabric of society' (p. 9). Rizvi (1990) refers to the complexities of modern racism and its links to a populist nationalism with an emphasis on uniformity and conformity. To challenge culturally biased forms of education and to recognise the powerful, 'non-neutral' role of the teacher requires more than descriptive accounts and inevitably limited (and potentially trivialising) accounts of the minority culture (Rizvi 1992). It also requires more than 'reflective practice' which Smyth (1992) sees as conforming and individualistic, lacking a 'politically informed' analysis (p. 292).

In New Zealand I believe that the complexity of racism needs to include an examination of how the dominant political ideology, through the deliberate creation of poverty, has increased material differences between ethnic and cultural groups. Also, the dominance of the New Right agenda in New Zealand has created a new cultural discourse that, with few exceptions, tells us that there is (still) 'no alternative' to a market model for structuring our educational and other social services. It is utterly clear that in New Zealand such markets create inequality.

The complexity, shifting nature, pervasiveness and significance of racism require our personal response if we are to state a belief in social justice. A colonising discourse creates stereotypes. These justify the dominance of particular 'other(s)' (Bhabha 1994) and maintain the dominant in their 'culture of contentment' (Galbraith 1992). In New Zealand this includes race/ethnic issues but, as economic disparities increase, also includes issues of social class that may, as in England, result in experiences of classist exclusion in teacher education and in schools (Maguire 1999).

If we are to pursue such issues in teacher education programmes, then we may need to challenge ethnic, gender and other discrimination in our institutions – e.g. who is represented on our staff; who gets appointed (and who does not); and how may we actively recruit and support people of minority backgrounds. How might we change our educational environment to make it appropriate and safe for a diversity of staff and students? We should strive to build a climate of trust (Malin 1999) in which issues of social justice and injustice may be addressed by students and staff. We also may need to recognise that work in this area will be difficult and will make our lives uncomfortable. When you challenge the dominant paradigm you will experience a backlash (Heshusius and Ballard 1996). Ideas, ideologies and behaviours that are harmful operate in complex ways. To resist and overturn them requires ongoing analysis and planned strategies for change.

Amongst the various possibilities and imperatives I think there is a need for those of us who are in a majority culture to strive to be aware of oppression and to work toward understanding and action. In that regard I suggest that story (fiction and non-fiction) has a role in communicating complex issues and in linking thought and feeling (Ballard 1994) so long as we are cautious about 'whose stories are used and in whose interest' (Cochran-Smith 2000: 174). There is, I think, something important in identifying with a harmed person. Emotion – including pain and outrage – has a role in prompting people to confront harmful policies and practices.

In a hotel room in Singapore in July 2000, I watched a television interview with French lawyer and writer Serge Klarsfeld who, with his wife Beate Klarsfeld, has brought many Nazi criminals to justice. He talked about his book on the 11,400 Jewish children arrested by French police of the Vichy government and deported from France to be killed at Auschwitz and elsewhere. Klarsfeld, who as a child in 1943 was hidden from the Gestapo by his parents (Klarsfeld 1996: xii), found that some of the murdered French children were recorded only as a number, and 'died nameless to the world'. He said that he prepared the memorial book of their names, addresses and as many photos as could be found to 'strike a blow against anti-Semitism, racism and xenophobia'. In this important and almost unbearable memorial, the 2,500 photographs include images of mothers and their babies awaiting death. On page 29, three infants sit in front of a barbed wire fence. One looks about to crawl toward the photographer. They are in a French concentration camp set up by the anti-Jewish Vichy regime (pp. 4–5).

Klarsfeld (1996) records how more than 75,700 Jews were deported from France to Auschwitz and other Nazi death camps (p. 8). The last convoys left France on 22 August 1944, a few days before Allied troops liberated Paris (p. 92). In the television interview, Klarsfeld was asked how he could comprehend the killings of Nazi Germany, and replied: 'It is six million, but it is one, plus one, plus one, plus one' (interview with Tim Sebastian, BBC World 'Hardtalk', 5 July 2000).

Each child, each person, matters. Dewey (1902: 3, cited in Noddings 1992: 180) suggested that what we want for our own children we should want for the children of others. If we live a privileged life in a culture of contentment, we will not do that.

To challenge a cultural ideology that creates poverty and sustains institutional racism requires, I suggest, political action. We may each have to decide how to respond to that idea and the implications of that for our role in teacher education.

References

Alcorn, N. (1999) 'Initial teacher education since 1990: funding and supply as determinants of policy and practice', *New Zealand Journal of Educational Studies* 34(1), 110–20.

Alton-Lee, A., Rietveld, C., Klenner, L., Dalton, N., Diggins, C. and Town, S. (2000) 'Inclusive practice within the lived cultures of school communities: research case studies in teaching, learning and inclusion', *International Journal of Inclusive Education* 4(3), 179–210.

Alton-Lee, A., Towns, S., Stevenson, M., Diggins, C. and Molloy, C. (2000) 'Making a difference? A role/requiem for classroom research', paper presented by G. Nuthall to the Biannual Congress of the German Educational Research Association, Göttingen, September.

Ballard, K. (ed.) (1994) *Disability, Family, Whänau and Society*, Palmerston North: Dunmore Press.

Barclay, P. (1995) *Joseph Rowntree Foundation Inquiry into Income and Wealth* (Vol. 1), York: Joseph Rowntree Foundation.

Barker, A. (1995) 'Standards-based assessment: the vision and broader factors', in

Peddie, R. and Tuck, B. (eds) *Setting the Standards: The Assessment of Competence in National Qualifications*, Palmerston North: Dunmore Press.

Barton, L. (1997) 'Inclusive education: romantic, subversive or realistic?' *International Journal of Inclusive Education* 1(3), 231–42.

Baxter, J. (1998) 'Culture and women's mental health', in Romans, S. (ed.) *Folding Back the Shadows*, Dunedin: University of Otago Press.

Bhabha, H.K. (1994) *The Location of Culture*, London: Routledge.

Bishop, R. and Glynn, T. (1999) *Culture Counts: Changing Power Relations in Education*, Palmerston North: Dunmore Press.

Blaiklock, A. (1999) 'Seen and not heard? The place of children and young people in Aotearoa New Zealand', paper presented to the Seventh Early Childhood Convention, Nelson, 27–30 September.

Booth, T. and Ainscow, M. (1998) 'From them to us: setting up the study', in Booth, T. and Ainscow, M. (eds) *From Them To Us: An International Study of Inclusion in Education*, London: Routledge.

Boston, J. (2000) 'Book review of Riske, E. and Ladd, H. (2000) *When Schools Compete: A Cautionary Tale*, New York: Brookings Institution Press, *New Zealand Education Review* 19 May, p. 11.

Brantlinger, E. (1997) 'Using ideology: cases of non-recognition of the politics of research and practice in special education', *Review of Educational Research* 67, 425–59.

Bronfenbrenner, U. (1979) *The Ecology of Human Development: Experiments by Nature and Design*, Cambridge, MA: Harvard University Press.

Campbell, G. (2001) 'How to run the country, Part one', *New Zealand Listener* 24 November, pp. 15–17.

Cantillon, B. (1998) 'The challenge of poverty and exclusion', in Hennessy, P. and Pearson, M. (eds) *Family, Market and Community: Equity and Efficiency in Social Policy. Social Policy Studies No. 21*, Paris: Organisation for Economic Co-operation and Development.

Cochran-Smith, M. (2000) 'Blind vision: unlearning racism in teacher education', *Harvard Educational Review* 70(2), 157–90.

Codd, J. (1999) 'Educational reform, accountability and the culture of distrust', *New Zealand Journal of Educational Studies* 34(1), 45–53.

Consedine, R. and Consedine, J. (2001) *Healing our History: The Challenges of the Treaty of Waitangi*, Auckland: Penguin Books.

Davies, L. and Nicholl, K. (1994) *A Statistical Profile of the Position of Māori Across the New Zealand Education System*, Wellington: Ministry of Education.

Department of Education (1988) *Tomorrow's Schools: The Reform of Educational Administration in New Zealand*, Wellington: Government Printer.

Durie, M.H. (1997) 'Identity, nationhood and implications for practice in New Zealand', *New Zealand Journal of Psychology* 26(2) 32–8.

Easton, B. (1997) *The Commercialisation of New Zealand*, Auckland: Auckland University Press.

Evison, H.C. (1987) *Ngai Tahu Land Rights and the Crown Pastoral Lease Lands in the South Island of New Zealand* (3rd edition), Christchurch: Ngai Tahu Māori Trust Board.

Galbraith, J.K. (1992) *The Culture of Contentment*, London: Penguin Books.

Grace, G. (1988) *Education: Commodity or Public Good?* Wellington: Victoria University Press.

Harker, R. (2000) 'The impact of de-zoning on New Zealand secondary schools', paper presented to the New Zealand Association for Research in Education Annual Conference, University of Waikato, 2 December.

Heshusius, L. and Ballard, K. (eds) (1990) *From Positivism to Interpretivism and Beyond: Tales of Transformation in Educational and Social Research (The Mind-Body Connection)*, New York: Teachers College Press.

Higgins, N. (2001) 'Blind People: A Social Constructivist Analysis of New Zealand Education Policy and Practice', Ph.D. thesis, University of Otago.

Jesson, B. (1999) *Only Their Purpose is Mad: The Money Men Take Over New Zealand*, Palmerston North: Dunmore Press.

Kelsey, J. (1993) *Rolling Back the State: Privatisation of Power in Aotearoa/New Zealand*, Wellington: Bridget Williams Books.

Kelsey, J. (1997) *The New Zealand Experiment: A World Model for Structural Adjustment?* Auckland: Auckland University Press/Bridget Williams Books.

Kissen, R.M. (1991) 'Listening to gay and lesbian teenagers', paper presented at the Annual Meeting of the National Council of Teachers of English, Seattle.

Klarsfeld, S. (1996) *French Children of the Holocaust: A Memorial*, New York: New York University Press.

Maguire, M. (1999) 'A touch of class: inclusion and exclusion in initial teacher education', *International Journal of Inclusive Education* 3(1), 13–26.

Malin, M. (1999) '"I'm rather tired of hearing about it . . ." Challenges in instructing an effective anti-racism teacher education program', *Curriculum Perspectives* 19(1), 1–11.

Mathews, P. (1999) 'Right on: the generation who have inherited the Rogernomics revolution come of age', *New Zealand Listener* 9 October, pp. 19–22.

Ministry of Education (1998) *Nga Haeata Matauranga. Annual Report on Māori Education 1997/1998 and Direction for 1999*, Wellington: Ministry of Education.

New Zealand Council of Christian Social Services (1999) *Facts and Figures about Food Banks and Income Inadequacy,* Wellington: NZCCSS.

Noddings, N. (1992) *The Challenge to Care in Schools: An Alternative Approach to Education,* New York: Teachers College Press.

O'Dea, D. (2000) cited in New Zealand Press Association report, 'Income gap widens', *Otago Daily Times* 10 June, p. 2.

Orange, C. (1989) *The Story of a Treaty*, Wellington: Allen & Unwin/Port Nicholson Press.

Rizvi, F. (1990) 'Understanding and confronting racism in schools', *Unicorn* 16(3), 169–76.

Rizvi, F. (1992) 'Racism, multiculturalism and the cultural politics of teaching', in Logan, L. and Dempster, N. (eds) *Teachers in Australian Schools: Issues for the 1990's*, Canberra: The Australian College of Education.

Saul, J. R. (1997) *The Unconscious Civilization*, Ringwood, Victoria: Penguin Books.

Scott, D. (1975) *Ask That Mountain: The Story of Parihaka*, Auckland: Reed/Southern Cross.

Skrtic, T.M. (1995) 'Deconstructing/reconstructing public education: social reconstruction in the postmodern era', in Skrtic, T.M. (ed.) *Disability and Democracy: Reconstructing (Special) Education for Postmodernity,* New York: Teachers College Press.

Smith, L.T. (1999) *Decolonizing Methodologies: Research and Indigenous People,* London/Dunedin: Zed Books/University of Otago Press.

Smyth, J. (1992) 'Teachers' work and the politics of reflection', *American Educational Research Journal* 29(2), 267–30.

Smyth, J. (1993) 'Introduction', in Smyth, J. (ed.) *A Socially Critical View of the Self-Managing School*, London: The Falmer Press.

Sylvia, C. and White, B.C. (1997) 'Diversifying the curriculum: a moral imperative', *International Journal of Inclusive Education* 1(3), 283–301.

Tapp, J. (1998) 'Hidden poverty and education', paper presented to the Fourth National Foodbank Conference "Hidden Poverty in New Zealand", Wellington, 13–14 November.

Te Puni Kōkiri: Ministry of Māori Development (1998) *Progress Towards Closing Social and Economic Gaps Between Māori and Non-Māori*, Wellington: Te Puni Kōkiri.

Te Puni Kōkiri: Ministry of Māori Development (1999) *Fact Sheet 3: Māori Unemployment*, Wellington: Te Puni Kōkiri.

Te Puni Kōkiri: Ministry of Māori Development (2000) *Progress Towards Closing Social and Economic Gaps Between Māori and Non-Māori: A Report to the Minister of Māori Affairs*, Wellington: Te Puni Kōkiri.

Te Puni Kōkiri: Ministry of Māori Development (2001) *Fact Sheet 14: Te Māori i Nga Kura Tuatahi: Māori in Primary Schools'*, Wellington: Te Puni Kōkiri.

Te Puni Kōkiri: Ministry of Māori Development (2001) *Fact Sheet 16: Te Māori i Ngä Kura Tuarua: Māori in Secondary Schooling*, Wellington: Te Puni Kōkiri.

Teachers Council (2002) 'Summary of institutions whose teacher education programmes have teacher registration board approval', Wellington, 10 April.

Temm, P. (1990) *The Waitangi Tribunal: The Conscience of the Nation*, Auckland: Random Century.

Thompson, S. (2000) 'Moving into higher gear', *Foundation* March, No. 39, p. 2.

Thrupp, M. (1998) 'The mapping schools in an international market', paper presented to the 'Mapping the Cumulative Impact of School Reform' Symposium, New Zealand Association for Research in Education Conference, Dunedin, University of Otago, 3–6 December.

Vincent, K. and Ballard, K. (1997) 'Living in the margins: lesbian experience in secondary schools', *New Zealand Journal of Educational Studies* 32(2), 147–61.

Waldegrave, C. (1998) 'Balancing the three E's, equality, efficiency and employment', *Social Policy Journal of New Zealand* 10 (June), 1–14.

Waldegrave, C., King, P. and Stuart, S. (1999) *The Monetary and Consumer Behaviour in New Zealand of Low Income Households*, Wellington: Family Centre Social Policy Research Unit.

Waldegrave, C., Stephens, B. and Frater, F. (1995) *Most Recent Findings in the New Zealand Poverty Measurement Project,* Wellington: Family Centre Social Policy Research Unit.

Wards, I. (1968) *The Shadow of the Land: A Study of British Policy and Racial Conflict in New Zealand 1832–1852*, Wellington: Government Printer.

Weisman, E.M. (1998) 'Preparing teachers to transform the world: Freire's pedagogy and teacher education', in Darder, A. (ed.) *Teaching as an Act of Love: Reflections on Paulo Freire and his Contributions to our Lives and Work*, Los Angeles: California Association for Bilingual Education.

Wyatt-Smith, C. and Dooley, K. (1997) 'Shaping Australian policy on cultural understandings: alternative approaches to inclusive education', *International Journal of Inclusive Education* 1(3), 267–82.

Chapter 5

'Sometimes I two-times think . . .'

Competing interpretations of inclusion for language minority students

Thor Ola Engen

> If one were to choose one key word to sum up the many political goals that Norwegian educational policy in our century has aimed for, it would have to be equity.[1]

Introduction

In this chapter, I will argue that inclusion has been interpreted in at least two ways, emerging from two separate discourses on equity. While one is connected to the mainstream school, the other is associated with a striving for equity for minorities. As the mainstream interpretation is dominant, it has, however, been implemented also among minorities, with considerable negative pedagogical effects. I will argue that the interpretation associated with a discourse on equity for minorities should be implemented among minorities, and could, in principle, function as a more comprehensive interpretation. This, however, presumes that it is understood and accepted in schools. Teacher educators have a formidable task introducing the concept of equity, so that it can be reinterpreted in the context of a multicultural society.

Inclusion as an ideology for the arrangement of general education has received considerable support during the last decades. The history of Norwegian primary education indicates, that a striving for inclusion has been the dominant tendency (cf. Dokka 1967: 403–9; Nilsen 1993: 163; Vislie 1990; Haug, this volume). For more than a century the school system has been systematically developed to function as an equitable institution, because it has been conceived as the central instrument in a more comprehensive process of changing society. The concept of inclusion, however, as well as perspectives on the process, have changed over the decades and vary in different educational contexts. For these reasons, inclusion may be ambiguous, especially in practising teachers' minds.

One reason for the ambiguity can be found in the special nature of teachers' professional knowledge, which is shaped to a great extent by organising principles which may lie in the past and can become lost from view.

Eisner (1991) analyses teachers' professional knowledge according to the concept of 'connoisseurship', the mix of experience and knowledge, habits of mind and talents of improvisation that teachers bring into play as they teach or observe the teaching of others. 'Connoisseurship' is influenced by teachers' fundamental theories and perspectives. Theories and concepts create windows through which teachers observe life in the classroom, locating certain phenomena in the centre of attention and moving others to the background.

Similarly, the 'craft knowledge' possessed by teachers is neither simply a technical skill, the application of general principles to practice, nor critical analysis. It involves 'situated-practice', a 'teaching sensibility' which is adapted to learners, curriculum content and local procedures. (Grimmet 1991; Leinhardt 1990). Craft knowledge and connoisseurship are learnt gradually in the course of a career of teaching (Goodson and Ball 1985; Nias 1989; Sikes *et al*. 1985). Attitudes, points of view, values and interests which inform teachers' professional identities do not disappear when new and competing ideologies are introduced and receive verbal support. Established frames of reference only move into the background, or 'freeze', being contained in the structure as 'frozen ideologies'. Thus they become one of the many layers of historical premises which influence institutional life (Liedman 1997).

Below, I aim to show that while inclusion as a term appeared rather late in pedagogical discourse in Norway, the processes it refers to are familiar. It was introduced into a strong tradition, with both ideological and practical aspects, that constituted a historically determined context for the interpretation of the concept. Thus, there may be a lack of correspondence between inclusion as a 'sent message' – as it is presented in this volume – and inclusion as 'received message', as it has been practised in schools.

Two phases in the development of inclusion

A striving for inclusion has been dominant for more than a century. Two distinctive phases may be identified in this process, the first focusing on equal rights and equal possibilities for social groups of varying backgrounds, the second focusing on social integration of individuals, not least pupils with special needs.

The first phase

From the beginning of the nineteenth century the school system of Norway was dual. The governing classes and the city bourgeois attended 'the learned school' which qualified students for the university and the most important work opportunities. Children of farmers, fishermen and workers attended the ordinary state school (*almueskolen*), which qualified them first for Christian confirmation, and then for marriage and life. The school system thus consolidated the class divisions in society and made social mobility by means of education almost impossible.

From around the middle of the nineteenth century a strong opposition against this dual system emerged. The so-called 'school opposition', proposed a common school for all children, a *'folkeskole'*, to embody the acknowledgement and establishment of equal rights and equal educational possibilities for all pupils, quite independent of their social and regional backgrounds. In 1889 the main principles of this philosophy were realised, as an Education Act was passed, making the first five years of the ordinary state school in urban municipalities a foundation for the middle-school stage of the learned school. In 1920 the common school was expanded to all the seven years of the *'folkeskole'* (Ness 1989: 111), and up to the 1950s even the rural ordinary state school was strengthened to such a degree that it qualified students fully for secondary education, opening the doors to the universities for children of all social and regional backgrounds (Ness 1989: 220–1). Moreover, by the end of the '1960s all sorts of organised streaming had been removed from the lower secondary level, so that the common school for all was expanded to nine years. The principle of equal rights and equal possibilities were therefore secured, and the idea of *the unitary school* had been established as far as social and regional backgrounds were concerned (Telhaug 1970). By this stage of development the idea of the 'unitary school', had practically become a moral category (Nilsen and Qureshi 1991: 92ff.) and hardly open to challenge.

However, equal rights and equal opportunities were restricted, in practice, to pupils with sufficient intellectual ability to reach a certain minimum academic standard, corresponding to the entry requirements of the learned school (Stang Dahl 1978; Haug 1998). Children with special educational needs were not allowed to attend (Ness 1989: 193).

As the development of the unitary school was looked upon as the central instrument in the general process of changing society, teacher recruitment and teacher training naturally were of central concern during the whole period. It has been argued that the teachers in Norway were an avant-garde in the struggle for equity, especially in the first half of the twentieth century, when what Slagstad calls 'the Liberal Party State' emerged as a framework for social and cultural improvement. Accordingly, Norwegian teachers were trained in the spirit of the unitary school, and a large majority of them dedicated themselves to the realisation of the programme. Thus Norwegian teachers of this period were called the 'Liberal Party Teachers' (Slagstad 1998).

The identification of teachers with the central causes of the Liberal Party, however, created yet another characteristic of Norwegian teachers and teacher education. In the middle of the eighteenth century Norwegian schools were still Danish institutions on Norwegian ground, both as far as language and cultural content were concerned. The second most important consideration for the school opposition and the 'Liberal Party Teachers' was therefore to develop a national educational system built on Norwegian culture and language. The school was considered a main instrument in the project of building a Norwegian nation in its own right, as well (Hvenekilde *et al.* 1996). Cultural homogeneity was to be promoted by the new unitary school, and curricula were developed to support such a process (Angell 1998: 167).

The strength and appeal of the project dedicated to one culture, one language and one people, created deeply rooted egalitarian *and* nationalistic attitudes in the Norwegian mentality. All ethnic groups apart from '*det nasjonsbærende folket*'[2] were considered 'strangers', the voice of minority groups being overlooked or even suppressed. While the Sami population, the indigenous population in Northern Norway and elsewhere in Northern Europe, had been taught by means of textbooks in religion written in the Sami language as early as in the seventeenth century, and while bilingual textbooks were developed and distributed in the eighteenth century, Norwegian authorities in the 1880s decided that all instruction should take place in Norwegian, and that all teaching in Sami should be prohibited. Sami-speaking pupils were not even allowed to use their own language in private conversation (cf. Darnell and Hoëm 1996; Ness 1989). The important decision made by Norwegian authorities in the 1880s, that all children had a right to receive instruction in their own regional language was not considered relevant for Sami children (Darnell and Hoëm 1996: 100–1). But as the nation-building project was in articulate opposition to Danish (and Swedish) cultural colonialism, Norwegian nationalism was openly and clearly associated with ideas of emancipation. Norwegian teachers were not opposed to the assimilative strategy, but carried it out with dedication, precisely because the unitary school was so closely associated with cultural emancipation and democracy.

As the nation-building process introduced a long period of severe assimilation of minority groups (Eitinger 1978, 1981; Haagensen *et al.* 1990), the early organisation of the Norwegian primary school may be considered as a prototype of what Baker (1996) calls a submersion programme, or what Skutnabb-Kangas *et al.* (1986) call a strategy of strong, brutal assimilation. The consequences were poor achievement and a low sense of well-being and self-esteem among Sami pupils. And while assimilation was dominant in most other western societies in the same period as well, it lasted longer in Norway than in most comparable societies. For example, the Norwegian Parliament decided that Finnish no longer could be used as a pedagogical aid as late as in 1936.

As this long-lasting paradigm received almost unconditioned support and identification from teachers, it is reasonable to believe that it constituted both their professional thinking and their perspectives on the organisation of schooling. My suggestion is that Norwegian teachers were trained to identify with the principles of equity *and* cultural homogenisation as twin values which occupied such a position in the teacher culture and in individual teachers' minds, that they functioned as a self-evident background for connoisseurship. Thus these twin values also constitute core principles of the historical context in which Norwegian teachers develop their situation-dependent praxis, as the theory of 'situated practice' suggests.

The second phase

During the twentieth century two parallel discourses emerged, both influencing the agenda for a further development of the unitary school. On the one side Sami activists along with a few social scientists and teachers built up a gradually stronger argument for an educational system built on Sami culture and language for Sami children, which began to receive recognition politically in the 1960s. The use of the Sami language and culture in school was thus given a legal platform and even some room in the curriculum in 1972. In the national curriculum of 1987 a more comprehensive plan for Sami education was introduced, with functional bilingualism formulated as an objective, while the curriculum of 1997 was even published in one Norwegian and one Sami version, leaving substantial room for Sami cultural content (cf. Darnell and Hoëm 1996; Øzerk 1997, 1999). This development has been followed by proposals for reforms in Sami teacher education.

On the other hand, as children with special educational needs were not accepted in the unitary school from the beginning, a debate on this injustice also grew gradually stronger, reaching a peak in the 1960s. There was widespread participation in this debate from politicians, as well as educationalists, teachers and parents, and there was a gradual reduction in the numbers of children excluded from the mainstream, until by 1975 laws on special and mainstream education were integrated to support a single system. This changed the character of the mainstream unitary school to a degree, and it may be considered as introducing a second phase in its development. According to Haug (this volume) one important aspect of this process was the adoption of the inclusive school idea.

Two perspectives on inclusion

The change of perspective as far as the education of Sami pupils is concerned indicates that the ideological paradigm for school development had been changed in a less homogenising direction. It seems that Norwegian educational authorities had learned a lesson, not least from the poor school results of Sami pupils. In support for this argument, we may add that a pluralistic ideology was introduced as a framework for including other pupils with a linguistic minority background, who began to appear in small numbers in Norwegian elementary schools in the late 1960s and early 1970s. Formally the new strategy of inclusion was labelled *integration*, but the concept was defined in explicit opposition to the former strategy of assimilation (Kommunal-og arbeidsdepartementet 1973: 17; Kirke-utdannings- og forskningsdepartementet 1995a: 12). As the children should no longer simply be treated as foreign-language speakers in a majority-language speaking mainstream school, the new strategy of integration may be called 'incorporation' (Eidheim 1971), implying that the school is adjusted both structurally and with regard to content, to the pupils' collective needs as an ethnic group, and that Sami pupils should be integrated as a group, not as individuals (Engen 1996). This strategy was not, however, followed by national guidelines concerning pupils with a linguistic minority background (Bjørkavåg 1990: 178).

On the other hand, the changes growing out of the parallel debate on the inclusion of pupils with special needs had a somewhat more ambiguous character. Haug (1998) has identified two central characteristics of the inclusive school emerging in this period. Social integration seems to be the superior consideration, in the sense that all children were expected to receive instruction in one and the same mainstream classroom, even when they were in need of special education. Further, mere physical integration of individuals was considered insufficient. Any pupil – without regard to individual dispositions – should have a right to be integrated socially and functionally as well (cf. Haug, this volume). This particular strategy thus seems to contain two interdependent and successive stages, desegregation followed and completed by functional social interaction between pupils, at least in theory (cf. Sletta 1984: 218). In practice withdrawal of children from mainstream lessons for special attention remained commonplace.

The other important consideration as far as the second phase of the unitary school is concerned was that pupils no longer should be expected to reach a certain minimum level of achievement, as was the case earlier in school history (Tønnessen 1995: 103; Tønnessen og Telhaug 1996). Further, instruction should no longer be considered a collective enterprise administered for groups of children, but should have an individual direction, being adjusted to the disposition of each individual child. As all decisions concerning subject matter, teaching methods, progression and other aspects of the concrete arrangement of instruction were considered a matter for negotiation at the same time, the code of instruction was fundamentally changed. A new and superior principle guiding all teaching was formulated in the terms of individually adjusted instruction (Haug 1998).

From this analysis we may conclude that the social and functional integrating aspect of the old unitary school was firmly strengthened in its new version, as the school should be open for all, without any exception. As the minimum standard of achievement was removed, being considered unrealistic for some pupils, and as even subject matter was considered a matter for negotiation, the nation-building function of academic content became less evident. The superior challenge for the teacher was to arrange instruction so that pupils could participate in curricular activities at their own level of functioning. These characteristics are easily understandable in light of the context they emerged from, but applied to linguistic minority children, they may be problematic.

Adjusting to minority pupils' needs can be done, then, in two ways. The task may be conceived from an individual perspective, as in the case of pupils with special needs, the main challenge often being to identify a suitable level for instruction. But in the case of Sami children, however, inclusion may also be conceived from a mainly cultural perspective, emphasising the selection of a suitable cultural context for instruction as the primary concern.

The strategy adopted for pupils with special educational needs may imply that the mainstream majority cultural context as well as the language of instruction is taken for granted as a neutral framework for curricular participation. This is illustrated by Stangvik's statement: 'The problem is not to define what should be considered as a normal way of life, but what means are necessary to achieve it' (Stangvik 1987: 25). If this is true, the culturally homogenising aspect of schooling is still present, but in a more concealed shape, and the inclusion strategy will still have the old assimilative functions, making subject learning an equally challenging task for linguistic minority children, as it had been for Sami children. Following Skutnabb-Kangas *et al.* (1986), a strategy that takes majority culture for granted may be called soft, humane assimilation – soft and humane, because it offers instruction that is individually adjusted as far as level is concerned.

This argument shows why the strategy growing out of the debate on the inclusion of pupils with special needs is ambiguous. It is not obvious from Haug's analysis (cf. Haug, this volume) that the mainstream majority culture should be taken for granted, especially as even subject matter is supposed to be a matter of negotiation. But since the task of selecting a suitable content seems to be left to a majority teacher, without any support from the National Curriculum, it is reasonable to suspect that majority culture will be assumed. There are, however, two additional arguments to support the assumption that the dominant Norwegian inclusion strategy actually does take the majority culture for granted. I will go on to present those two arguments.

Governmental guidelines

In a paper for Parliament in 1995, the government outlined central principles for the education of Sami children as well as for children with a linguistic minority background (Kirke-utdannings- og forskningsdepartementet 1995). In an analysis of this paper I have compared the guidelines to a set of criteria corresponding to the concept of incorporation, introduced earlier (Engen 1995). The analysis showed that even if the government paper uses the term integration as an overall term for both the Sami and other linguistic minority contexts, concept content varies fundamentally. As far as Sami children are concerned, all the criteria of the concept of incorporation are satisfied. As far as pupils with a linguistic minority background are concerned, however, none of the criteria are satisfied. Even if the government paper talks about equal participation and equal rights in both cases, equality seems to be connected to linguistic minority pupils as individuals only. They are not granted any rights as members of a minority group. Further, all parameters are satisfied if we compare the governmental guidelines for linguistic minority pupils to a set of criteria for assimilation. The term integration therefore has different conceptual connotations in the two contexts. In the Sami context it corresponds to incorporation, in the context of other linguistic minorities, it comes very close to assimilation, i.e. participation on majority cultural terms.

Further, it seems that incorporation as a strategy towards Sami pupils is chosen because of the educational needs of Sami pupils, as the government paper emphasises that pupils should be allowed to develop bilingualism, bicultural competence and ethnic identity. If this rhetoric were to be taken seriously, however, one would expect that it be made relevant for linguistic minority pupils in general, as they may be considered to have exactly the same educational needs. But as we have seen, this was not the case.

The real reason for the distinction made between the two groups seems to be that other linguistic minority children do not have the same legal rights as Sami children. This is owing to the fact that Norway has signed a number of international agreements concerning the civil rights of indigenous people, agreements that later have been confirmed in national legislation. The actual background for choosing incorporation as a strategy in the Sami context therefore seems to be of a formal and legal character.[3]

In my opinion, this indicates that the government actually did not acknowledge the principle of incorporation as a pedagogical strategy, and that its fundamental preference for a strategy of inclusion was (soft, humane) assimilation. Thus the government indirectly supported the idea that elementary schooling should preferably have a culturally homogenising, if not necessarily a nation-building function. Under such conditions it would not be surprising if schools felt free to take the majority culture for granted. Let me take a look at this option.

Teachers' understanding of integration

My second argument for the assumption that the prevailing Norwegian inclusion strategy takes the majority culture for granted, is empirical, deriving from a study where I interviewed a sample of teachers and analysed community level curricular documents (Engen 1994a, b). The results of the study showed that the respondents both explicitly and implicitly supported an interpretation of integration corresponding to assimilation. At the same time they were explicitly in opposition to a concept of integration as incorporation. This was the case even if the respondents probably knew – or at least were supposed to know – that integration as incorporation at that stage was the official national policy (cf. above).

My interpretation of the data was that local authorities and teachers did not openly oppose national policies. However, their understanding of the integration concept emerged from their context of interpretation, which was the strong, almost moral tradition of the unitary school, where the core twin values were equity, without concern for social or regional background, interwoven with cultural homogenisation.

Thus the teachers were not conscious proponents of assimilation, a term deriving from an ideological context they were unfamiliar with, but strong opponents of any kind of segregation. They accepted cultural homogenisation as a latent function, as long as the minority pupils were allowed to work at their own speed, according to the principle of individually adjusted instruction. The respondents showed no awareness that initiatives established from this perspective could discriminate culturally and pedagogically against minority pupils. Teachers and local authorities thus interpreted integration spontaneously in a way corresponding closely to the characteristics identified by Haug, taking for granted the majority culture as a common frame of reference.

It therefore seems that a strategy of inclusion corresponding to the concept of incorporation has little general support in the Norwegian school system, even if it is accepted in the Sami context. This paradox is supported by Juell (1992: 45), who suggests that all work concerning linguistic minorities has been a side track in the administrative system. It further seems that the dominating strategy objectively – if not subjectively – has strong assimilative connotations. As in the EU-countries and the USA, Norwegian authorities may have been tempted by the positive connotations of pluralism, at the same time considering minority languages – and cultures – as associated with differentiation, not unity, and segregation, not integration (cf. Baker 1996; Engen and Kulbrandstad 1998). I will argue, however, that incorporation has important advantages for all linguistic minority children.

Home language competence

> Sometimes I two-times think . . . I think like in my family and in the house. And then I think like in school and other places. Then I talk. They aren't the same, you know.[4]

Most linguistic minority children grow up in bilingual contexts. The home language is their main tool of communication in domains covering family and everyday domestic affairs, not to mention everyday culture and values. Thus they practise the majority language to a minimal and the minority language to a maximal degree in situations where existentially important topics are discussed, and in situations where conversation and linguistic requirements exceed everyday language. This naturally affects both the quality and quantity of language exposure and practice.

The use of the majority language will be determined first by what majority domains are actually open to minority children and, second, by the degree of their involvement in these domains. It seems, however, that minority preschool children's majority language practice is often restricted to informal inter-ethnic peer activity, in or outside kindergarten (cf. Øzerk 1992). Participation in informal activity is still sufficient to enable minority children to develop a certain majority linguistic competence. Phonology and even morphology will be quite well developed, as these aspects of linguistic competence are established relatively early. Vocabulary, however, will probably be restricted. According to Schmitt and McCarthy (1997: 103) the 2000 most frequent words in a language provide approximately 96% coverage of spoken discourse, even with adult speakers. Thus a maximum vocabulary of 2,000 words will be sufficient for effective communication in any everyday conversation. Similarly, syntax will be restricted by the narrow expectations of informal peer communication. Thus minority children's majority language skills are described as restricted to Basic Interpersonal Communication Skills (BICS) (Cummins 1980, 1983), defining a level of competence that majority children practice in informal activity, and that minority children need only a couple of years to develop. The concept further indicates that minority children relatively fast may become quite proficient within the range of the 2,000 most frequent words.

Minority children's' majority language BICS, however, reflects only a narrow range of their total linguistic competence (see Lundberg et al. 1994; Høien et al. 1994; Kulbrandstad 1997: 143–4), as they have coded most of their basic experiences by means of the home language. Only if their two languages are counted together do minority children have a size and depth of vocabulary that equals the average level of monolingual majority peers (Romaine 1995; Saunders 1983). In a study of school beginners in Oslo, Bjørkavåg (1990) observed that minority pupils had better home language than majority language skills, and they scored considerably lower than their majority peers in the majority language. In a recent study Sand and Skoug (2002) confirmed that minority children were far behind majority peers in majority language development, even if they were able to communicate quite well. This difference will affect minority children's readiness to take up the fundamental task of the first years of education, which is literacy development.

Development of literacy skills

As Oakhill and Graham (in Kulbrandstad 1996: 74ff.) point out, there are two principal aspects of becoming a skilled reader; acquiring *decoding* skills and learning to go beyond the decoded words to extract the author's message. As Wong Fillmore and Valadez point out:

> Decoding is obviously an aspect of reading, but few of us would call it 'reading'. By reading, we refer . . . to the act of *reconstructing the meaning of a text* as intended by the writer, and through this process, *gaining access to the information that is encoded in the text.*
>
> (Wong Fillmore and Valadez 1986: 661)

Acquiring technical decoding skills is most efficient when children are allowed to read material that reflects a world that is familiar to them, in a language that they already know (cf. Vygotsky 1978: 117–18). Text-based discussions not only make fragments of the past more available, but also establish a new method of uniting the elements of past (and distant) experience with the present. As private spontaneous experiences are being articulated and coded, they create conscious awareness, i.e. of the situation or the context and language. Even through reading instruction, conscious awareness is developed, confirming Baker's (1996: 301) proposition that one's cultural heritage is discovered and internalised through reading. But the basic and tacit prerequisite is that meaning, vocabulary and language structures can be taken for granted when reading.

If reading materials, however, are based on a taken-for-granted majority cultural background and are introduced in the majority language, minority children are doubly disadvantaged. Linguistically their disadvantage is illustrated by the interval between a majority language BICS of about 2,000 everyday words, compared to about 8–10,000 words, which according to Viberg (1993, cf. Crower and Wagner 1992), is the average vocabulary of a majority school beginner. Culturally they are disadvantaged because reading materials not only reflect unfamiliar majority cultural experiences, but also do so without acknowledging it.

While the silent presuppositions of such reading texts will be easily reconstructable for most majority children, they will be unfamiliar to minority children, awakening few associations. Following an argument of Bøggild Mortensen for Denmark:

> . . . one cannot claim that [Turkish pupils] feel alienated by the open message which they like the Danish pupils, learn to acquire if they have sufficient linguistic familiarity with Danish to participate functionally in the learning process. What they feel alienated by is the silent language, which conditions the 'spirit' of the classroom, and which the Danish pupils have internalised during their primary socialisation in the family (Bøggild Mortensen 1989: 162, 163). . . . For this reason: '. . . immigrants . . . struggle hard to grasp the "basic narrative", which is an organic condition of life in the host country. They see only the "simple story" . . .'
>
> (Bøggild Mortensen 1989: 156, after Houggaard, my translation)

The dominant strategy of Norwegian schools is to make introductory reading material as simple as possible, both linguistically and with regard to substance. This may, however, have a rather paradoxical effect as far as minority pupils are concerned. On the one hand elementary language use makes 'the open message' relatively easy to decode mechanically. Further, as the Norwegian national curriculum for the elementary level recommends that instruction should be organised in a way that allows pupils to interpret communication by means of non-linguistic contextual cues, even minority pupils should be able to participate in classroom discourse, creating an impression of adequate linguistic proficiency. On the other hand even linguistically simple introductory texts will be heavily dependent on their implicated context. One may even suggest that the more simple texts are made linguistically, the more their meaning will rest on a silent language or a basic narrative. This means that the comprehension of simple texts is more dependent on a shared context with the reader than more complicated texts, written in a more decontextualized language, which makes some of its presuppositions explicit. The simpler the text is made within a given majority cultural context, the more minority students therefore are at a risk of lacking the kind of knowledge that spontaneous comprehension presupposes.

Minority pupils may thus have insufficient comprehension primarily due to unfamiliarity with the text's implicated majority cultural context. This affects their ability to develop efficient decoding skills. But as they may know the majority language well enough to acquire technical decoding skills, the nature of the reading problems will not be obvious for teachers. The ambiguity of the problem will be reinforced because minority pupils create an impression of sufficient language mastery. Because teachers are trained to believe that reading material *is* simple, taking the cultural context of texts for granted, they might – like Norwegian special pedagogues (Böyesen 1987) – easily interpret reading problems as due to undeveloped technical skills (cf. even Skrtic 1995: 250).

Accordingly, teachers may concentrate individually adjusted instruction on pupils' decoding skills, gradually changing reading instruction to a mainly mechanical enterprise (cf. Bergman 1994: 20–1), so that minority pupils will have to concentrate even more on the 'simple story'. In this way they will lead attention further away from content comprehension and verbalisation of cultural experiences, be it minority or majority based, reinforcing minority pupils' initial handicap.

The gap is widened

I do not argue, then, that minority pupils will not make any progress in reading, particularly since a large proportion of them can be expected to work really hard (Engen *et al.* 1996), but they will have to invest their effort in mechanical decoding. Erstad (1990: 176, 202) shows that even older, strongly motivated minority children are often left to learn their lessons by heart. And as efficient decoding is dependent upon comprehension, minority pupils' reading skills will develop more slowly than those of majority pupils, with a risk that they will not develop fluency. In this way, minority pupils have a reduced opportunity to develop a deeper comprehension of the majority culture by means of reading, reinforcing their initial lack of linguistic competence. Where majority pupils by means of reading begin to develop a conscious awareness of the language and the situation, minority pupils struggle with efficient decoding skills and comprehension.

It is not surprising that Kulbrandstad (1997: 143–4) finds that minority pupils have severe problems reading and writing fluently in Norwegian, both after three and eight years of systematic majority language instruction (cf. Kulbrandstad 1996: 167; Engen *et al.* 1997).

The distance between the groups regarding reading skills will therefore not decrease by means of individually adjusted instruction, which is the most widespread expectation, but increase (cf. Thomas and Collier 2002). Individually adjusted instruction which takes the majority culture as given is so inefficient that it is tempting to agree with Baker (1996: 127), that certain literacy teaching strategies may function as a mechanism of suppression.

Consequences for inclusive school development and teacher education

If the educational programme places no emphasis on the minority language, or on minority cultural topics, submersion will be its function (Tosi 1988; Hvenekilde *et al.* 1996). A paradigm allowing differentiation only according to individually conditioned needs is therefore also insufficient. Some grouping according to minority pupils' bilingual and bicultural predisposition must be permitted. I only have room to mention two ways in which this can be done (for a more comprehensive discussion, see Baker 1996).

At the initial elementary level it seems most reasonable to enable minority pupils to learn reading and writing in their home language. Home language-based literacy training should, however, last for longer than it takes to be able to crack the reading code. It should last for as long as it takes to establish fluent reading skills. Generally, one may suggest that the longer the period, the better the chances are to succeed (cf. Thomas and Collier 2002)[5]. An estimated minimum period for such a task may be four years.

The main advantage of this model is precisely that it allows minority pupils an opportunity to establish fluent decoding skills by enabling them to take comprehension for granted, at the same time as they develop conscious interpreting skills and conscious awareness of language and the situation. Giving introductory literacy instruction in the home language will, however, also require that the pupils receive parallel instruction in the majority language as a second language.

Further, it seems reasonable to give minority pupils home language support when they study subject matter, administered through so-called bilingual subject instruction (see Wong Fillmore and Valadez 1986: 654), requiring either a bilingual teacher instructing bilingual (and monolingual) pupils, or two co-operating teachers in one classroom (see Øzerk 1997, focusing on Sami experiences). Bilingual subject instruction allows minority pupils to utilise their home language to develop scientific conceptual tools. For example they can develop concepts in arithmetic by means of the home language, and then quite easily transform them to the majority language, when their second language competence has developed sufficiently. One need not learn to multiply twice.

These consequences have, in fact, been recognised formally in the Norwegian 1997 National Curriculum for the primary school, in accordance, however, with a strategy of soft, humane assimilation (Øzerk 1997). But they have been implemented in the classrooms only to a modest degree (Engen 1994b; Nedberg 1997; Engen and Kulbrandstad 1998: 215–17; Andersen 2002; Engen and Ryen 2002) and seem to have close to no room at all in the curriculum of teacher training (Engen and Ryen 2002).

One restriction attached to bilingual subject instruction is that the minority pupils' home cultural experiences are ignored, communicating an implicit message that they are of secondary value. This may alienate the pupils from curriculum content, and reduce motivation. In any case, it will make it difficult for them to interpret, comprehend and articulate their own cultural background by means of curriculum contents. If the monocultural curriculum which is taken for granted were reformulated, however, to reflect a variety of cultural backgrounds, and even adding a comparative perspective to classroom discourse (Engen 1989), both majority and minority pupils' cultural background would be recognised more completely. This strategy has been implemented in the latest Norwegian elementary school curriculum in religion and philosophy.

Acknowledging minority pupils' bilingual and bicultural predisposition, however, requires that teachers develop an understanding of how the cultural background of children can be used and recognised in ways that promote learning. As shown earlier, teachers' craftsmanship must be adjusted, whenever conditions change, as theories and concepts function to organise and enlighten the school landscape, at the same time as they also move certain areas in the background. To enlighten new areas and change the perspective of the teachers' professional perception, thereby bringing new phenomena into perceptual focus, one needs new theories and concepts. According to Jordell (1986) socialisation to the challenges in school may take place almost unconsciously, as long as one is only expected to make minor adjustments. But when the challenge is to develop an understanding and acceptance of integration as incorporation, my argument indicates that minor adjustments are not sufficient. In this particular case, a more fundamental shift is required, more like what Kuhn (1972) calls a shift of paradigm.

At least three major consequences may be suggested for teacher education. First, teacher training students need to be educated to understand and accept cultural diversity in general, not only variation related to ethnicity, but variation related to all kinds of subgroups in (post)modern society. It is important to develop an understanding that even majority culture is a highly heterogeneous entity. Therefore focusing exclusively on individualised instruction, at the same time as the mainstream majority culture is taken for granted, is an insufficient paradigm for teachers, even if it may be an inherent function of the old unitary school's homogenising paradigm, influencing thinking as a frozen ideology.

Second, all the subjects of the teacher-training programme – from religion to mathematics – need to be perceived from a multicultural perspective. This argument is illustrated by the way literacy is analysed in this chapter, and how the subjects of religion and philosophy have been reformulated in Norway. Even majority pupils will, however, profit from such an approach (Collier and Thomas 2002). Studying Norwegian as a second language will raise majority students' consciousness of their language, and studying Christianity as compared to Islam or Hinduism will raise their awareness of religious values and practices in general, hopefully making majority teachers better prepared to teach both majority and minority pupils, and all groups of pupils more culturally conscious and tolerant.

Third, all teacher-training institutions should seriously try to recruit bilingual students and staff, for at least two reasons. On the one hand, teachers who share minority pupils' cultural and linguistic backgrounds will be more sensitive to minority pupils' reactions and have an intuitive readiness for adjusting instruction to minority pupils' educational motives and needs (cf. Au and Jordan 1981; Romaine 1995: 280). This will be the case not only when teachers with a minority background support majority teachers during bilingual subject lessons, but also, for example, in intro-ductory literacy teaching, not least if and when teaching has to be conducted in the majority language. Moreover, it is of fundamental importance for both majority and minority pupils, and not least for democracy, that minority representatives hold visible and valued positions in the educational system. Recruitment of minority background teachers should therefore be a major concern of any inclusive ideology.

Notes

1 Lars Roar Langslet, former conservative secretary for church and education.
2 Translated this means something like 'the population carrying the task of building a nation forward in Parliament and various official positions'.
3 Romaine 1995: 246 mentions a parallel case from the Netherlands, referring to the education of children from Friesland as compared to other minority groups.

4 Buffy, 5 years, cited in Walsh 1991: vii.
5 Anders Bakken, personal communication, paper in press.

References

Andersen, S.I. (2002) *Loven, læreplaner og den flerkulturelle virkeligheten, hovedfag i flerkulturell og utviklingsrettet utdanning*, Høgskolen i Oslo.

Angell, S.I. (1998) 'Norsk målungdom : har NMU vorte ein organisasjon berre for dei som er "omvende" til nynorsken?', *Syn & Segn* 104(2), 166–71.

Au, K.H.P. and Jordan, C. (1981) 'Teaching reading to Hawaiian children : finding a culturally appropriate solution', in Trueba, H.T., Au, K.H.P. and Guthrie, G.P. (eds) *Culture and the Bilingual Classroom: Studies in Classroom Ethnography*, Rowley, MA.: Newbury House.

Baker, C. (1996) *Foundations of Bilingual Education and Bilingualism* (Bilingual Education and Bilingualism, 1), Clevedon: Multilingual Matters.

Bergman, P. (1994) 'Invandrareleverna och deras förutsetningar', in *Att undervisa invandrarelever i svenska: kommentarer till kursplaner i svenska och referensmaterial i svenska som andraspråk*, Stockholm: Statens skolverk: Liber Distribution.

Bjørkavåg, L.I. (1990) *Rapport fra førsteklasseundersøkelsen i prosjektet 'Språk og undervisningsmodeller'*, Oslo: Utdannings- og forskningsdepartementet.

Bøggild Mortensen, L. (1989) *At være eller ikke være: tyrkisk ungdom i København og Ankara*, København: Akademisk forl.

Crower, R.G. and Wagner, R.K. (1992) *The Psychology of Reading: An Introduction*, New York: Oxford University Press.

Cummins, J. (1980) 'The entry and exit fallacy in bilingual education', *NABE: The Journal for the National Association for Bilingual Education* 4(3), 25–59.

Dahl, T.S. (1978) *Barnevern og samfunnsvern: om stat, vitenskap og profesjoner under barnevernets oppkomst i Norge*, Oslo: Pax.

Darnell, F. and Hoëm, A. (1996) *Taken to Extremes: Education in the Far North*, Oslo: Scandinavian University Press.

Dokka, H.J. (1967) *Fra allmueskole til folkeskole: studier i den norske folkeskoles historie i det 19. hundreåret*, Oslo: Universitetsforlaget.

Eidheim, H. (1971) *Aspects of the Lappish Minority Situation*, Oslo: Universitetsforlaget.

Eisner, E.W. (1991) *The Enlightened Eye: Qualitative Inquiry and the Enhancement of Educational Practice*, New York: Macmillan.

Eitinger, L. (1981) *Fremmed i Norge*, [Oslo]: Cappelen.

Engen, T.O. (1989) *Dobbeltkvalifisering og kultursammenlikning: utkast til en oppdragelses- læreplan- og planleggingsmodell*, Vallset: Oplandske bokforlag.

Engen, T.O. (1994a) 'Lærerskjønn og bedømmelse', in Hvenekilde, A. *Veier til kunnskap og innsikt*, Oslo: Novus.

Engen, T.O. (1994b) 'Integrering – som normalisering eller inkorporering, in Hvenekilde, A. *Veier til kunnskap og innsikt*, Oslo: Novus.

Engen, T.O. (1995) 'Integrering og likeverdig deltakelse?: et kritisk blikk på Stortingsmelding nr 29', *Norsk pedagogisk tidsskrift* 79(6), 319–24.

Engen, T.O. and Ryen, E. (2002) *Senter for kompetanseutvikling i den flerkulturelle skolen (SEFS): en underveisvurdering utført på oppdrag av UFD: foreløpig og fortrolig rapport*, Hamar: Høgskolen i Hedmark.

Engen, T.O. and Kulbrandstad, L.A. (1998) *Tospråklighet og minoritetsundervisning*, Oslo: Ad Notam Gyddendal.

Engen, T.O., Sand, S. and Kulbrandstad, L. A. (1997) *Til keiseren hva keiserens er?: om minoritetselevenes utdanningsstrategier og skoleprestasjoner: sluttrapport fra prosjektet 'Minoritetselevers skoleprestasjoner'*, Vallset: Oplandske bokforl.

Erstad, K. (1990) *Norge som flerkulturelt samfunn: kulturelle og samfunnsmessige faktorer av betydning for utvikling av kunnskaps-, verdi- og identitetstilknytning hos barn av pakistanske foreldre i Oslo*, Oslo: Universitetet i Oslo.

Goodson, I. and Ball, S.J. (1985) *Teachers' Lives and Careers*, Issues in Education and Training Series, 3, London: Falmer Press.

Grimmet, P.P. (1991) 'Teacher's craft knowledge as a basis for theorizing about practice in teacher education: keynote address', Research Conference of the Norwegian National Council for Teacher Education on Mentoring New Teachers in Teaching Education, Elverum, Norway.

Haagensen, E., Kvisler, L. and Birkeland, T.G. (1990) *Innvandrere: gjester eller bofaste?: en innføring i norsk innvandringspolitikk*, Oslo: Gyldendal.

Haug, P. (1998) *Myrlandet: spesialundervisning i grunnskulen 1965–1991* (Spesialundervisning og lærarutdanning, 1), Volda: Høgskolen i Volda og Møreforskning, Volda.

Hvenekilde, A., Hyltenstam, K. and Loona, S. (1996) 'Språktilegnelse og tospråklighet', in Engen, T.O. and Hvenekilde, A. (eds) *Minoritetselever og språkopplæring*, Vallset: Oplandske bokforl.

Høien, T., Tønnessen, F.E. and Lundberg, I. (1994) *Kor godt les norske barn?*, Stavanger: Senter for leseforskning.

Juell, N. (1992) *Flyktninger: nasjonalt ansvar, lokal utfordring*, Oslo: Kommunenes sentralforbund: Kommuneforlaget.

Jordell, K.Ø. (1986) 'Lærersosialisering – yrkessosialisering av voksne, in Vaage, S.G., Mandal, G. and Jordell, K.Ø. (eds) *Hvordan lærere blir til*, Oslo: Universitetsforlaget.

Kirke-utdannings- og forskningsdepartementet (1995) *Om prinsipper og retningslinjer for 10–årig grunnskole: ny læreplan* (St.meld, 1994–95: 29), Oslo: Departementet.

Kirke-utdannings- og forskningsdepartementet (1995a) *Opplæring i et flerkulturelt Norge*, Oslo: Nov.

Kommunal- og arbeidsdepartementet (1973) *Innvandringspolitikk* (Norges offentlige utredninger, 1973: 17), Oslo: Universitetsforlaget.

Kommunal- og regionaldepartementet (2000) *Nasjonale minoritetar i Noreg: om statleg politikk overfor jødar, kvener, rom, romanifolket og skogfinnar* (St.meld, 2000–2001: 15), Oslo: Departementet.

Kuhn, T.S. (1972) 'Scientific paradigms', in Barnes, B. (ed.) *Sociology of Science: Selected Readings*, Harmondsworth: Penguin Books.

Kulbrandstad, L.A. (1996) *Lesing på et andrespråk – en studie av fire innvandrerungdommers lesing av læreboktekster ter på norsk*. Avhandling for dr. art.-graden, Oslo: Universitetet i Oslo.

Kulbrandstad, L.A. (1997) *Språkportretter: studier av tolv minoritetselevers språkbruksmønstre, språkholdninger og språkferdigheter*, Vallset: Oplandske bokforl.

Leinhardt, G. (1990) 'Capturing craft knowledge in teaching', *Educational Researcher*, 19(2), 18–25.

Liedman, S.E. (1997) *I skuggan av framtiden: modernitetens idéhistoria*, Stockholm: Bonnier Alba.

Lundberg, I., Høien, T. and Tønnessen, F.E. (1994) *Norsk leseundervisning i internasjonalt lys*, Stavanger: Senter for leseforskning.

Nedberg, A. (1997) *Lite, men godt?: en rapport om tilrettelegging av undervisning for elever fra språklige minoriteter i Troms*, Tromsø: Høgskolen i Tromsø, Avdeling for lærerutdanning.

Ness, E. (1989) *Det var en gang: norsk skole gjennom tidene*, Oslo: Universitetsforlaget.

Nias, J. (1989) *Primary Teachers Talking: A Study of Teaching as Work*, London: Routledge.

Nilsen, S. (1993) *Undervisningstilpasning i grunnskolen – fra intensjoner til praksis : en kildeanalytisk og deskriptiv-analytisk studie*, Oslo: Universitetet i Oslo, Institutt for spesialpedagogikk.

Nilsen, S. and Qureshi, N.A. (1991) *Utfordringer i sosialt arbeid med flyktninger og innvandrere*, Oslo: Kommuneforlaget.

Resnick, L. (1991) 'Situations for learning and thinking', recipient's address for the award for distinguished contributions to educational research 1990, American Educational Research Association, Chicago.

Ricoeur, P. (1971) 'The model of the text: meaningful action considered as a text.' *Social Research* 38(3), 529–62.

Romaine, S. (1995) *Bilingualism*, Oxford: Blackwell.

Sand, S. and Skoug, T. (2002) *Integrering – sprik mellom intensjon og realitet?: evaluering av prosjekt med gratis korttidsplass i barnehage for alle femåringer i bydel Gamle Oslo: rapport 1*, Elverum: Høgskolen i Hedmark.

Saunders, G. (1983) *Bilingual Children: Guidance for the Family*, Clevedon, Avon: Multilingual Matters.

Schmitt, N. and McCarthy, M. (1997) 'Editors comment', in Schmitt, N. and McCarthy, M. (eds) *Vocabulary: Description, Acquisition and Pedagogy*, Cambridge: Cambridge University Press.

Sikes, P.J., Woods, P. and Measor, L. (1985) *Teacher Careers: Crises and Continuities*, London: Falmer Press.

Skrtic, T.M. (1995) 'Deconstructing/reconstructing public education: social reconstruction in the postmodern era', in Skrtic, T.M. (ed.) *Disability and Democracy: Reconstructing (Special) Education for Postmodernity*, New York: Teachers College Press.

Skutnabb-Kangas, T., Kangas, K. and Kangas, I. (1986) *Minoritet, språk och rasism*, Stockholm: Liber.

Slagstad, R. (1998) *De nasjonale strateger*, Oslo: Pax.

Sletta, O. (1984) 'Sosial inkludering og ekskludering i skoleklasser', in Skaalvik, E.M. (ed.) *Barns oppvekstmiljø*, Oslo: Aschehoug/Tanum-Norli.

Stangvik, G. (1987) *Livskvalitet for funksjonshemmede: normaliseringsprinsippet som grunnlag for forbedring av livskvalitet*, Oslo: Universitetsforlaget.

Thomas, W. and Collier, V. (2002) 'A national study of school effectiveness for language minority students' long-term academic achievement', CREDE, http://www.crede.vcse.edn/research/llaa/1.1_final.html

Tosi, A. (1988) 'The jewel in the crown of the modern prince: the new approach to bilingualism in multicultural education in England', in Skutnabb-Kangas, T. and Cummins, J. (eds) *Minority Education: From Shame to Struggle*, Clevedon: Multilingual Matters.

Tønnessen, L.K.B. (1995) *Norsk utdanningshistorie: en innføring*, Oslo: Universitetsforlaget.

Viberg (1993) 'Andraspråksinlärning i olika åldrar', in Cerú, E. (ed.) *Svenska som andraspråk. Mera om språket och inläringen*, Lärarbok 2, Stockholm: Utbildningsradion, Natur och Kultur.

Vislie, L. (1990) 'Evaluation and political governing in a decentralized educational system', in Granheim, M., Kogan, M. and Lundgren, U.P. (eds) *Evaluation as Policymaking: Introducing Evaluation into a National Decentralised Educational System*, London: J. Kingsley.

Vygotsky, L.S. (1978) *Mind in Society: The Development of Higher Psychological Processes*, Cambridge, MA: Harvard University Press.

Vygotsky, L.S. (1987) *The Collected Works of L.S. Vygotskii: Problems of General Psychology* (including the volume *Thinking and Speech*), New York: Plenum Press.

Walsh, C.E. (1991) *Pedagogy and the Struggle for Voice: Issues of Language, Power, and Schooling for Puerto Ricans*, New York: Bergin & Garvey.

Wong Fillmore, L. and Valadez, C. (1986) 'Teaching bilingual learners', in Wittrock, M.C. (ed) *Handbook of Research on Teaching*, New York/London: Macmillan/CollierMacmillan.

Øzerk, K.Z. (1992) *Tospråklige minoriteter: sirkulær tenkning og pedagogikk: presentasjon og drøfting av teorier, hypoteser og forskningsresultater*, Haslum: Oris.

Øzerk, K.Z. (1997) 'Tospråklig opplæring og funksjonell tospråklighet', in Sand, T., Bøyesen, L., Øzerk, K.Z., Stålsett. U.E. and Grande, S.Ø. (eds) *Flerkulturell virkelighet i skole og samfunn*, Oslo: Cappelen akademisk forl.

Øzerk, K.Z. (1999) *Opplæringsteori og læreplanforståelse: en opplæringsteoretisk, læreplanteoretisk og pedagogisk-filosofisk tilnærming til grunnskolens opplæringspraksis og de nye læreplanverkene L97 og L97 Samisk*, Vallset: Oplandske bokforlag

Chapter 6

Qualifying teachers for the school for all

Peder Haug

Introduction

The main issue discussed in this chapter is the extent to which teacher education qualifies new teachers for working with absolutely all pupils in the compulsory school, with a focus on special education. The chapter presents a particular understanding of inclusive education. This is used as a reference in the presentation and discussion of a study of Norwegian teacher education, with a focus on how teachers are prepared for implementing the inclusive ideas. The results from this study are not very promising when it comes to the competence of new teachers for meeting the heterogeneity of the pupil population in a school for all. In the last part of the chapter these results are analysed and discussed.

Inclusive education

Inclusion and the school for all are really difficult to define formally. There are many examples of definitions being closely questioned and discussed (Barrow 2000; Thomas 2000; Vislie 2000; Wilson 2000). There are at least two different levels of definition. One concerns the ideology- and value-orientation in inclusive education. The other deals with how these should influence educational practice. I concentrate my efforts on the latter aspects, leaning heavily on among others Howe (1997) and Persson (2001) when it comes to fundamental value questions.

Booth (1996) argues that inclusion involves two processes, namely increasing pupils' participation within the culture and curricula of school, and decreasing exclusion from school culture and curricula. I share his understanding, but want to identify some crucial and more detailed aspects of the inclusion process as well. I argue for four important tasks for the school for all to address and to continually develop for each student:

- To increase fellowship. All children should be a member of a school class and take part in social life at school together.

- To increase participation. Genuine participation, as distinct from being an onlooker, involves two processes: the creation of opportunities for everyone to be involved socially with others, and the active encouragement to be involved.
- To increase democratisation. All voices should be heard. All students shall have the opportunity to comment upon and to influence matters concerning their own education.
- To increase benefit. All students should have an education that enables them to learn and participate.

During the last part of the twentieth century children who for different reasons had been excluded from ordinary classes and schools in Norway, as in many other nations, were gradually moved from homes, institutions, special schools and special classes and into the neighbourhood school. Without exception, all pupils in Norwegian compulsory school (age 6–16), at present, must be a member of a regular class, where ordinary teachers have the main responsibility for the teaching. To teach all children together under the concept of the school for all has become one of the most basic aspects of schools in Norway (Vislie 1990), and it has long enjoyed support from a majority of politicians, teachers' unions, teachers and parents. This is the consequence of adopting the inclusive school concept, or the school for all, the end of a long process of development in Norwegian educational policy. Research being done indicates that there still is some way to go before these ambitions are achieved in the Norwegian compulsory school (Dalen and Skårbevik 1999).

A decisive question is whether, and if so how, this development should affect teacher education, here explicitly referring to teacher education for the compulsory school. There are many reasons for discussing whether teacher education more or less passively should mirror the full activity of the compulsory school. One most important objection to this is that teaching is not a technical and rational implementation of what at any given time is politically decided nationally or locally. Teaching presupposes advanced values, skills and knowledge that cannot be changed by way of single and simple measures. Teacher education also prepares teacher students for an occupational career lasting 30 to 40 years, involving the need for a much wider and more general approach to qualification than for what goes on in compulsory school at any given point in time. Nevertheless, the inclusive school concerns fundamental values and goes to the root of questions concerning education. Therefore, the significance of this issue for teacher education cannot be neglected or argued against under the cover of instrumentalism or because it is thought to be of short-lived importance. It is my belief that a premise for realising the inclusive school is that all general teachers must be prepared to meet, recognise and understand all sorts of pupils and classroom situations and act accordingly, irrespective of the children's ability, interests, talent, gender, class and ethnic background. This educational policy should concern teacher education, and this has in fact also been official policy in recent years. Departmental circulars and the prevailing national curriculum for teacher education have formulated expectations indicating that all programmes and activities in teacher education are to prepare the students for these tasks.

This does not mean that all teachers should acquire full competence in whatever specialities are required for meeting all the children's needs and idiosyncrasies. This is not practical, it is not possible, it is not necessary and it is a misunderstanding. It is my opinion that very few pupils will be in a situation where their education is dependent upon their daily meeting advanced specialist competence. Instead, teacher education must give all the teacher students a competence that makes them able to meet and teach the range of variation in or the heterogeneity of the pupil population, and when it is a necessity, be able to receive counselling from people with specialist competence.

In this article I view these fundamental questions from the vantage point of special education. This is not done because special education is necessarily a more important matter than other challenges in the school for all. Neither has special education heavier responsibilities than other areas when is comes to implementation of the school for all, although individuals representing the field of special education have shown greater interest than most others in the inclusive school (Allan 1999; Christensen and Rizvi 1996; Clark *et al.* 1997; Clarke *et al.* 1995; Dyson and Millward 2000; Pijl *et al.* 1997). The term special education actually need not exist in a school based on inclusive ideologies. There every pupil should be challenged according to individual interests, aptitude etc. together with all the other pupils in the class or group. To place a tag on some pupils because, for some reason, they have different needs of support than most others should be of no interest. Yet special education continues to exist as an individual legal right and as an academic field of its own. To what degree and how students in teacher education are being prepared for teaching pupils with special needs could be treated as an important indicator for the position of the inclusive concept of schooling. The assumption is that how teachers have been educated to deal with one of the large vulnerable groups of pupils in school gives a clue to how they are prepared to meet and teach the complete heterogeneity of pupils and therefore the inclusive school.

The present state of affairs

Even though the state of affairs in teacher education concerning this issue has not recently been studied scientifically, long experience of teacher education tells me that the situation is not what it ideally should be. There is no independent central or local evaluation of the competence newly qualified teachers actually possess when they leave the faculty of education. To avoid my own subjective bias in determining the matter, I carried out a survey with teacher students and I did interviews with lecturers on these questions. A sample of 272 students from 8 out of 18 Faculties of Education in Norway answered a questionnaire and I interviewed 18 staff-members from three of these Faculties (Haug 2000a). I studied the compulsory part of teacher education that was common to all teacher students. I did not include options in which at least some students could specialise in teaching children in need of special support. Effectively, the research involved case-studies which provided insight into the influences on the content and teaching approaches within teacher education (Yin 1994).

Both groups of respondents agree that within the general and compulsory programmes, the necessary standards are not achieved when it comes to qualifying the students to teach pupils with special needs and to meet the ideal of an inclusive school. The students, however, are much more negative in their evaluation than the staff members, a general trend in studies of other areas of teacher education (Jordell 1986). Knowledge about how the pupils who are in need of special support may benefit from teaching is very often not included in the preparation of the teachers. Whether the students were given lectures or read prescribed books dealing with special education varied between groups and subjects within a faculty as well as between faculties.

To the extent that the students were studying issues with relevance to special education, the perspectives were out of date. That is, what I have called the first regime of special education (Haug 2000b) and what Dyson (1999) describes as the first wave of special education dominates. The students learned about individual pathology, about individual problem categories and even about different categories of disabilities. The solutions, how to teach these children, were found in diagnoses and individual treatment very often outside the classroom, and not in changing the teaching and learning conditions for the same pupils to create a classroom inspired by the ideas of inclusion. The general picture shows that the students (falsely) learned that they as teachers could leave the children with special needs to the special education support system. They learned about special organisational arrangements for these pupils, and that the special education teachers were to have the full responsibility for their education, not the general teacher.

It seemed quite arbitrary whether students in teacher education were involved in programmes with the intention to make them capable to teach in compulsory school in accordance with the approved and formulated inclusive ideals presented above. So much so, that where the concepts of inclusion and inclusive school were in use, they had got another meaning in teacher education, different from, for instance, that in the national curriculum and in most of the international literature. In some of the interviews with the lecturers in the faculties of education, the respondents believed that they were preparing the students for the school for all. I found the word 'all' to be vague, unclear and ambiguous. When the expression 'school for all pupils' was used, there was always an implicit exception. 'All' would usually mean 'all pupils that can profit from the teaching that goes on'. This I take to mean that the pupils were supposed to adapt to the teaching, not the other way around. Another unifying expression for the understanding of 'all' is that the students of teacher education become qualified for teaching the pupils within the 'normal variation'. This implies that there is a 'not normal variation', dealing with children with different forms of learning problems or facing other problems. One of the respondents put it this way:

> I think that for most pupils with disabilities, you have to be more spec-
> ialised than is possible in general teacher education. I therefore believe
> that it is irresponsible of society to give ordinary teachers the respon-
> sibility for a number of children they are not qualified to teach in the
> best possible way. It is not right for the children or the teachers. As I see
> it, we can try to qualify them to teach within a sort of normality, plus
> and minus.

Another example of how to define 'all' is the perspective given on how to organise the teaching in the compulsory school. In teacher education collective-oriented teaching dominates. The main focus for the teacher students is how to teach whole groups and classes as uniform audiences. The children in need of special support do not necessarily benefit very well from this mode (Kavale and Forness 1999). They are much more dependent upon individually adapted teaching, in class. According to official intentions, for instance, in the national curriculum of the compulsory school this should be the most dominant and most important method of teaching, but it gets less attention in teacher education. In the introduction to this article, I presented four processes in inclusive education to increase fellowship, participation, democratisation and benefit. These are to be understood as crucial develop-ment tasks in all education, to create a school more in agreement with the ideas behind inclusive education. In teacher education all four seem to be neglected when it comes to preparing for the complete heterogeneity of pupils.

Why neglect the inclusive elements?

The results from the study are not very satisfactory, seen from the viewpoint of inclusive education. My own a priori prejudice gained status as a valid conclusion. We are not far from the situation reported by Evans and Lunt (2002). They found considerable obstacles in meeting the wide range of individual needs when striving to move school closer to the ideals of inclusive education. In my case, the lecturers seem not to be especially aware of inclusive education at all. At best the situation can be compared with what Cuban (1993) has named hybrids, a combination of different approaches, a little of everything.

A relevant question is why teacher education in Norway has neglected this very important element. Why have we not been able to realise what has been formulated in the national curriculum for the compulsory school since 1974, and in the national curriculum for teacher education since the 1980s? I have at least two reasons for asking this question. One is that this is not the only case where one can register similar conditions, lack of change. Intellectually I am curious as to why this very central issue of educational policy has not been followed up. The second is that to be able to produce strategies for how to proceed to improve the situation, it is important to understand and explain these findings as well as possible. Only a broad and thorough understanding of internal and external processes in teacher education would suffice as a background for developing teacher education. It is my intention here to give some initial explanations of my findings. One must also have in mind that no simple or easy way exists by which to reach the ultimate goal of the inclusive school. Several paths could lead forward, therefore it is important to allow for diversity and openness in the development of both the school and teacher education.

I will try two different approaches. First, could it be that the members of the faculties of education do not have the knowledge, the capacity or the will to become involved in this issue of the inclusive school? Are they, in one way or another, against the construction of it, or the ideology behind it? The other approach is wider. To develop inclusive education is a big challenge. Has teacher education on an institutional level developed adequate strategies for continually implementing new external expectations and duties?

In my research there are examples of both. I find several examples of individual resistance towards qualifying teacher students for the school for all, as well as a more general lack of interest in and commitment to change. In the coming presentation and discussion I take both perspectives with me as points of departure. The general issue is change and lack of change in teacher education; to understand this seems to me to be the most fundamental task.

Stability or change?

Is it the case that teacher education does not appear to be especially oriented towards reform or change, and that this could be the reason behind the discouraging results of my study? This question has been raised on general grounds in the research literature many times. I met two different but parallel opinions from my respondents. On one hand, there is no doubt that teacher education has gone through a period of extensive change since the early 1970s. Among other things I would mention that the faculty system has been reorganised. We have introduced new national curriculum plans on four occasions (1974, 1980, 1992 and 1998), partly as consequences of expansion of teacher education, partly because of new political initiatives. New subjects have been made compulsory. The grading system has been changed twice. Lecturers are supposed to spend some of their time doing research. Students must take more responsibility for their own learning. The number of lessons has been reduced. To qualify as a teacher the students have to study twice the length of time (two years' study time before 1974, four years after 1992) etc. With reference to issues like this, some respondents said that teacher education is changing too fast, a reason for not complying with developments: 'We do not recognise the institution from one day to the next. It is impossible to take an active interest in it all.'

A lecturer returning to teacher education as a member of staff 25 years after her own graduation from the same faculty of education gives a second opinion. She described her experience like this:

> It has a very strong tradition. When I started I got a shock. It was almost the same as when I graduated 25 years earlier. I felt that it is the same now as it was then. I simply became surprised.

This lack of change corresponds to what has been found in international research and in recent Norwegian research as well (Adams and Tulasiewicz 1995). If one studies the fundamental conditions, teacher education appears to conform relatively closely to tradition, and to be characterised by a stable collective culture responding slowly to change.

> In looking at the impact of change on teacher education at the macro-level, we are confronted with a lack of significant differences in how teachers have been prepared for their profession since the 1930s.
>
> (Freiberg and Waxman 1990: 622)

In his study of qualifying for occupational ethics in teacher education Bergem (1993) reports similar results. When she analyses student participation in teacher education Kvalbein (1998) concludes in the same way, as is also the case in other research reports (cf. for instance Michelsen *et al.* 1998; NOU 1996: 22).

Notions of too extensive change and almost complete lack of change in teacher education stand side by side. One way of explaining this contradiction is to make a distinction between *arenas of formulation* and *arenas of realisation*. One approach to reform is to formulate intentions about change, without necessarily following this up with action. The arenas of formulation could shadow what actually goes on in an institution in the arena of realisation. Many of the changes being referred to can be understood as formulated intentions, but at least a part of them have not been followed up in practice. They are represented in teacher education texts and discussion, giving the impression of processes of rapid change. It could also be appropriate to introduce the concepts *incremental reform* and *fundamental reform*. Incremental reform is to improve the efficiency and effectiveness within existing structures of schooling. Fundamental reform is permanently to alter the structures of schooling or grammar of schooling (Cuban 1993; Tyack and Cuban 1995). In my study, most of what can be said to be new in teacher education seems to be incremental. Similarly, the changes observed by others in teacher education are also incremental: they are distinct, but they are not far-reaching. This is for instance the situation when it comes to changing subject matter, changing the grading system and most of the other examples given above. It can further be argued that it is a matter of chance whether and to what extent fundamental changes take place in teacher education, no matter how central or important they are, and irrespective of their being formulated in the national curriculum of teacher education. Inclusive education presupposes fundamental change, something completely new.

Explaining lack of change

How can it be explained that teacher education is characterised by fundamental stability. There is no single or simple answer. I will present several different perspectives in the next part of the chapter.

The prevailing reform perspective

In what has been called 'the prevailing reform perspective' (Brunsson and Olsen 1990) change is seen as a result of rational choice, where organisations like teacher education institutions are characterised by a hierarchical view of leadership, steering and power. To make decisions and to implement decisions are seen as two distinct and different matters. The first is an issue for the few politicians. The latter concerns the many, working in, for instance, teacher education. The fact that the expected action is not realised, or does not function is explained with reference to personal and individual weaknesses; among other things it could be bad leadership, lack of will, low interest or competence, lack of clarity in curriculum texts etc. The effort to improve the situation is most often concentrated upon educating or motivating the individuals engaged in the matter. In the research material I find lots of explanations of this kind, referring to individual and technical rationality. Respondents have passed on that:

- The formulations in the national curriculum are not clear or distinct enough.
- The staff are not acquainted with the expectations in the national curriculum.

- They do not know the meaning of different concepts such as adapted teaching, inclusion or for that matter, special education.
- They disagree with what is written in the national curriculum.
- They disagree that special education could be an important matter for teacher students.
- They are negative towards special education and any insights that can offer.
- To develop the necessary competence in qualifying teachers is a matter for other subjects than their own.
- They are not qualified to educate teacher students in this respect.
- There is not time for this part of the syllabus.
- This part of the syllabus is less important than other tasks and issues in teacher education.
- They do as well as they can, this is the result.
- The existing knowledge on how to succeed in developing an inclusive school is not sufficient, there is little to tell the students about the matter.
- It is an impossible task to qualify all the students to teach all pupils in compulsory school.
- To qualify all the students to teach all pupils in compulsory school is a matter for further education for specially interested teachers.
- The dimension of educational science in teacher education is too restricted.
- The students have too little formal knowledge when they start to study.
- The students have no interest in this particular matter.

A key message is that the national curriculum is not very useful as a tool in the world of realities to direct content or methods in teacher education. Curriculum is interpreted very freely by each of the lecturers and from their personal perspectives. He or she considers a series of circumstances other than is signalled in the curriculum text. Many of these have in common one very important element, that is personal interest and involvement. From the interviews, I conclude that a theme in which the members of staff have a burning interest, is almost guaranteed a central position in course literature and in teaching, even if it is not important from the perspective of the national curriculum. A theme in which no one on the staff is interested will not be present in literature or teaching, even if it is very central in the formulations in the national curriculum. This is what I have named 'anarchy', giving teacher education the character of a private enterprise. This explanation is related to a whole series of research results dealing with the relationship between policy intentions and practice (Crowson *et al.* 1996; March and Olsen 1976).

From this analysis follows the fear that many valuable, necessary and important issues and perspectives in the qualification of teachers could suffer an identical fate as special education and inclusion. The detailed content of teacher education seems to be relatively arbitrary and dependent upon the individual lecturer's teaching. To change teacher education then, you have to convince and motivate the lecturers.

However, it seems difficult to explain the stability and lack of fundamental change typical of teacher education, simply by referring to personal and individual matters. We know that the differences both within and between the faculties of education are great, and that they are as typical as the similarities (Michelsen *et al.* 1998). That gives reason to believe that the results presented here also can be interpreted as consequences of institutional peculiarities. Over the last 40 years or so, teacher education in Norway has moved from a very tightly controlled system into one enjoying relatively broad professional autonomy, and most probably this has resulted in far more variation in teacher education. The different faculties of education themselves define and amplify how to teach and qualify the students within the framework laid down nationally in legislation and in the curriculum. The way this is done is an important issue to look into.

Steering signals from the state

Although there are very few steering signals emanating from the state concerning qualification for special education and inclusion in the national curriculum for teacher education, taken on their own, those that do exist are clear and unambiguous. Viewed in isolation, they cannot be misunderstood, as is the case with other issues in the national curriculum for teacher education. Seen in connection with each other, however, as for instance with regard to gender, ethnic minorities, children from immigrant families, local culture, bullying, etc., the steering signals give contradictory and diffuse messages. Teacher education is supposed to do all the 'right' and 'good' things, where little is given preference and priority. It is not clear for instance what is expected and how teacher education should react when special education and inclusion are seen in connection with all the other tasks that also should be carried out. I also suspect that many lecturers do not know the meaning of several of the fundamental concepts used to describe teacher education and practice.

The ideals are high, the curriculum promises a great deal, probably too much. According to the lecturers I have interviewed it is not possible to accomplish the ideals formulated for teacher education with the available resources and competence. I quote one of them: 'There is a kind of impossibility in all these objectives presented as imperatives, with the short time we have to our disposal . . . it is a ridiculous framework . . .' In policy it is common to formulate higher intentions and expectations than education is able to reach. That is one reason why I prefer to characterise the national curriculum as overdressed and swag gering. This is an example of advanced commercialism and overselling, to borrow concepts from another area

(House 1974). When the actors agree that it is impossible to do what is expected of them, this legitimises the fact that they must do what they themselves think is best, and what it is possible to accomplish. This legitimises a situation in which both individuals and institutions can choose to understand what is meant differently. In the faculties of education within the different subjects taught, there is a sort of competition and tug-of-war as to which themes and issues should have priority, and behind them all we find different individuals.

The fact that curriculum formulations do not necessarily function very well as steering signals should be expected, in general. The content of the curriculum is the result of the efforts of many different contributors with differing interests and views (Pinar *et al.* 1995). In constructing curriculum texts, it is not uncommon to manage conflicting views by including them all in a text, but at a very general level. To really change teacher education, then, curriculum texts have to be more unambiguous, with a clearer and more explicit set of priorities and they must be more practicable.

Professional autonomy

Teacher education is organised as a loosely coupled system both in the relation between faculty and state, as well as the relations within the different structures in the faculty itself (Scott and Meyer 1994). Faculties are organised with different departments. Within this organisation we find many different subjects about which no single person could have total knowledge about. Each of these subjects has its own distinctive character, known only to a very small number of lecturers. Therefore, in practice, common aims and common understanding are difficult to develop. Teacher education becomes fragmented into separate subgroups competing with each other according to their own special interests and traditions. Hargreaves (1995) describes this as 'balkanising'. Under the cover of autonomy, the faculties of education consist of a series of satellites defined by the different subjects flying freely and independently around, where the professional core is difficult to observe.

It seems unrealistic and undesirable to produce curriculum texts telling the lecturers in teacher education in detail what to do and what to think. There must be greater room for professionalism, to avoid instrumentalism. To make local autonomy in teacher education function properly, it is necessary to have what Pinar *et al.* (1995: 848) describe by using the metaphor 'a very complicated conversation'. How to understand the national curriculum must be a part of a living conversation, where everyone whom it concerns participates. From this it follows that everyone lecturing in teacher education together with their students should take an active part in a comprehensive local discussion about what to teach and how to teach to prepare the students in the best possible way for working in school. In this conversation questions dealing with qualifying students for teaching pupils with special needs of support and how to function in the inclusive school should be of utmost importance.

My research and experience indicate that local discussions and co-operation on these matters only take place to a very limited extent. That is, I find active and informal discussions and conflicts of opinion between lecturers within the individual subjects taught in the faculties, but to a far lesser extent between staff representing different subjects within the faculty as a whole. I found no examples where all staff in a faculty had discussed issues dealing with the ideological foundation of teacher education, how best to qualify students for being a teacher, about the meaning of inclusive education, etc. Matters dealing with teacher education in general, and special education in particular, are seldom talked about on an institutional level in teacher education. Partly this is because people are not comfortable in managing the disagreements and conflicts that exist, so that these tensions are rarely brought out into the open. This avoidance of the examination of conflict and hence its resolution is a dominant feature of the cultures of higher education. A more open approach may be discouraged, paradoxically, by the way the national curriculum seeks to establish as a key ideal that there should be harmonious communities, with shared aims and values, in both teacher education and schools. Such institutions may take care to avoid revealing a lack of harmony.

Local autonomy becomes a personal task. It is (mis)understood as an individual responsibility. It therefore becomes very much up to the individual lecturer to formulate and realise his or her own ideology, learning content and practice about how best to qualify future teachers. And since not one of the faculties I have been into has any form of independent internal quality control, except subject exams, which on top of everything they themselves control to a large extent, this can go on without interruption. To change teacher education, then, you have to connect the different interests and institutes more closely, you have to develop an arena for discussion, a culture for managing conflicts and disagreements and internal quality control.

Tradition and collective culture

Teacher education is relatively dominated by tradition. There are beliefs historically situated, widespread and deeply rooted about the nature of knowledge, how teaching should occur and how people should learn. They steer the thinking in teacher education towards certain forms of behaviour. This both strengthens and moderates the 'anarchy'. Tradition is one of the most important elements in keeping the anarchy going, and tradition defines the limits of the anarchy. To put it bluntly, one notion is that things are ordinarily done either very close to the way or in the way that they have always been done in teacher education. This is combined with each lecturer's own definition of what is important from within his or her own subject culture. When new persons are employed, they very quickly become socialised into the established course of action, and represent it in their own teaching (Michelsen *et al*. 1998). When a member of staff for his or her own sake develops an appropriate content and a teaching method that works within this tradition, they very often last for years, and even for a whole career (Bergem 1993; Kvalbein 1998). In this way a collective culture has gradually developed during many years (Kvalbein 1998). Should the curriculum or other important elements of teacher education change, it is not very difficult to reformulate what is new so that it suits what is already done in the faculty and has been done for a long time. In this way education changes the reform, and not the other way around (Tyack and Cuban 1995).

Teacher education becomes filled with what has been called frozen ideologies, traditions and its own specific culture strongly influencing the teaching (Liedman 1997). The faculties appear as both conservative and conserving. One dominating part of this tradition has been not to be very preoccupied with qualifying students to teach pupils with special needs. The general part of teacher education has never actually shown any interest in children with special needs for support. This has been the case since the eighteenth century. At one time this was rooted in the assumptions that some children should be segregated, and were not to be a part of every teacher's responsibility. This notion has also continued to exist in practice, contrary to more recent decisions and intentions. For this reason, teacher education has never in its practice been especially preoccupied with the ideas of inclusive education either. To change teacher education you have to reduce the influence of the established teacher education tradition, and you have to develop the collective cultures in teacher education to incorporate the new ideas you want to develop.

Education development and research

In an analysis of the history of special education in the Norwegian compulsory school (Haug and Tøssebro 1998), I have concluded that no one has developed the necessary knowledge and skills that could enable us to come near to achieving the ambitions of the school for all. The closer we approach the classroom, the less knowledge and fewer skills we have access to that could be of help. To change this is, of course, a responsibility for many parties. In general it is expected that the faculties of education should produce new knowledge through the engagement of lecturers in development and research. The national curriculum also states that the teaching in teacher education should be research-based. If teacher education is to play a part in creating the school for all, faculties can contribute to this intention by doing some of the research and development that is needed, but there are barriers. In general, teacher education has no tradition of or competence in doing research. That this should be a part of the faculties' responsibilities was laid down in the Teacher Education Act of 1973, but it is still a controversial question in the faculties whether it is appropriate to tie up working hours developing new knowledge. The alternative view is that in teacher education teaching is the only important task. Some of my respondents admit that they have great problems living up to academic standards in their research. As argued by Zeichner:

> It is ironic how unscholarly the process of teacher education reform has often been even in institutions that pride themselves on their scholarships and research.
>
> (Zeichner 1999: 12)

This can at least partly be explained by the quality of this research. In an analysis of educational research Lagemann (2000) concludes that Dewey's characteristics of educational research from 1929 has still remained central until the end of the century. His words – *an arm-chair science* – indicate research far removed from practice. What is needed is research that assists practical teaching, executed in close coalition with schools and teachers. However, to change teacher education you have to give research a more dominant role in the analysis and discussions of how to teach and what to teach both in teacher education and in school. Not that research could or should have a monopoly in overcoming these challenges, but it could be redefined so that it makes essential contributions.

Contradictory developments

Power in teacher education can be explicit or more usually implicit. Sarason (1990) claims that to implement reforms, you have to change some of the power structures in education. To do that, you have to master a thorough knowledge about the enterprise to be reformed, and that also presupposes a certain kind of courage. Only then will you touch some of those aspects of culture and tradition necessary for moving towards the ideal of an inclusive school. During the last ten to twenty years we can find several examples of a slow and partly hidden change of power structures in teacher education. At least some of these oppose inclusion. I will give a few examples illustrating the confusion and antagonism in teacher education. If teacher education is to be changed, you have to give power to forces that represent the perspectives that should dominate in inclusive education.

Basic understanding

There is a movement in an instrumental and technical direction in the dominating basic understanding of teacher education at the present time (Telhaug 1997). This occurs at the expense of introducing the students to the general values and historical conditions that are the basis of the school of today. Teacher education gives the students less insight into the foundations of the teaching profession. Yet to work in a school without knowing the assumptions behind its aims will be difficult, perhaps meaningless. How is it possible to know if one is on the right track, or if one is working against important intentions and values that it has taken generations or more to develop? Without this kind of knowledge, how is it possible to be aware of what to fight for or against in order to achieve the highest standards?

The shift in the content of teacher education from principles to the more pragmatic and instrumental will make newly qualified teachers less able to bring about the school for all. The idea of the school for all is the result of more than one hundred years of struggle. During this period many different arguments and solutions have been tried, and many of them rejected. When lecturers and students are not acquainted with this, it is easier for them to be tricked by populist political rhetoric.

Educational theory

Educational theory is one of several compulsory subjects in teacher education, but during the last ten years, less importance has been attached to it. It was here one would find discussions with the greatest relevance for inclusive education through issues like increasing fellowship, participation, democratisation and benefit in a wide sense (see the introduction of this chapter). Instead, more emphasis is given to school-subject learning and school-subject didactics. This has moved the focus in teacher education from this vast pedagogical interest to a much narrower academic subject orientation. As a result, it is likely that newly qualified teachers may be better able to communicate basic subject knowledge to those pupils who are motivated and capable of receiving their message. Pupils who experience difficulties will be the losers, because the teachers will not master the pedagogical part of their duties as well as they should. The counter-argument, of course, is that the prioritising of ways of teaching school-subject should more than compensate for this. My study indicates that this is not the case. This is poorly developed for most school-subjects, at least when it comes to pupils with special needs. Some studies also underline that the main problem in teaching is not that the teachers lack subject-knowledge, but that they have problems organising and practising teaching for the diversity of the pupil population (Engelsen 2000; Ogden 1998).

Special education knowledge

A third example can be found in the development of special education knowledge for the last 25 years. An examination of the research and development work shows two very clear trends over time (Haug 2000b). The research community has not been able to develop sufficient knowledge to carry through differentiated teaching within the class, which is a pre-supposition for inclusive education. Research in these areas has only to a small extent been built on an inclusive perspective. The first generation of special education research as it is described earlier still dominates. There have been power struggles around these interests, of course. Some academics and institutions have actively prevented the new perspectives from gaining precedence in research. Very few seem to be interested in or have the opportunity to study what should or could be done to promote an inclusive school. There are no clear alliances, and there is no distinct centre of power to promote such research. Therefore it is difficult, for those who support the school for all, to promote its development.

From private to public enterprise

The starting point for this chapter was how teacher education qualifies its students to teach all pupils in school, according to the ideas of an inclusive school and the school for all. I approached this issue by studying how teacher students were educated to deal with one of the most vulnerable groups of pupils in school, those receiving special education, which indicates how they are taught to meet the heterogeneity of pupils. What I found was disappointing, both when it comes to what is being done and as regards attitudes and points of view. The school for all does not enjoy strong support in teacher education.

Most attempts to change education and education policy are based on the prevailing and dominating reform perspective. The notion is that formulations in a national curriculum will lead to new content, organisation, practice and quality in teacher education. The study reported here indicates that this is not the case, at least when it comes to qualifying future teachers to teach all children in a school for all. Educational policy makers fail to recognise that what is written and said are not necessarily being put into effect. The results are not unexpected or sensational, they have been repeated in many studies concerning the national steering of education.

That the organisation, content and teaching in faculties of education are far more random than the formulations in the curriculum should imply. It is the circumstances of individual lecturers in the faculty that determine what really goes on in teacher education. I have used the metaphors 'anarchy' and 'private enterprise' about the power and processes which produce the learning content that qualifying teachers are supposed to master. *Seen in isolation,* this can be understood as the consequences of individual choices. This, however, will not explain the more basic question: what allows this personal factor to penetrate an institution like teacher education? To explain this, I needed to look into other mechanisms.

I had to consider a series of factors that regulate the scope for action in teacher education, and which represent the collective teacher education culture and tradition. These include: diffuse national steering signals, local autonomy, organisational 'balkanisation', teacher education tradition, limited education research, and weak strategic use of power. Taken together these elements legitimise a situation in which every lecturer is able to make his or her interpretation.

In summary, I conclude that to change teacher education so that it supports greater inclusion you have to do the following:

- Convince and motivate the lecturers.
- Make curriculum texts about inclusion less ambiguous and more practical.
- Connect the different interests and institutes more closely together, develop an arena for discussion, a culture for managing conflicts and disagreements and internal quality control.
- Reduce the influence of teacher education tradition, and develop collective cultures to incorporate the new ideas you want to develop.
- Give research a more prominent role in the analysis and discussions of how to teach and what to teach both in teacher education and in school.
- Give power to forces that represent the perspectives that should dominate in inclusive education.

References

Adams, A. and Tulasiewicz, W. (1995) *The Crisis in Teacher Education: A European Concern?* London: Falmer Press.

Allan, J. (1999) *Actively Seeking Inclusion. Pupils with Special Needs in Mainstream Schools*, London: Falmer Press.

Barrow, R. (2000) 'Include me out: a response to John Wilson', *European Journal of Special Needs Education* 15(3), 305–13.

Bergem, T. (1993) *Tjener-aldri herre. Om lærerutdanning og yrkesetiske holdninger.* Bergen: NLA-forlaget.

Booth, T. (1996) 'Stories of exclusion: natural and unnatural selection', in Blyth, E. and Milner, J. (eds) *Exclusion from School: Inter-professional Issues for Policy and Practice*, London: Routledge.

Brunsson, N. and Olsen, J.P. (1990) *Makten att reformera*, Stockholm: Carlssons.

Christensen, C. and Rizvi, F. (1996) *Disability and the Dilemmas of Education and Justice*, Buckingham: Open University Press.

Clark, C., Dyson, A., Millward, A.J. and Skidmore, D. (1997) *New Directions in Special Needs. Innovations in Mainstream Schools*, London: Cassell.

Clarke, C., Dyson, D. and Millward, A. (1995) *Towards Inclusive Schools?* London: David Fulton Publishers.

Crowson, R.L., Boyd, W.L. and Mawhinney, H.B. (eds) (1996) *The Politics of Education and the New Institutionalism*, Washington, DC: Falmer Press.

Cuban, L. (1993) *How Teachers Taught. Constancy and Change in American Classrooms 1880–1990*, 2nd edition, New York: Teacher College Press.

Dalen, M. and Skårbevik, K.J. (1999) 'Spesialundervisning på grunnskolens område 1975–1998.' in Haug, P., Tøssebro, M. and Dalen, M. (eds) *Den mangfaldige spesialundervisninga. Status for forsking om spesialundervisning*, Oslo: Universitets-forlaget.

Dyson, A. (1999) 'Important recent developments in special education research', speech, Oslo: Norwegian Council of Research.

Dyson, A. and Millward, A. (2000) *Schools and Special Needs. Issues of Innovation and Inclusion*, London: Paul Chapman Publishing.

Engelsen, B.U. (2000) 'Enkeltfagenes didaktikk: En amputert skolefagsdidaktikk', Norsk pedagogisk tidsskrift.

Evens, J. and Lunt. I. (2002) 'Inclusive education: are there limits?' *European Journal of Special Needs Education* 17(1), 1–14.

Freiberg, H.J. and Waxman, H.C. (1990) 'Changing Teacher Education', in Houston, W.R. (ed.) *Handbook of Research on Teacher Education*, New York: Macmillan.

Hargreaves, A. (1995) 'Realities of Teaching.' in Anderson, L.W. (ed.) *International Encyclopedia of Teaching and Teacher Education*, 2nd edition, New York: Pergamon.

Haug, P. (2000a) *For alle elevar? Lærarutdanninga og spesialundervisninga i grunnskulen,* Volda: Høgskulen i Volda og Møreforsking Volda.

Haug, P. (2000b) 'Regimes of special education research, trends in special education research in Norway', paper at European Educational Research Association, Edinburg 20–23 September 2000.

Haug, P. and Tøssebro, J. (eds) (1998) *Theoretical Perspectives on Special Education Research*, Kristiansand: Høyskoleforlaget.

House, E.R. (1974) *The Publics of Educational Innovation,* Berkley: McCutchan Publishing Corporation.

Howe, K.R. (1997) *Understanding Equal Educational Opportunity. Social Justice, Democracy and Schooling*, New York: Teachers College Press.

Jordell, K.Ø. (1986) *Fra pult til kateter. Om sosialisering til læreryrket, Universitetet i Tromsø*: Rapport Nr. 1, 1986.

Kavale, K.A. and Forness, S.R. (1999) *Efficacy of Special Education and Related Services*, Washington: American Association of Mental Retardation.

Kvalbein, I.A. (1998) *Lærerutdanningskultur og kunnskapsutvikling*, Pedagogisk forskningsinstitutt: Universitetet i Oslo.

Lagemann, E.C. (2000) *An Elusive Science. The Troubling History of Education Research*, Chicago: University of Chicago Press.

Liedman, S.-E. (1997) *I skuggan av framtiden. Modernitetens historia*, Stockholm: Bonnier Alba.

March, J. G., and Olsen, J. P. (1976) *Ambiguity and Choice in Organizations*, Oslo: Universitetsforlaget.

Michelsen, S., Dahl, J. and Homme, A. (1998) *Lærerutdanningen under høgskolere-formen*, Oslo: Norges forskningsråd.

NOU (1996) *Lærerutdanning. Mellom krav og ideal.*

Ogden, T. (1998) *Elevatferd og læringsmiljø*, Oslo: Kirke-, utdannings- og forsknings-departementet.

Persson, B. (2001) *Elevers olikheter och specialpedagogisk kunskap*. Stockholm: Liber.

Pijl, S.J., Meijer, C.J.W. and Hegarty, S. (eds) (1997) *Inclusive Education. A Global Agenda*, London: Routledge.

Pinar, W.F., Reynolds, W.M. Slattery, P. and Taubman, P.M. (1995) *Understanding Curriculum*, New York: Peter Lang.

Sarason, S.B. (1990) *The Predictable Failure of Educational Reform*, San Francisco: Jossey-Bass Publishers.

Scott, W.R. and Meyer, J.W. (1994) *Institutional Environments and Organizations*, Thousand Oaks: Sage.

Telhaug, A.O. (1997) 'Forty years of norwegian research in the history of education', *Scandinavian Journal of Educational Research* 41(3–4), 347–64.

Thomas, G. (2000) 'Doing injustice to inclusion: a response to John Wilson', *European Journal of Special Needs Education* 15(3), 307–10.

Tyack, D. and Cuban, L. (1995) *Tinkering toward Utopia. A Century of Public School Reform*, London: Harvard University Press.

Vislie, L. (1990) 'Evaluation and political governing in a decentralised educational system', in Granheim, M., Kogan, M. and Lundgren, U.P. (eds) *Evaluation as Policymaking*, London: Jessica Kingsley.

Vislie, L. (2000) 'Doing justice to inclusion: a response to John Wilson', *European Journal of Special Needs Education* 15(3), 311–13.

Wilson, J. (2000) 'Doing justice to inclusion', *European Journal of Special Needs Education* 15(3), 279–304.

Yin, R.K. (1994) *Case Study Research. Design and Method,* Thousand Oaks: Sage Publications.

Zeichner, K. (1999) 'The new scholarship in teacher education', *Educational Researcher* 28(9), 4–15.

Chapter 7

Creating structures for inclusive development in teacher education

Kari Nes and Marit Strømstad

Introduction

In this chapter we will first discuss our approach to inclusion in schools and how this relates to the Norwegian legislation. Second, we explore the inclusiveness of teacher education in our institution and how that may influence the students. We will then outline how inclusion is taught formally in pre-service and postgraduate education. Finally we will describe and discuss how staff from the institution have been involved in creating more inclusive schools through a school development project, which functioned as in-service education for teachers who took part. We argue that though policies in many ways are inclusive, the cultures and practices of teacher education are less inclusive. Our suggestion is that inclusion should be put on the agenda through discursive conversations, which may strengthen the consciousness of teacher educators regarding inclusion. A tool in such conversations may be the development of an 'Index for Inclusive Teacher Education'.

Inclusion

In 1997 inclusion was introduced in Norway through 'The curriculum for the 10-year compulsory school' (hereafter L97) (The Royal Ministry of Education, Research and Church Affairs (hereafter RME), 1999a). One of the forerunners of the notion of inclusion was integration. Integration proved to be narrowly interpreted as being mainly concerned with children with special needs. (See Peder Haug's Chapter 6 in this book.)

L97 lays down that schools should be inclusive and accommodate all students. This quote from L97 describes the school which is aimed at:

> The school is a workplace and meeting place for everyone. It is a place where pupils come together, learn from and live with differences, regardless of where they live, their social background, their gender, their religion, their ethnic origin, and their mental and physical ability.
>
> (RME 1999a: 63)

Our experience is that inclusion is interpreted and practised in different ways. We therefore find it useful to present our understanding, which we see as in tune with L97. For three years we have been engaged in a project aiming at evaluating the inclusiveness of Norwegian schools after the implementation of L97. Because we needed to know what to look for in an inclusive school, it was necessary to have a view of the implications of inclusion for the detailed activities in a school. In that process we were informed by the specific questions in the *The Index for Inclusion* (Booth and Ainscow 2000), which we translated and adapted for use in Norway. The Norwegian title is the *Handbook for Inclusion* (hereafter 'the Handbook', Booth and Ainscow 2001). As the Handbook was applied in the school development project described later in this chapter and in our analysis of teacher education, we would like briefly to mention basic concepts from the book as well as our own concretisation of inclusion.

Inclusion in the Handbook

The Handbook invites schools to explore their cultures, policies and practices through a series of indicators and specific questions. Cultures have to do with values. Inclusive cultures create 'a secure, accepting collaborating community' (Booth and Ainscow 2000: 8). Such a community guides decisions about policies, which must be permeated by inclusion. Inclusive practices reflect the inclusive cultures and policies. Such practices reduce barriers to learning and participation for students as well as carers and staff.

When learning does not take place as expected in school, the established view is to look for reasons for the failure in the child. The Handbook consistently avoids the categorisation of students which is an inevitable consequence of focusing on individual needs. It is replaced by the concept of 'barriers to learning and participation'. All participants in a school community can experience such barriers. Focusing on individual categorised needs can impede the school's ability to recognise the properties of their organisation, choice of teaching materials, ways of communicating, etc. which can be real barriers to a learning community for students, carers or staff. An inclusive school aims at identifying and removing such barriers to give optimal conditions for all.

In the Norwegian Handbook 'adapted education' is a significant notion meaning everything a school does to adjust teaching to the diversity of students. Adaptation involves planning the content and teaching material so that it motivates the students to participate in the academic community according to their aptitudes. Two teachers co-teaching in the classroom is an example of adaptation because that makes it easier to give individual support. Another example of adaptation is to divide classes or to teach in groups. Adaptation is essential for success with inclusion. Schools can, however, choose means of adaptation which are not inclusive by giving segregated lessons to some students over an extended period and thus isolate them from the community. Resources traditionally earmarked for special groups should be seen in the total context as contributions to adapted education for all.

Concretisation of inclusion in schools

Related to our project aimed at evaluating inclusion in schools after the implementation of L97 we needed to decide what to look for to appraise inclusive practice. The outcome of this work was a selection of characteristics based on L97, which is consistent with the Handbook. According to L97 students are to be included in a social, academic and cultural community. In order to achieve an academic community where every student has the opportunity to learn according to his or her abilities, teaching has to be adapted. Adapted education is not a new demand in Norwegian schools; it has been an issue in former Norwegian curricula. But to meet the challenge of inclusive education 'adaptation' is a key concept. Adaptation is not only about what to teach and how, but also the ways of evaluating student efforts and achievements. Traditionally, the phrase 'all students' has not necessarily meant all. It is therefore necessary to stress that when we talk about inclusion, 'all' literally means all. Though in our opinion categorisation of students is inconsistent with inclusion because it pre-supposes pathology, it is widely practised not least because a diagnosis may release extra resources. Categorised students and students from minority groups are vulnerable, and schools have to be committed to their right to learn.

If all students are to be part of a shared social and cultural community they require a classroom and school environment which supports the participation of all students regardless of their abilities. The school must realise that every student can experience exclusion, not only students with special needs or students from ethnic minorities. Gender and social class are also issues not to be overlooked.

In the inclusive school students should learn to cooperate together and take responsibility for others as well as for themselves. This implies that students must learn democratic principles through practice. The formally chosen student councils are important areas for democratic learning. So is real participation in decision-making concerning their own learning and the learning environment for other students in schools and classes (Strömstad 2003).

But inclusion does not relate only to students. Parents and carers too, should be given opportunities to take part in decisions concerning their children's situation at school. On the one hand, they have the main responsibility for their children and should have real influence on their learning in schools. On the other hand they represent the local culture which is an important resource for the schools.

Finally the staff plan and perform their teaching in an inclusive environment where they learn from one another, and develop and enrich the community through their active participation. Diversity of both staff and students is regarded as a resource.

Inclusion in teacher education

It takes a lot of knowledge and skills to realise the vision of the inclusive school as formulated in the Norwegian National Curriculum. Teachers are a key factor in such a development. What are the roles of institutions for teacher education in preparing teachers for inclusive schools and supporting schools that want to develop more inclusive practice? The main influences determining teachers' actual practice include their own experiences in school, what they learn theoretically from their lecturers and practically from practice supervisors. The nature of the institution in which they learn to teach also creates messages that they carry with them into their schools. In this section of our chapter we discuss the inclusiveness of the cultures, policies and practices of teacher education.

National prescriptions

'General plan and regulations for General Teacher Education' (RME 1999b) lays down the organisation and subject matter of teacher education in Norway. In its general part, inclusion is mentioned only once with clear reference to students with special needs: 'Teacher trainees should understand how teachers can contribute to inclusive schooling in such a way that students with special needs take part in the social, academic and cultural community in an equitable way' (ibid.: 21, our translation). In the chapter on pedagogy the scope is extended: 'At the core is the discussion on how teacher attitudes, knowledge and skills contribute to the development of an inclusive school by giving good opportunities for social engagement and learning to all students' (ibid.: 41). Inclusive education is not mentioned in any of the other chapters on different subjects in teacher education. However, this cannot be interpreted to mean that pedagogy alone is responsible for teaching inclusion and inclusive practice. The general part of the plan states that the responsibility of teacher education is to 'meet society's need for qualified teachers who can work towards the realisation of the educational intentions and aims' (ibid.: 9). The curriculum also states that teacher education must reflect what is common for all educational work. As inclusion is an important characteristic of the schools described in L97, it seems that teacher education also should be inclusive.

Several of the characteristics listed in our concretisation of inclusiveness are mentioned in the curriculum. The need for adapted education is stated both generally and in chapters on particular subjects. During their education teacher students also should realise the individual student's right to be part of a community and the necessity of cooperation with students, colleagues, and carers. Though no detailed description is given, it is evident that teacher education is meant to prepare for the realisation of inclusive practices in schools.

From August 2003 teacher education in Norway will have a new curriculum. The background is presented in a white paper (RME 2002). As far as inclusion is concerned, this white paper does not seem to signal any significant differences. Adapted education in one school for all is still emphasised, as is participation and cooperation. The multicultural perspective is more emphasised, in general and in all subject areas.

Admission to teacher education in Norway is relatively open. This means that there is no lower qualification limit as long as applicants meet general entry criteria for higher education, irrespective of grades. Students must, however, present police certification establishing that they have never been charged, prosecuted or sentenced for sexual abuse, serious violence or possession of illegal drugs. Apart from these restrictions there are no other selection procedures such as interviews. Thus access to teacher education is regulated by market mechanisms only. Some might say entrance ought to be more exclusive. This open admission policy, however, does not imply that all entrants become teachers. Apart from passing their exams, students must prove fitness to teach. According to prescriptions from RME (1999c) evaluation of students' fitness to teach must run continuously through the four years of education. Both lecturers and practice supervisors are responsible for this. There is a set of criteria for evaluation and these are generally concerned with the students' fitness to work with children in the future. If the student shows a lack of commitment and interest to plan for and work with a group of children, he or she has to be offered supervision and possibilities for development. Possible reasons for the student's non-fitness are not specified. If the student does not improve, a committee is assembled to make a final decision. The student must be informed and given the opportunity to speak for himself or herself. If the committee decides that the student is unfit, he or she can be excluded from teacher education for three years after which he/she is permitted to try anew. These prescriptions cannot in our opinion be regarded as exclusive, but as a necessary guarantee of quality. As there are specific rules for the whole procedure, the chances for arbitrary treatment are relatively small.

Inclusion in our college

The documents quoted above are prescriptive for all teacher education in Norway. They express an inclusive policy, which should influence the practice in all the colleges of teacher education. But colleges also have their local cultures, policies and practices, which may not be quite consistent with various central signals.

A formal evaluation of the inclusiveness of teacher education in our college has not yet been carried out. This part of our chapter is therefore tentative. It is based upon our own experiences, observations and informal conversations with colleagues.

Documents

The college has three local documents worth mentioning because they have to do with our own strategies. One is the strategic plan. It states that our institution should be based on 'the democratic principles developed in our culture: The inviolability and dignity of the individual, freedom of expression, and honesty' (Høgskolen i Hedmark (hereafter Hihm) 2000a: 1).[1] The college shall also have a multicultural perspective and an international basis. In many ways the document reads as if the intention is to be inclusive, though inclusion is not mentioned specifically.

Directed by the state, colleges must have a locally approved 'plan for strategy and actions with regards to disabled students' (Hihm 2000b). The plan in our institution has this vision: 'The college shall be accessible for disabled students so that they can make use of their abilities and possibilities on a par with all other students' (p. 2). It also states that a good college for disabled students is good for everybody. A programme of initiatives to secure the well-being and achievement for disabled students is described. This ranges from physical access to support during lessons and exams. An important issue is to make college staff more conscious of the problems disabled students may face during their study. A social understanding of disability is emphasised. Even then the authors have found it necessary to mention five categories of disability which the college has to accommodate. In spite of this the plan by and large reads as inclusive, apart from the fact that nothing is said about how to encourage disabled students to come to our institution. There is nothing about how to recruit disabled persons, only how to adapt conditions to those who are already admitted. There is no document or evident strategy concerning disabled staff. The reason is presumably that this is taken care of in Norwegian legislation through the law concerning working environment (Arbeids- og administrasjonsdepartementet 1997).

'Action plan for gender equality' (Hihm 1999) differs from the plan concerning disabled students in that central aims in the gender equality plan are to strengthen the position of females in the institution by recruiting female researchers and leaders. There is no formal plan for attracting students or lecturers from minority cultures, but some initiative is taken in that field. New qualification programmes for bilingual early childhood, primary and secondary school staff are also being planned.

Cultures and practices

Central and local documents cited above show that the institution has policies and strategies aimed at inclusion in certain fields. What about cultures and practices? The Department of Teacher Education has so far had very few students with disabilities, and one may wonder why. In our experience this group of students are given at least some support, but they are in no way invited to come. Though the plan is there, the consciousness of the fact that we have disabled students is not always present. A student who was temporarily in a wheel-chair had to be carried downstairs by her fellow students because the elevator was locked at 3.30pm. Though lessons ordinarily finish at that time, students are welcome to stay in the buildings and some even have lessons in the evening. Access was, however, denied to those who could not use the stairs.

We also know that colleagues are doubtful as to the future work of disabled teachers and pre-school teachers. They are not confident that a person who cannot see or hear well can be trusted with a group of children. Educators from the Norwegian language department are currently discussing whether or not students with dyslexia are fit to teach Norwegian. Presumably there is no general answer to this question.

Gender equity is also lacking in practice. The majority of teacher students are female and concerns are sometimes articulated about the failure to recruit more male students into teacher eduction. However, our leaders are mainly men. All the directors and deputy-directors are men. Some 52% of the staff are women, but only 41% of lecturers and professors are women. In our institution only 31% of research reports etc. are written by women.

The authors of this chapter both teach what is called 'pedagogy' in Norwegian teacher education. In our sub-department inclusion is often informally debated. We do not know to what extent inclusion is on the agenda outside our section. With Peder Haug's findings in mind (see Chapter 6), we invited ten colleagues from different sub-departments (mathematics, Norwegian, arts, ICT and others) to an hour's discussion on inclusion. None of the negative attitudes to which Haug refers were voiced during that hour, like resenting the prescriptions in the national curriculum about the school for all or reducing the issue to a matter of special education. We found that our colleagues were positive about inclusion, but that they at the same time felt unclear about what it is and wanted opportunities to discuss it. Among the points emphasised were the following:

- Teachers have to be generous to words, and tolerant of, a diversity of ability, culture and behaviour.
- All children must be heard and recognised as persons in schools.
- Every child must feel that his or her presence is important to others.
- It is important that the child is met with positive expectations.

- Student teachers must learn to realise that some children think differently, but that their thinking is not necessarily wrong.
- Low expectations are exclusive.
- It is important that everybody feels responsible for the well-being and development of the school – students, teachers, other staff, and carers. Cooperation is necessary to succeed.
- Not only students, but staff must feel respected and included.
- Inclusion is a fundamental attitude towards other people.
- It is important to emphasise students' success.
- Student teachers must learn to encourage the participation of their peers.
- It is a challenge to make student teachers take responsibility for their own learning.

The conversations revealed that in our colleagues' personal experience, our institution, in many respects, does not encourage the participation of staff. The institution has democratically elected boards at different levels, but employees feel that their voices are not heard when decisions concerning their workplace are made.

Apart from occasional courses there is no forum for conversations on teaching methods or syllabuses, nor for debating fundamental issues of educational philosophy such as inclusion. In that respect individuals are left either to make their own choices or cooperate with colleagues on their own initiative. Both staff and students complain about the lack of cooperation between lecturers. As future teachers our students are expected to cooperate with colleagues and orchestrate their teaching so that subjects are not only taught separately but linked across the curriculum as well. In our college, subjects are mostly taught separately, but less so in early childhood teacher education than in teacher studies for primary and secondary schools. Collaboration within or across the disciplines varies, but it is possible for lecturers who teach Norwegian, mathematics or other subjects to give their lessons with minimal cooperation with each other. True to the curriculum, the leadership has tried to change this by establishing new frameworks for collaboration, and it is slowly changing towards a more collaborative practice. This year some students have three weeks of interdisciplinary work in which lecturers from different departments are involved. All students take part in one interdisciplinary project each year.

Our colleagues' general view was that inclusion is not sufficiently emphasised in teacher education. They found the lack of cooperation in our department regrettable. Though we are obliged to teach about inclusion, each can do as he or she prefers: there is no demand for a common practice.

Our colleagues have a positive attitude to inclusion, but some speak about it in a very general way. The notion of barriers to learning and participation is absent. The need for adapted education was mentioned only with regards to 'those who are different from others'. They emphasised the necessity for teachers to recognise students as persons and understand them, but they did not, in this short conversation, prove any practical understanding of how an inclusive school is realised.

Our experience from other discussions is that for some of our colleagues it is difficult to realise that inclusion is not limited to special education, but challenges a school as a whole. Some are of the opinion that inclusion is unrealistic. Arguments are: 'There are students who need to be taken out of the class-room' or 'What about the other students?' Some actively oppose it. As spokespeople of inclusive schools we are not regularly invited to meet all students and explain our views. Many of our colleagues know about the Handbook, but as far as we know few refer to it in lessons.

Our conclusion from what we have seen and heard then is that there is a lack of an overall vision and direction for our teacher education concerning inclusion. Lecturers are left to teach what they prefer and in the way they prefer. In this respect our institution is not inclusive and does not present a good example for our students, to be future teachers in an inclusive school.

Teacher education has a long tradition and changes very slowly. Those who have been at the institution for many years teach new staff how to act and teach. A new colleague in the college was asked how she was doing, and she said 'Fine, but . . .'. And then she spoke about friendly offers to inform her about how we do things around here, and about comments she received if she did not do things as they usually had been done: 'Everyone answers when I ask, but no one has asked me about anything – about my experiences or my opinions'. It is interesting to note that the Handbook refers to exactly the same phenomena. It asks how new teachers are welcomed and how their possibilities to explore the school with fresh eyes are utilised (Nes 2000).

Open conversations in our institution might challenge the school's prevailing conceptions of teaching, learning, students and school. Senge (1991, 2000) refers to such conceptions as mental models and claims that such models control our behaviour. Referring to Argyris, Senge characterises them as our theories-in-use (Senge 1991: 178). Tacit and unconscious models can be dangerous. Not submitted to change through open dialogue, they can be effective barriers to necessary changes in any system.

Teaching inclusion

Though inclusion is imperfectly practised, the institution is obliged to teach it. How far do we succeed in that respect?

In pre-service training for primary and lower secondary school the students work with L97 and thus get to know the notion of inclusion. What they are taught in other lessons we do not know, but there are reasons to believe that the interpretation of inclusion is affected by the traditional understanding of integration as (at least partially) welcoming those who formerly did not belong. Such a belief is strengthened by looking through the chosen text-books. In the basic book concerning lesson planning, inclusion is only mentioned in one paragraph related to children with special educational needs. This paragraph even concludes with a quotation from a white paper stating the possibility of educating students in special schools for a 'shorter or longer time' (Engelsen 2002: 152). The need for adapted education for all in mainstream classes is emphasised throughout the book, although the contradiction with the above statement is not noted.

Adapting to cultural diversity has been an important issue in our college for many years: 'We want to give our students a basis for developing a cultural awareness concerning their own identity and related to their future roles as teachers and cultural transmitters' (Sand 1999: 12, our translation.) Intercultural competence is an aim. Other issues concerning the relationship between the cultural majority and minorities are also explored in lessons and textbooks in pedagogy and to some extent in social science, but not much, if at all, in other subjects. Our impression is that student attitudes in this area are being challenged and are changing towards more inclusive thinking. This, however, has to do with the fact that some lecturers have taken a special interest in the question of cultural diversity in Norway. This corresponds to Haug's view that initiatives in teacher education result more from individual autonomy than from planned development (cf. Chapter 6).

For the last 15–20 years, areas of special education have been regarded as an integral part of every student teacher's programme in Norway. The belief is that knowledge of 'special' children is necessary for all teachers in order for them to be able to respond to student diversity. The mathematics curriculum in teacher education demands that students should learn to assess and remedy problems experienced in learning mathematics. The lecturer in mathematics as well as the practice teacher is supposed to deal with dyscalculia and learning problems in this subject. In a similar way the teaching in other subjects in teacher education should prepare future teachers to meet children of all abilities at any particular age. The Norwegian language lecturer should teach about dyslexia, and the lecturer in education should present the general themes of special education. But to what extent have these lessons actually taken place, and what is the implicit message?

The basic textbook on special education in use for all students preparing to teach in the compulsory school (Asmervik et al. 1999) is clearly in the tradition of the psycho-medical paradigm in special education, locating deficits within individual children (Clark et al. 1995). There are separate chapters on mental retardation, behaviour problems, etc. Inclusion is not an issue in this book. In their last chapter the authors admit to this and comment upon the fact that the book says very little about how to change the school system towards being more inclusive. Inclusion then, is totally left to the lecturer, and we do not know to what extent it is taught and debated in classes.

In their practice periods, students may have supervisors who really try to develop inclusive practice, and students get acquainted with well-working models for adapted education. But they may also meet teachers who more or less oppose inclusion and tell students that 'this is theory, they cannot all be included'. Fundamental concepts may be given various interpretations by the supervisors: when a student teacher in a school asked about a child missing from the class, the teacher in charge explained that 'he is out because he is integrated'. The boy in question was categorised as having special educational needs and had a pull-out programme.

As part of their pre-service education students in their fourth year can choose to study special education (1/2 year/30 credits). This course has a focus on individual problems and needs, but a systems approach and inclusion are also on the agenda. With one exception the chosen text-books give a very short and incomplete presentation of inclusion.

Relatively new in our college is a year's post-graduate study in special education focusing on inclusion. It was developed and marketed as special education studies and therefore gives some attention to individual needs. However, the emphasis is on a whole school approach and adapted education for diversity. As part of their qualification students have to do some development work in pre-schools or schools. The focus of this work is inclusive cultures, policies, and practices.

Inclusion and teacher development

It may be that the present structures and traditions of teacher education at our institution are – at least at the moment – not ideal for teaching students how to be inclusive. It takes time to change, and meanwhile there are other ways of working to participate in the bringing about of inclusive schools. One way is to work directly with schools and teachers who want to change their cultures, policies and practices. In-service education is also teacher education. As part of our research we have been working with the *Handbook for Inclusion* in different Norwegian schools. Here we shall briefly present a case of how competences in teaching inclusively can improve through goal-oriented school development.

In-service education has many advantages compared to pre-service education. Teachers are experienced and they are familiar with the demands of school life. They are responsible teachers, not students faced with problems they may regard as more or less artificial and constructed by a lecturer. On the other hand they can be tired, resistant to 'all these reforms' and bound by traditions and habits they are reluctant to change.

In the Handbook, inclusion is specified in a series of indicators and questions about the school's cultures, policies and practices. Exploring the school with the help of these makes possible exactly the kind of conversations that we described as lacking in our institution. Like lecturers in our institution, teachers in schools also complain that they have no time for open discussions about students, school and the nature of teaching and learning. Systematically working with the Handbook makes this possible, and it provides a useful aid.

In our project, eleven different schools volunteered to carry out school evaluation and development supported by the Handbook (Nes and Strömstad 2002). An important issue in the Handbook is to involve not only teachers, but students, carers and all staff in evaluation and development of the school. Engaging people other than teachers in such work was new to most of them. The outcome was diverse and interesting. In some schools teachers were surprised by what students, carers and non-teaching staff had to say. In other schools, students and parents reported more bullying than teachers were aware of. One school unexpectedly learned how satisfied carers were. Some found they agreed more than they had presumed, whilst others found more controversies than they were prepared for. One staff described their cooperation as idyllic until an anonymous questionnaire disclosed that new staff felt ignored and not welcomed by those who had been there for years. They were never asked what their opinions were, and the fact that they saw the school with fresh eyes was not cashed in on. They were expected merely to learn from the others. Several schools concluded that they did not offer sufficiently adapted education because they had not formerly realised the barriers to learning and participation created by their own organisation, learning materials or teaching methods. Students complained that they were exposed to a fake democracy. Teachers repeatedly said that students had a voice, but in the end students' experience was that it was the teachers who decided.

Such findings made staff question their traditional ways of organising students, teaching methods, choice of material, etc. Having explored their schools in different ways, staff made plans for improvement. In some schools we observed that action plans changed substantially. They were more specific, with goals that could be evaluated. Teachers wanted to try new methods and ways of working. The first evaluations show that though changes are not sensational, the work with the Handbook has brought some development towards inclusion. Staff are more conscious of their cultures, policies and practices, which is perhaps the most important outcome. This kind of awareness will create new development and competence in staff.

Implications for teacher education

One outcome of using the Handbook in schools is that its many concrete questions enhance more conscious attitudes and make people question the theories behind their own practice. We ask ourselves how these experiences from developmental work in schools can influence the ways of working in undergraduate teacher education. One suggestion is that the Handbook could be used in connection with teaching practice. Teacher students should be asked to explore the schools and classes with the help of the Handbook. It would make them more conscious, and it would inspire the supervisors to explore their own practices. Thus the Handbook might have a double effect. On the one hand it would help to qualify the students for the inclusive school. On the other hand it would promote an awareness of inclusion in the schools where students have their teaching practice.

Experience from the school development project may have several implications for our institution. Working with the Handbook brought forward a discursive conversation aimed at finding solutions. Interacting with members of school communities other than teachers made it difficult to hide real problems and defend practices based only on tradition. Our very fragmented description of the way things are in our institution for teacher education shows that we have many of the same problems that the project schools have.

Perhaps we need a Handbook for inclusive teacher education. At least we need a forum for dialogue and discursive conversations about what we are actually doing in teacher education. Involving the students as well as teachers and other staff would be a challenge. Students are asked to evaluate our teaching and the outcome of their learning, but these evaluations are only systematised to a limited extent. Students are not involved in an overall evaluation of their education and the institution as such. A Handbook might be useful to guide us through such a process. Perhaps inviting the whole college to participate in developing a Handbook for inclusive teacher education could be a way forward.

Note

1 The translations from these documents are our own.

References

Arbeids- og administrasjonsdepartementet (1997) *Lov om arbeidervern og arbeids-miljø*, Oslo.

Asmervik, S., Ogden, T. and Rygvold, A.-L. (eds) (1999) *Innføring i spesialpeda-gogikk*, 3rd edition. Oslo: Universitetsforlaget.

Booth, T. and Ainscow, M. (2000) *Index for Inclusion. Developing Learning and Participation in Schools*, Bristol: Centre for Studies on Inclusive Education.

Booth, T. and Ainscow, M. (2001) *Inkluderingshåndboka*, Vallset, Norway: Oplandske bokforlag.

Clark, K., Dyson, A., Millward, A. and Skidmore, D. (1995) 'Dialectical analysis, special needs and schools as organisations', in Clark, C., Dyson, A. and Millward, A. (eds) *Towards Inclusive Schools?*, London: David Fulton Publishers. pp. 78–95.

Engelsen, B.U. (2002): *Kan læring planlegges?*, Oslo: ad Notam Gyldendal.

Hihm, Høgskolen i Hedmark (1999) *Handlingsplan for likestilling 1999–2003*, Hedmark, Norway.

Hihm, Høgskolen i Hedmark, (2000a) *Strategisk plan i perioden 2000–2004,* Hedmark, Norway.

Hihm, Høgskolen i Hedmark (2000b) *Strategier og handlingsplan for studenter med funksjonshemning,* Hedmark, Norway.

Nes, K. (2000) 'The inclusive school and teacher education: about curricula and cultures in initial teacher education', in Ainscow, M. and Mittler, P. (eds) *Including the Excluded. Proceedings of 5th International Special Education Conference,* University of Manchester.

Nes, K. and Strømstad, M (2002) 'Skoleutvikling og inkludering', in Haug, P. and Monsen, L. *Skolebasert vurdering,* Oslo: Abstrakt forlag, pp. 115–35.

RME, The Royal Ministry of Education, Research and Church Affairs (1999a) *The curriculum for the 10-year compulsory school in Norway,* Oslo.

RME, The Royal Ministry of Education, Research and Church Affairs (1999b) *Rammeplan og forskrift for allmennlærerutdanningen/ General plan and regulations for General Teacher Education,* Oslo.

RME, The Royal Ministry of Education, Research and Church Affairs (1999c) *Forskrift om skikkethetsvurdering i lærerutdanningene,* Oslo.

RME, The Royal Ministry of Education and Research (2002) *St.meld.nr.16 (2001–2002) Kvalitetsreformen. Om ny lærerutdanning Mangfoldig – krevende – relevant,* Oslo.

Sand, S. (1999) 'Oppgaven er kulturformidling', in *Nord syd,* Copenhagen: October 18.

Senge, P. (2000) *Schools that learn,* London: Nicholas Brealey Publishing.

Senge, P. (1991) *Den femte disiplin,* Oslo: Egmont Hjemmets bokforlag.

Strömstad, M. (2003) 'Democracy in Norwegian Schools', to appear in Allan, J. (ed.) *Inclusion, Participation and Democracy: What is the Purpose?,* The Netherlands: Kluwer Academic Publishers.

Chapter 8

Inclusion and exclusion in the university

Julie Allan

Introduction

This chapter offers a deconstruction of two important documents which dictate teacher education practice within Scotland. The *Code of Practice for Students with Disabilities*, issued by the Quality Assurance Agency for Higher Education (QAA 1999) is part of a whole 'suite of inter-related documents' (ibid.: 1), on the basis of which all UK higher education establishments are held to account. The General Teaching Council of Scotland's *Medical Examination Standards for Admission to Courses of Initial Teacher Education and Training . . . and for Admission to the Register of Teachers* (GTCS 1995) establishes the legally binding standards of 'fitness to teach' (ibid.: 1) and therefore governs entry into teacher education and the profession. Deconstruction of these documents reveals some of the exclusionary pressures they create for the disabled students they claim to be encouraging into higher education and into teaching. The process of deconstruction is intended to operate here as playful, positive and generative: 'it's not a question of calling for the destruction of such institutions, but rather of making us aware of what we are in fact doing when we are subscribing to this or that institutional way of reading' (Derrida 1983: 125).

The chapter then shifts to teacher education practice and explores some recent experiences of exclusion by newly qualified teachers in Scotland. The focus on barriers encountered by disabled students and beginning teachers within this chapter illustrates the wide-ranging nature of exclusion within the policy and practice of teacher education, but represent only two of the many arenas of exclusion within it. Gender, ethnicity and social class are rarely acknowledged as arenas of exclusion within teacher education. Instead, these are silenced within establishments which are race blind (Almeida-Diniz and Usmani 2001) by individuals who cannot handle multiple oppressions and who are intent on equipping new teachers (only) with skills. This 'teacher training imperative', as it is presently configured, is far from inclusive and so student teachers have few examples to draw upon. Furthermore the policies which drive teacher education institutions (TEIs) and the universities in which many of them are housed espouse values of inclusivity and participation, while actively discouraging these in practice.

Inevitably, a paper of this kind, which adopts deconstruction as its main approach, cannot bear to end itself, but instead will pause with some discussion of the destabilisation generated, and will explore the possibilities for a more responsible form of teacher education. This takes the form of a series of double-edged questions which seek to acknowledge, rather than resolve, some of the contradictory obligations which face teacher educators. In addressing these questions, it may be necessary to ignore some of the haunting voices in the choices that we make (Levinas 1979).

Teacher education in Scotland

Scotland has six teacher education establishments, all of which have become absorbed into universities in recent years. Teacher 'education' has been the nomenclature used to describe the establishments' activities rather than the term 'training' adopted in England and Wales. Five of the establishments provide primary teacher education through a B.Ed. route and offer a one-year postgraduate diploma to secondary teachers. The University of Stirling is the only institution to provide concurrent secondary teacher education to students alongside subject degree programmes. Newly qualified teachers in Scotland become provisionally registered with the General Teaching Council for Scotland and, following a successful probationary period, are granted full registration. The recommendations of the McCrone Committee (2001), charged with examining the pay and conditions of service of teachers, including beginning teachers, have recently been put into place and these have created considerable confusion and dissatisfaction within the system. Among those most likely to be disadvantaged are the students of the University of Stirling, and the exclusionary pressures created by what amounts to contempt for diversity are examined later in the chapter.

Deconstruction and the ghostly presence of inclusion

Both the *Code of Practice* and the General Teaching Council's *Standards* can be read constructively as attempts to ensure quality of provision in higher education for disabled people (QAA 1999) and to safeguard the health, safety, welfare and educational progress of young people who are in the care of teachers (GTCS 1995). On the other hand, they can be read as yet another example of *missing the point* about inclusion, evidenced in the language and the assumptions about practice. A deconstructive reading of these documents suggests, not so much an absence of inclusion, but rather a ghostly presence, since inclusion *appears to be there*. The spectral nature of inclusion can be likened, in Derrida's terms, to the unread text which allows for the displacement of authority: 'not read, not yet read, awaiting reading' (Wolfreys 1999: 280). We are still citing inclusion as our goal; still waiting to include, *and* speaking as if we are already inclusive. Taking this 'peculiar abdication' (Royle 1999: 302) of authority to its logical end, inclusion can only be achieved by 'ex-citation' (p. 305), that is when inclusion is no longer cited, but has passed spectrally into our language and practices.

Deconstruction does not ignore context entirely, since, as Derrida urges, 'we still have to think through what is happening in our world' (Derrida 1991a: 274). It does, however, call into question assumptions that a text 'exists in a stable system of reference to other texts of *information* – its *context* – which, ideally at least, can be fully represented' (Kamuf 1999: 255; original emphasis). According to Derrida (1991b) 'writing has a possibility of functioning cut off, from a certain point, from its original meaning and from its belonging to a saturable and constraining context' (ibid.: 97). This chapter forges a link from text to context by following the deconstruction of the two documents with an exploration of the barriers experienced in practice by beginning teachers. The point is neither to synthesise the two perspectives nor to make spurious distinctions between policy and practice, but to try to illustrate the pervasive nature of exclusionary pressures within the text and talk of teacher education.

The Quality Assurance of Disability

The Quality Assurance Agency *Code of Practice* was established in response to the UK-wide National Committee of Enquiry into Higher Education (the 'Dearing' and 'Garrick' reports). The Code is intended to 'identify a comprehensive series of system wide expectations' (QAA 1999: 1) and 'authoritative reference points for institutions as they assure, consciously, actively and systematically, the academic quality and standards of their programmes, awards and qualifications'. Section 3 of the Code relates to students with disabilities and 24 'precepts' have been established with the expressed aim of providing quality assurance 'safeguards' (ibid.: 2). These precepts, the QAA insists, are neither a charter, nor a blueprint, but merely offer 'some pointers towards good practice' (ibid.: 3). In the four precepts examined below, the apparition of inclusion is both conjured and expelled. First, however, it is worth noting what the QAA regards as its constituency of disabled students.

Who is disabled?

'There are many different ways of defining who is disabled' (ibid.: 5), according to the Code, which claims to follow no particular model, but instead goes for coverage, listing the various impairments including medical conditions and health problems. The fluctuating nature of disability, arising for example from illness or injury or needs changing during the course of study, is highlighted, with goal of 'developing an environment within which individuals feel able to disclose their disability' (ibid.: 11). The under-representation of disabled people is reflected upon and attributed, in part, to problems of access, teaching methods and attitudes and in this move, inclu-sion is conjured as a wish to be more 'welcoming' to disabled students. But it is also banished by the very notion that disabled students need to be welcomed, like some guest who would otherwise not be there. The document claims that it 'recognises that disabled students are an integral part of the academic community' (ibid.: 3). It also acknowledges their problematic status, however, and in so doing, expels inclusion once again:

> It may appear that the needs of disabled students are not central to institutional survival and should therefore give way to issues of 'higher' priority.
>
> (Ibid.: 3)

The quotation marks around 'higher' are intriguing and suggest possibly that the QAA is daring institutions to consider anything of greater significance than the needs of disabled students. This dare is immediately followed by a clear threat:

> When setting their priorities, however, institutions will want to take into account that the quality of their overall provision will be measured, in part, on how well they meet the expectations of this code.
>
> (Ibid.: 3)

Inclusion, then, is swiped twice here, first of all by the insistence on demon-strating measurable outcomes, then by the unspecified threat of a negative QAA report. The effect is not to remove inclusion entirely, but to leave a trace of it which amounts merely to a set of technical solutions to personal troubles (Wright Mills 1979).

Precept 1: general principles
Institutions should ensure that in all their policies, procedures and activities, including strategic planning and resource allocation, consider-ation is given to the means of enabling disabled students' participation in all aspects of the academic and social life of the institution.

> (Ibid.: 6)

This precept calls up inclusion, in terms of enabling disabled students' 'participation in all aspects of . . . academic and social life' (ibid.), yet also banishes it, by inviting institutions merely to give 'consideration' to the means of achieving this. What follows is a series of active verbs: 'implementing' (procedures); 'ensuring' (information and understanding of the legal framework); 'providing' (staff development) (ibid.: 6–7). Again, however, institutions are only asked to consider enacting these.

Precept 4: information for applicants, students and staff
The institution's publicity, programme details and general information should be accessible to people with disabilities and describe the opportunities for disabled students to participate.

(Ibid.: 9)

Disabled students, according to this precept, are only supposed to participate where there are 'opportunities', and only when these are 'described' (ibid.) to them. Institutions are asked, in this case, to 'consider implementing arrangements which ensure that' (ibid.) information is clear, accurate and accessible. The verb to 'consider' cancels out any requirement to 'ensure' and simultaneously cancels out inclusion.

Precept 10: learning and teaching
The delivery of programmes should take into account the needs of disabled people or, where appropriate, be adapted to accommodate their individual requirements.

(Ibid.: 13)

The undecidability within this precept is interesting: it offers an either-or scenario: either the needs of disabled people are taken into account, or the 'delivery' of programmes is adapted 'where appropriate'. It is difficult to envisage doing the latter without the former, but the presentation of these two options in this way leads to a displacement of responsibility, or a licence to do nothing. Inclusion does not even exist here as an apparition; it remains uninvited by inertia. Yet, it makes a rare appearance, of sorts, in the enjoinder to institutions to ensure staff 'plan and employ teaching and learning strategies which make the delivery of the programme as inclusive as is reasonably possible'. The question of how much inclusion 'is reasonably possible', together with the recommendation that staff 'know and understand the learning implications of any disabilities of the students whom they teach' allows inclusion, once again, to be spirited away.

Precept 13: examination, assessment and progression
Assessment and examination policies, practices and procedures should provide disabled students with the same opportunity as their peers to demonstrate the achievement of learning outcomes.

(Ibid.: 15)

This particular precept appears relatively unproblematic and is potentially inclusive. Again, however, in the recommendations, institutions are asked only to 'consider implementing procedures for agreeing alternative assessment and examination arrangements' and only 'when necessary'. Institutions are asked both to be flexible in their conduct of assessment and to apply procedures 'consistently across the institution'. 'Rigour and comparability' must also be upheld. These points of guidance are, of course, only what institutions 'should consider'. An apparently subsidiary set of recommendations, relating to the provision of extra time, equipment and alternative assessment formats is provided, and flexibility is mentioned again, but these suggestions are given as those which institutions 'may wish to consider'. Inclusion is ghosted out of the assessment process out of respect for institutional preferences.

Fit to teach?

In Scotland, no individual can teach in schools unless he or she is on the General Teaching Council of Scotland's Register of Teachers. The *Medical Examination Standards for Admission to Courses of Initial Teacher Education and Training in Relevant Institutions Leading to the Award of a Teaching Qualification and for Admission to the Register of Teachers* (GTC 1995) establishes medical standards for a person's eligibility for registration and for entry into teacher education. The Standards are expected to cover both processes, although it distinguishes between them only in relation to the timing of the medical examination.

The Standards function as a legally binding document, although the GTC points out that its Standards cannot have the same legal imperative as applied to individuals not trained in Scotland, but who are seeking GTC registration. It also contains guidance on procedures for assessing 'applicants who have significant motor, sensory or other impairment' (ibid.: 1), which it insists 'is not a legally binding direction'. The Standards are accompanied by a series of comments, which are nevertheless separated from them by their enclosure within a shaded box. It is the comments which inflict the greatest damage, by appearing as a reasonable voice which both conjures and disappears inclusion. Like the QAA document, the GTC Standards can be read at one level as an inept piece of disablism, which excludes through its medicalising discourses and insensitivity to its own exclusionary language. At another level, however, this spectacular display of missing the point can be examined to see how inclusion is both there and not there within the document and how this is possible. So another spectral analysis is called for.

Risk, hazard and the unfit teacher

The teacher who is unfit to teach is placed in the text as the embodiment of the apparition of inclusion which is both feared and revered:

The principal concern of these Standards is to safeguard the health, safety, welfare and educational progress of children and young people who are in the care of teachers. In this context fitness to teach and to be in charge of children and young people covers a number of overlapping domains which include physical health, mental health, motor, sensory and other impairment.

(Ibid.: 1)

The Council recognises that one of the many roles of education is to combat irrational fears, discrimination and prejudice and to improve public attitudes to illness and impairment. Council accepts that such a role should not be impeded by procedures which exclude from the teaching profession well-qualified and strongly-motivated individuals who have a disability. They make valuable contributions in all parts of society. In education, they may in addition increase the understanding of the wider community, challenge prejudice and stigma, and raise the aspirations of those pupils with a disability. It follows that illness, impairment or disability should not be regarded as inevitable barriers to a career in teaching.

(Ibid.: 2)

The GTC acknowledges the 'strong wish' of 'many people with impairments . . . to distance themselves from a medical model' (ibid.: 1). It also denies them this, by presenting impairments as a problem of functionality, judgements about which will determine an individual's inclusion or exclusion from teaching and/or teacher education. Risk and hazard is the fear which chases inclusion away almost as soon as its presence is invited, although it is acknowledged that the dangers vary between subjects and school sectors. In calling for 'a realistic assessment of risk . . . [and] fairness and flexibility', the GTC suggest that:

What may be an acceptable risk in a Mathematics or language classroom may be unacceptable for Technology, Home Economics, Science or Physical Education. Although primary teachers work in all areas of the curriculum, it can be argued that the degree of risk inherent in primary sector technology, for example, is much less than in secondary. Also, because the amount of a primary teacher's time spent on potentially hazardous activities is likely to be small, it may be possible to circumvent any perceived risk through, for example, having another adult present for these limited instances.

(Ibid.: 5)

The ghostly presence of inclusion, conjured up in the shape of the unfit teacher, is a 'phantasm' (Derrida 1998: 143), an image of a dangerous subject, who threatens the well-being of children. The image, the would-be teacher and inclusion, therefore, all have to be disavowed.

Assessing potential

The 'educationally meaningful assessment' (ibid.: 2) is posed as a means of escaping the tyranny of the medical model, even though 'to be in accordance with the Regulations, the final judgement about fitness to teach must be with the medical officer' (ibid.: 10). The 'assessors', appointed by the principal of the teacher education establishment could consist of 'some combination of the following . . . subject/sector teacher (school); subject/sector tutor, course leader etc. (institution); educationist with expertise in the specific area of impairment (e.g. teacher of visually impaired); teacher with similar impairment to the applicant' (ibid.: 10). This form of symbolic representation ventriloquises inclusion, that is, gives it a presence, but only as its own 'empty shell, the accident of a substance' (Derrida 1991c: 588). Or to use Derrida's language as applied to Joyce, inclusion is made to experience the 'gramophone effect' (ibid.: 576) in which it is affirmed, reproduced, mechanised and committed to. Without ever being there.

Teacher education is governed by competences and takes place in institutions which both produce and are subjected to an audit culture (Strathearn 1997). Critiques of the development of competences (e.g. Hustler and McIntyre 1996) have drawn attention to their highly technicist nature and the threat to teacher autonomy, while Stronach *et al.* (1996: 74) have argued that the competences are a form of 'de-skilling'. The assessors, however, are expected to ignore the competences and to judge only an individual's 'potential to be a teacher' (QAA 1999: 10). This involves assessing whether an individual will be able, in the future, to 'meet the essential requirements of teaching – to communicate effectively with children, to manage classes, and to secure effective learning'. It does not require consideration of the competences nor observation of the applicant's performance *in the classroom*. The guidance suggests that such opportunities for applicants to spend time at a school and/or for a period of observation 'may be helpful'. Beyond that, however, the assessment process is expected to determine the *likelihood* of a person's capacity to communicate effectively with children, manage classes and secure effective learning.

Excluding the unfit

The GTC operates a binary categorisation of those who are either 'fit to teach' or 'unfit to teach' (ibid.: 7). If designated unfit, the candidate has to be told of the Council's decision and must:

- be informed of the reasons and his/her right of appeal where this exists;

- in the case of an applicant with a significant impairment, be given a full account of his/her strengths and limitations, indicating ways in which functioning might be improved;
- be informed of any conditions to be met before reapplication could be considered;
- be informed about any relevant sources of support or vocational guidance (ibid.: 8).

The legislative obligations of the Council clearly dictate the tone of these conditions; yet, the phrase 'indicating ways in which functioning might be improved' could require them to spell out impossibilities to particular individuals. Not only could this be distressing to the individuals concerned; it is also a total relinquishment of authority. So inclusion is completely absent here, since the Council, by this point, appears to be unwilling even to try.

Inclusive teacher education: not yet there?

The QAA and GTC documents both claimed to be inclusive, yet managed to avoid this in ways which appeared, on the surface, to be rational and well intentioned. Inclusion, in both documents, has been 'there without being there. It was not yet there. It will never be there' (Derrida 1998: 144). Yet it cannot exist in this state without a certain 'uncanniness, without the strange familiarity of some specter' (ibid.). In other words, it is our own conviction that we are moving towards inclusion – and that we know what this is – that stops us in our tracks. Deconstruction of these texts reveals a form of exclusion which is sinister, because it is hidden behind the platitudes and good intentions of widening participation in higher education. The experiences of the beginning teachers in the following example represent a more blatant and punitive kind of exclusion.

From text to context: disappearing diversity

The McCrone Committee, established in 1999 to examine the pay and conditions of service of teachers, made its wide-ranging recommendations in 2001. A key concern of the Committee was the experience of newly qualified teachers, many of whom had been forced to work in supply posts. Although the supply work counted towards the beginning teacher's probation and final registration, the inconsistency of their experiences, the multiplicity of schools they often had to teach in and the lack of support was regarded as 'little short of scandalous' (McCrone 2001: 7) by the Committee:

> It is no way to treat a new entrant to any profession, let alone one that is as demanding and of such public importance as teaching, where help and wise counsel are essential. It is difficult to think of circumstances

more likely to lead to discouragement and to new recruits leaving the profession for other jobs.

(Ibid.)

The Committee proposed that a formal induction period, commencing in August of each year and supported by a training programme, be introduced. Students of the University of Stirling, who graduate from a concurrent teacher education programme in December of each year, suddenly became an anomaly which could not be accommodated within the new arrangements. The key players, the Scottish Executive, the General Teaching Council and the main teachers' union, were all sympathetic to the proposition that there might be a second entry point to the induction year in January, but no one was prepared to guarantee this. Several local authorities appeared willing to have such flexibility, but the Secretary of the Association of Directors of Education in Scotland sent a clear message that the University of Stirling was the problem and needed to change its provision to fit the new arrangements. Furthermore, it became clear that there was going to be an overall shortage of induction places, so authorities' concerns were understandably with trying to honour the guarantee given by the Scottish Executive that every new teacher would be given a place at the start of the induction year.

Stirling students, then, were faced with the prospect of taking a supply post for six months, at a newly introduced probationer rate, until they could join the new scheme in August. There was much anger and frustration among the students:

I for one do not relish the prospect of unemployment because of a collection of narrow minded bureaucrats.

I would like to meet Professor McCrone to 'congratulate' him on the fine mess we are in. I would also be interested to be 'enlightened' concerning his vision of education and to ask those who commissioned his reports about the rationale behind this farce. When I started on the ITE programme in September 2000, there was a shortage of teachers. Two years on, it seems that the authorities can afford to train new teachers to throw them on the scrapheap. What happened? . . . The present situation of 'terminating' good teachers does not make sense.

Stories from the schools with which the students were associated did nothing to reassure them that they would be accommodated within the system. Among the most disconcerting of these were accounts of current probationers on temporary contracts not being given permanent posts because of the need to make way for new teachers joining the induction scheme. Students envisaged hostile environments in departments where they had taken the place of existing 'good' colleagues.

The students took matters into their own hands and sent a barrage of letters to local authorities, the Scottish Executive and Members of the Scottish Parliament (MSPs). One individual student provided some crucial leadership, communicating with each of the key players, keeping the students informed and encouraging a rational, rather than an emotive, response. Extensive newspaper coverage (*TESS* 2001, 2002) helped to publicise the situation and the involvement of one particular Member of the Scottish Parliament (MSP) led to a question being asked in the Scottish Parliament:

> As the deputy minister is fully aware, there is considerable concern among the Stirling University education students that when they enter the teaching profession in January 2003 they may not be able to join the teacher induction scheme, unlike other education students, who will join the scheme in autumn 2002. Does the minister agree that, if that is the case, Stirling education students are being discriminated against. What steps is he taking to ensure that the January 2003 entrants will be able to join the teacher induction scheme?
>
> (Scottish Parliament 2000)

The response from the deputy minister was the kind of bland non-committal statement which is customary from the Scottish Executive:

> It is true that the only guarantee in relation to the teacher induction scheme is for those joining the scheme at the start of the school year in August. The current scheme will be introduced in August this year and the plan is that the scheme will start in August in subsequent years for all students. However, as the problem has been drawn to our attention by local MSPs and others, we have examined the issue, as has the teacher induction group. Although there has been no change to the guarantee, there have been discussions with several local authorities that have indicated a willingness to take on student teachers as probationers earlier in the year. We would encourage that, we are pleased that those discussions are taking place and we hope that there is a satisfactory outcome for the students involved.
>
> (Ibid.)

When pushed further by another MSP to acknowledge that the Stirling students had been 'forgotten about', the deputy minister for education made it clear that the problem arose because of unacceptable levels of difference within the system. Put another way, it was the University of Stirling's fault:

> I have little more to add in relation to the Stirling students, except to say that I am aware from my time in the enterprise and lifelong learning department that a range of issues affect Stirling students because of the two-term system that the university operates. We are in regular

discussions with students and others from Stirling University, and we want to tackle and overcome those problems wherever possible.

(Ibid.)

Whether or not the Stirling students will be granted a reprieve from the tyranny of supply teaching which the new induction arrangements were supposed to resolve remains to be seen. The teacher education programme at Stirling is likely to succumb to the pressure for uniformity. But for the students about to exit from the system, the future, at least in the short term, appears bleak, as one remarked:

> At the risk of sounding negative, if something isn't done then January–August is going to be spent asking (awfully politely) 'Would you like fries with that?'

Responsible teacher education?

To ask why the point about inclusion continues to be so spectacularly missed within teacher education and more generally, in spite of the clear steers from many disabled and non-disabled writers (e.g. Barton 1997; Oliver 1996; Rieser and Mason 1992), is to risk lapsing into a frustrated lament. Furthermore, it is not enough to dismiss policy documents such as the two examined above as failing to be inclusive; rather, it is important to try to read these texts around their own 'blind spot' (Patrick 1996: 139), to disrupt their 'decidability' (ibid.: 140) or certainty and to begin to understand the role of misunderstanding (Biesta 2001). Inclusion, it appeared, was the particular blind spot which was both enunciated and denied in both these documents. They spoke of inclusion as if it was almost there, whilst actively ghosting it away. Because enunciation and denial were both partial, inclusion appears to be there, allowing for the displacement of authority. Thus, inclusion was avowed as being 'in place', yet remains outside, a spectator in its own wake. These policy documents represent significant barriers to inclusivity, sitting as they do within an accountability culture which encourages proving rather than improving (Ball 2000). The exclusionary pressures faced by the Stirling students were more blatant and, in the McCrone Committee's words 'little short of scandalous' (McCrone 2001: 7). The students' take on how this experience was likely to influence their development as inclusive teachers was disconcerting, even if it was not surprising.

Inclusion is like the piece of grafitti which reads 'do not read me' (Derrida 1979: 145), an order that has to be transgressed in order to be obeyed. Inclusion is conjured up in both documents, only to be dismissed, because its implications are too great. Yet the implications of explicitly denouncing inclusion are greater, so it is spirited quietly away. The frequency and intensity of the process of conjuring has a multiplicatory effect, so that we find a crowd of revenants waiting for us. Fuelled by our own guilt that inclusion is *not yet there*, the crowd has turned nasty:

> It is crawling with them . . . shrouds, errant souls, clanking of chains in the night, groanings, chilling bursts of laughter, and all those heads, so many invisible heads that look at us, the greatest concentration of all specters in the history of humanity.
>
> (Ibid.: 150)

Attempts to disperse the crowd are both reductionist and unsuccessful: we/they 'try to straighten things out, they seek to identify, they pretend to count. They have trouble'. Inclusion is thus further generated as a process of 'critical problematisation' which functions as a 'shield, an armor, a rampart as much as it is a task for the inquiry to come' (ibid.: 153).

One way out of this inertia is to find a more responsible form of teacher education. This is one which recognises that the quest for certainty creates closure in teacher education practices and profound injustices of the kind which have been seen here. Derrida (1997) suggests that injustice is a product of a pressure to reach a just decision, and the instant when this occurs is a 'madness' (Derrida 1992a: 26) because one is forced towards closure. Furthermore, he argues, the certainty with which recommendations – for example about what constitutes good practice – need to be made allows for the evasion of responsibility (Derrida 1992a). Teacher education might be viewed as consisting of a series of aporias or contradictory imperatives (Derrida 1992b), which are equally important and which cannot readily be reduced to a single decision or a recommendation:

> I will even venture to say that ethics, politics, and responsibility, if there are any, will only ever have begun with the experience and experiment of the aporia. When the path is clear and given, when a certain knowledge opens up the way in advance, the decision is already made, it might as well be said that there is none to make; irresponsibly, and in good conscience, one simply applies or implements a program . . . It makes of action the applied consequence, the simple application of a knowledge or know how. It makes of ethics and politics a technology. No longer of the order of practical reason or decision, it begins to be irresponsible.
>
> (Ibid.: 41–5)

The responsibilities faced by teacher educators appear to be contradictory, pulling them in different directions:

- How can student teachers be helped to acquire and demonstrate the necessary competences to qualify as a teacher *and* to understand themselves as in an inconclusive process of learning about others (Gregoriou 2001)?

- How can student teachers develop as autonomous professionals *and* learn to depend on others for support and collaboration?
- How can student teachers be supported in maximising student achievement *and* ensuring inclusivity?
- How can student teachers be helped to understand the features of particular impairments *and* avoid disabling individual students with that knowledge?
- What assistance can be given to student teachers to enable them to deal with the exclusionary pressures they encounter *and* avoid becoming embittered or closed to possibilities for inclusivity in the future?

There are clearly no quick and easy solutions to these 'double contradictory imperatives of a continuum of *double duty*' (Egéa-Kuehne 2001: 204, original emphasis). They are presented as a series of questions in order to foreground the ethical nature of the debate about inclusion in teacher education (Allan 1999) and are intended to accompany, rather than displace, more direct forms of action against exclusionary pressures. Direct action within teacher education might involve posing as a kind of 'cultural vigilante', seeking to expose exclusion 'in all its forms, the language we use, the teaching methods we adopt, the curriculum we transmit and the relations we establish within our schools, further education colleges and universities' (Corbett and Slee 2000: 134). The greatest responsibilities facing teacher educators, however, are to challenge the certainty and closure within policies and practices which produce exclusion for particular individuals, and to resist the temptation to neutralise educational processes 'through a translating medium which would claim to be transparent, metalinguistic and universal' (Derrida 1992a: 58). The inclusion project is now accepted as involving a mammoth task of restructuring schools, practices and attitudes (Barton 1997; Ainscow 1999). But if the confidence which surrounds the 'teacher training imperative' (Slee 2001: 173) and the accompanying guarantees of quality and standards cannot be subverted, then much will have been in vain.

References

Ainscow, M. (1999) *Understanding the Development of Inclusive Schools* London: Falmer.
Allan, J. (1999) *Actively Seeking Inclusion: Pupils with Special Needs in Mainstream Schools* London: Falmer.
Almeida-Diniz, F. and Usmani, K. (2001) 'Changing the discourse on race and special educational needs', *Multicultural Teaching* 20(1), 25–8.
Ball, S. (2000) 'Performativities and fabrication in the education economy: towards the performative society?' *The Australian Educational Researcher* 27, 1–23.

Barton, L. (1997) 'Inclusive education: romantic, subversive or realistic?' *International Journal of Inclusive Education* 1, 231–242.

Biesta, G. (2001) 'Preparing for the incalculable: deconstruction, justice and the question of education', in Biesta G. and Egéa-Kuehne, D. (eds.) *Derrida and education,* London: Routledge.

Corbett, J. and Slee, R. (2000) 'An international conversation on inclusive education', in Armstrong, F., Armstrong, D. and Barton, L. (eds) *Inclusive Education: Policy, Contexts and Comparative Perspectives*, London: David Fulton.

Derrida, J. (1979) 'Border lines'. In Bloom *et al.* (eds) *Deconstruction and criticism*, New York: Seabury Press.

Derrida, J. (1983) 'Deconstruction and the other: interview', in Kearney, R. (ed.) *Dialogues and Contemporary Continental Thinkers: The Phenomenological Heritage*, Manchester: Manchester University Press.

Derrida, J. (1991a) 'Letter to a Japanese friend', in Kamuf, P. (ed.) *A Derrida Reader: Between the Blinds*, New York: Columbia University Press.

Derrida, J. (1991b) 'Signature event context', in Kamuf, P. (ed.) *A Derrida Reader: Between the Blinds*, New York: Columbia University Press.

Derrida, J. (1991c) 'Ulysses gramophone: hear say yes in Joyce', in Kamuf P. (ed.) *A Derrida Reader: Between the Blinds*, New York: Columbia University Press.

Derrida, J. (1992a) 'Force of law: the mystical foundation of authority', trans. M. Quaintance, in Cornell, D., Rosenfield, M. and Carlson, D.G, (eds) *Deconstruction and the Possibility of Justice*, New York and London: Routledge.

Derrida, J. (1992b) *The Other Heading: Reflections on Today's Europe*, trans. P. Brault and M. Naas, Bloomington and Indianapolis: Indiana University Press.

Derrida, J. (1997) 'The Villanova roundtable: a conversation with Jacques Derrida', in Caputo, J.D. (ed.) *Deconstruction in a Nutshell: a Conversation with Jacques Derrida*, New York: Fordham University Press.

Derrida, J. (1998) 'Specters of Marx', in Wolfreys, J. (ed.) *The Derrida Reader: Writing Performances*, Edinburgh: Edinburgh University Press.

Egéa-Kuehne, D. (2001) 'Derrida's ethics of affirmation: the challenge of educational rights and responsibility', in Biesta, G. and Egéa-Kuehne, D. (eds) *Derrida and Education*, London: Routledge.

General Teaching Council for Scotland (1995) *Medical Examination Standard for Admission to Courses of Initial Teacher Education and Training in Relevant Institutions Leading to the Award of a Teaching Qualification and for Admission to the Register of Teachers*, Edinburgh: GTC.

Gregoriou, Z. (2001) 'Does speaking of others involve receiving the 'other'? a postcolonial reading of receptivity in Derrida's deconstruction of *Timaeus*' in Biesta, G. and Egéa-Kuehne, D. (eds) *Derrida and Education*, London: Routledge.

Hustler, D. and McIntyre, D. (1996) (eds) *Developing Competent Teachers: Approaches to Professional Competence in Teacher Education*, London: David Fulton.

Kamuf, P (ed.) (1991) *A Derrida Reader: Between the Blinds*, New York: Columbia University Press.

Levinas, E. (1979) *Totality and Infinity,* trans. A. Lingis, Pittsburgh: Duquesne University Press.

McCrone Committee of Inquiry into Professional Conditions of Service for Teachers (2001) *A Teaching Profession for the 21st Century*, Edinburgh: HMSO.

Oliver, M. (1996) *Understanding Disability: From Theory to Practice*, Basingstoke: Macmillan.

Quality Assurance Agency for Higher Education (1999) *Code of Practice for the Assurance of Academic Quality and Standards in Higher Education: Students with Disabilities*, Gloucester: QAA.

Patrick, M. (1996) 'Assuming responsibility: or Derrida's disclaimer', in Brannigan, J., Robbins, R. and Wolfreys, J. (eds) *Applying: to Derrida*, Basingstoke: Macmillan.

Rieser, R. and Mason, M. (1992) *Disability Equality in the Classroom: A Human Rights Issue*, London: Disability Equality in Education.

Royle, N. (1999) 'On not reading Derrida and Beckett', in Wolfreys, J. (ed.) *Literary Theories: A Reader and Guide*, Edinburgh: Edinburgh University Press.

Scottish Parliament (2002) Official Report, 30/5/02.

Slee, R. (2001) 'Social justice and the changing directions in educational research: the case of inclusive education', *International Journal of Inclusive Education* 5, 167–78.

Strathearn, M. (1997) '"Improving ratings": audit in the British university system', *European Review*, 5, 305–21.

Stronach, I., Cope, P., Inglis, B. and McNally, J. (1996) 'Competence guidelines in Scotland for initial teacher training: supercontrol or superperformance?', in Hustler, D. and McIntyre, D. (eds) *Developing Competent Teachers: Approaches to Professional Competence in Teacher Education*, London: David Fulton.

Times Educational Supplement Scotland (2001) 'Cold shoulder for the winter probationers', 1, 24/5/02.

Times Educational Supplement Scotland (2002) 'Left high and dry by the system', letters page, 31/5/02.

Wolfreys, J. (1999) 'Introduction: what remains unread', in Wolfreys, J. (ed.) *Literary Theories: A Reader and Guide*, Edinburgh: Edinburgh University Press.

Wright Mills, C. (1979) *The Sociological Imagination*, Harmondsworth: Penguin.

Chapter 9

Understanding disability and transforming schools

Linda Ware

> People are not cultural dupes of old structuralism frameworks. They do
> indeed, exhibit agency, struggle, and imagination as they grapple with
> structures wrapped around their located lives.
>
> (Lois Weiss, 1996)

Introduction

This chapter examines school reform in the instance of an inclusion
initiative, Understanding Disability and Transforming Schools (hereafter, the
Project). The *Project* was initiated by a large suburban school district[1] in
upstate New York that funded this author to develop a school-based
partnership with the School of Education at the University of Richland
(hereafter, SOEUR). One component of the research on the *Project*
consisted of a qualitative study, directed by this author, to document the
obstacles to its implementation. This research occurred over three years and
included field notes, interviews, observations and document analysis that
inform the episodes presented in this chapter. Due to the limitations of
space, only a fraction of the research that was conducted will be considered
in response to the question raised by the editors: how does inclusion affect
students, educators, curricula and pedagogies in the context of a school of
education? The question is explored by a close examination of the workings
of privilege, entitlement, elitism and exclusion embedded in SOEUR.

Mismeaning, mirage and the marketing of reform

Calls for reform of teacher education in the US are as frequent as calls for
reform of public schools. Demands for more testing or less, more rigid
standards or less, more local control or less, all of which ensure the
continuous cultivation of contested space in schools. The politics of education appointments whether at the level of building administrator, district
superintendent, state governor or executive authority, are often obscured by
this more-or-less approach, creating the mirage that simple equations for
equity fuel the very complex systems that underwrite schooling.

Recently the United States Secretary of Education, Rod Paige, echoed the call for more stringent standards for kindergarten through grade twelve (K-12) students, schools and teachers outlined in President George W. Bush's education law, No Child Left Behind (2002). Consistent with the rhetoric of previous administrations this campaign slogan-turned-law champions progress for all children, however it also has citizens literally 'singing' the praises of federal education policy. The *New York Times* (Schemo 2002) reports the Administration's marketing strategy to justify increased annual testing in grades three through eight includes the song, 'No Child Left Behind' written for a children's television show that receives a $4 million grant from the Education Department. The song suggests the 'mood of an upbeat gospel' and is currently piped into the phone system at the Department of Education in Washington, DC, where callers will hear:

> We're here to thank our president,
> For signing this great bill,
> That's right! Yeah,
> Research shows we know the way,
> It's time we showed the will!
> (Cerf and Durkee 2002)

No Child Left Behind includes penalties for schools that fail to erase the gap in scores between white students and black and Latino students within 12 years. Bush previously mandated similar policy during his reign as Governor of Texas. At that time, widespread scandals erupted across the state as educators and administrators, fearful of similar penalties, attempted to literally 'erase' the gap by falsifying an increase in the text scores of black and Latino students (see McNeil 2000 for a discussion of standardised testing in Texas schools).

Slogans and jingles often serve educational reform, but in this particular moment of rampant mismeaning through overt manipulation of facts and the covert 'spin' that 'glosses' over legitimate social, economic and cultural concerns, such myth and ceremony seem far more ominous. Nonetheless, it is likely that public relations personnel in local school districts, state education departments and schools of education will join the chorus to inveigle populist beliefs. Although schools of education may appear at the periphery of current education reform they are still susceptible to 'steering processes' described by Popkowitz (1993). These processes emerge from the 'coalescence of practices and epistemological patterns in multiple institutions [where] . . . seemingly discrete educational practices occurring in state governments, universities, and research communities produce a certain selectivity' (ibid.: 293). From this emerges a 'unique ensemble of procedures . . . [that] taken together embody patterns of social regulation' (ibid.). These regulatory practices inscribe teacher education through its reliance on processes of rationalisation and the creation of rules and standards by which reasoning about teacher education is practised. It is the latter that affords the use of knowledge in promotion of certain truths as they are 'inscribed in the problems, questions, and responses that are to secure and enhance professional life' (ibid.). In this instance a slogan might read: *The rhetoric of professionalism legitimates the practices that emerge* (with apologies to Popkowitz).

This chapter explores the need for schools of education to examine their own rhetoric in the example of reform for inclusion. Faculty must begin with self-critical reasoning about their institution's regulatory processes and the values that inform their version of professionalism before they can assume the authority to espouse claims of reform for inclusion. In much the same way that educational researchers have urged dialogue among teachers in the midst of various reform initiatives, research into the efforts of schools of education in the midst of similar changes is long overdue. In the section that follows I borrow from *Teacher Education in Transition: Collaborative Programs to Prepare General and Special Educators* (Blanton *et al.* 1997), a collection of case studies from ten American universities describing institutional efforts to transform teacher education through the creation of collaborative programs in support of inclusion.[2] These authors suggest the many challenges that inclusion poses for teacher education programmes, most notably, the challenge of initiating and sustaining dialogue on change.

Tensions, contradictions and silences

Collaboration has been touted for several decades as the fulcrum essential to support inclusion in K-12 schools. Most schools of education include faculty with research interests in K-12 collaboration, some write text-books devoted to collaboration, at a minimum, most universities offer course work in support of collaboration. However, few teacher education faculty have actually attempted collaboration within their own institutions, as such efforts often amount to little more than 'forcing unconsenting adults to perform unnatural acts' (Kirst 1991: 616). The case studies presented by Blanton *et al.* (1997) suggest the need for effective communication given that dialogue specific to attitudes, beliefs, and assumptions is not easily orchestrated among educators whether in K-12 or post-secondary settings. The mere act of discussing core content for all teachers can prove disruptive. For example, after years of conforming to a structure of separate programmes, faculty at the University of Cincinnati dismissed the need to identify 'core' coursework suitable for all graduates in their master's programme. Given the seeming inability to find language that would enable faculty to share their most basic beliefs about teaching and learning, their initial efforts were marked by frustration. Some reasoned that collaboration was not mandated reform and more likely, just another 'trend' that threatened to consume tremendous time and energy. Some wondered whether a unifying framework undermined the established norms of the two programmes; others experimented with team-teaching and integrated coursework; and still others quibbled about the ownership of courses and the uneven commitment to the development of a shared vision. Finally, 'over the course of several intense discussions, we learned about one another's views and participated in conversations that led eventually to refinement and redefinition of the shared philosophy of our program' (ibid.: 135).

Providence College cited the impetus for their collaborative efforts as predating the call for 'shared responsibility' in support of the Regular Education Initiative (REI 1986) by then Secretary of Education, Madeline Will. By 1986 Providence had already won faculty approval for a unified program that focused on diversity, collaboration, teacher professionalism and effective teaching practices.[3] Early exchange proved 'lively, exhausting and painful' as their discussions began by considering what teachers should know and be able to do, and how best to include it within a minimum number of courses (Blanton *et al.* 1997: 250). This unified program continues to thrive and now includes professional development partnerships and service learning opportunities within the curriculum, however faculty maintained that the challenge remains to build 'continuous study groups' into their current program.

Syracuse University, well known for their Inclusive Elementary and Special Education Program, also characterised their initial efforts as a lively exchange of ideas. Interest in a unified program traced back to a faculty retreat in 1987, thereafter, core faculty (five or six persons from two divisions in the college of education) began regular meetings that ultimately included the entire college of education. Merging core content proved to be one of the first hurdles as some faculty voiced concerns over the potential loss of enrolment should a pre-service student be unwilling to teach special education students and wanted only to teach non-disabled students. Remarkably, the Syracuse vision 15 years ago was such that the response offered was,

> Well, if a student feels that way, perhaps he or she should not be a teacher, as there is no longer any such thing as teaching elementary education without students with disabilities in the classroom. Perhaps the student does need to go elsewhere.
>
> (Ibid.: 23).

From its inception, teacher educators working in support of inclusion were well aware that inclusion would challenge many of the status quo assumptions of schooling. General education teachers who boldly refused special education students admittance to their classrooms were no longer able to justify their entitlement to teach 'some' but not 'all' students. That is not to say that covert ablist beliefs have been extinguished. Similar to racism, ablist normativity operates just beneath the radar where overt exclusionary assumptions and practices are renounced while simultaneously cultivating more covert mechanisms to 'outlaw' difference (Baker 2002; Campbell 2000). However, while many K-12 educators have moved toward understanding that inclusion begins with acknowledging the inherent exclusion in educational systems, such insight is sorely lacking in teacher education programs where selectivity and exclusivity are the norm.

Blanton *et al.* provide a glimpse into the processes undertaken by teacher education faculty as they began rethinking and restructuring for inclusive education. However too little analysis is provided in exploration of one of the most formidable barriers to inclusion reform in higher education – the discursive tensions inherent in teacher preparation programs. According to Gore (2001) most teacher educators can reach consensus regarding concerns about 'programs and purposes' but struggle is inevitable once faculty begin to probe the fundamental differences among the dominant discourses in teacher education and the influence of those discourses in lived practice. Gore calls for a 'distillation of what matters' (p. 133) in teacher education programs, although based on experiences in her own institution, she too concedes that such an exchange is unlikely. Reflection on actual practice and re-examination of established curricula often reveal the workings of privilege, entitlement, elitism and exclusion embedded in many teacher education programs. This contradiction recalls Sally Tomlinson's critique of the 'imagined moral framework' assumed by general and special educators (1982, 1996). Tomlinson suggests that, armed with a professional credential, teachers can 'claim a degree of altruism and a disinterestedness from wider social, political and economic considerations' (1996: 79). However, in the example of teacher education, claims of disengagement from the social, political and economic contexts of schooling are rare, particularly among those that espouse a social reconstructionist tradition. This tradition, according to Liston and Zeichner (1991), focuses on the preparation of teachers who can 'play a positive role in the making of a more just, equitable, and humane society' (p. 154). But do the actual practices of teacher educators follow? Certainly teacher education espouses the language of 'criticalness' as in the example of critical pedagogy, critical literacy, critical sociology, critical feminism, critical media literacy, critical special education and critical race theory. Webpages from schools of education are awash in slogan-rich recruitment propaganda that proclaims a commitment to diversity and social justice. *Why then were efforts to consider the hidden curriculum in teacher preparation so troublesome to many of these contributors?* How many more institutions would likewise be caught short when attempting to practise what they teach?

Real time, real talk, real politics

In their conclusion, Blanton *et al.* assert that collaboration in teacher education is possible, however, it assumes real time for communication and it inevitably forces a confrontation with new or alternative conceptions of teaching and learning. Real time dialogue, debate and a close re-examination of the distinctly different discourses that tend to separate general and special education teachers are urged as necessary and unavoidable. Given that inclusion is unavoidably political and conflictual, the actual narrative from these accounts would have been useful. Instead readers are left to read between the lines and to imagine the complex and, likely, contentious conversations about educational policies and practices that occurred. Such a contradictory approach by the authors points to assumptions of moral authority by those who willingly probe the motivations of teachers but refrain from similar intrusions and exposure in their own teacher education programs. The profession's silence on what it takes to begin and sustain this type of dialogue is evident in the paucity of research from teacher educators engaged in examination of their own attitudes, beliefs and assumptions regardless of the topic.

Inclusion, in the instance of teacher education reform, cannot be fully considered in the absence of contending with these historic tensions, contradictions and silences. As Barton suggests, 'inclusive education is part of a human rights approach to social relations and conditions. The intentions and values involved are an integral part of a vision of the whole society of which education is a part' (Barton 1997: 234). In his view, central demands in an inclusive society include, 'social justice, equity and democratic participation' and thus, 'barriers to their realization within an existing society need to be identified, challenged, and removed' (p. 233). Clearly, one such barrier is the absence of research into real-time dialogue in schools of education as they contend with the conflict that inclusion invites. Turning the tools of research upon ourselves would likely reveal 'both the limits and the permeable boundaries of our own cherished discourses' (Gore 2001: 126).

Research into the 'obstacles to implementation' of Understanding Disability and Transforming Schools provided a unique opportunity to examine many of these same tensions, contradictions, and silences. The *Project* was designed to support inclusive education reform that was simultaneously undertaken in a school district and SOEUR. Several episodes emanating from SOEUR serve as flashpoints to underscore the point raised earlier that 'the rhetoric of professionalism legitimates the practices that emerge' (Popkowitz 1993: 293).

Understanding disability and transforming schools

In the fall of 1998, the Graceland Central School District (hereafter, GCSD) invited SOEUR to draft a proposal to support state-mandated inclusion.[4] This 'speculative' conversation included me, the then chair of the teaching and curriculum department, and the then Associate Dean. As the most recent faculty hire and a newly transplanted New Yorker, my involvement in the *Project* as the only non-administrative faculty seemed ill advised for several reasons. Chief among them was my newly established commitments to three urban secondary schools in a nearby district under court-ordered inclusion (Ware 2000).[5] And because the university recruited me to develop a post-secondary interdisciplinary disability studies program with the college of arts and sciences, the medical school and the school of education – outreach efforts had just begun. Although the then Dean was sympathetic to my concerns, he urged a reprioritisation of my commitments to instead place GCSD on top. He was less concerned that SOEUR faculty had expressed no interest in the *Project*. However, my participation was essential given that: (1) this was a special education initiative and I was the only faculty in 'special education' (a term used by SOEUR faculty as if synonymous with disability studies), and (2) my prior experience with inclusion and district-wide reform far exceeded that of other SOEUR faculty. Months later when GCSD pledged fiscal support to underwrite a new master's program in inclusive education the Dean issued the directive that I take 'intellectual leadership' of the *Project*. Although the task before me initially seemed overwhelming, it soon became apparent that a unique opportunity existed to create a K-12 educational inclusion initiative informed by disability studies which would coincide with my efforts to promote disability studies in higher education.

Inclusion: a social-cultural approach

Understanding Disability and Transforming Schools would address both cultural variables (attitudes, values and beliefs) and systemic factors (structured time, resources and administrative support) to prepare the district for inclusion. Specifically, this proposal would allow teachers to obtain a master's degree for teaching in inclusive classrooms, or complete coursework with inclusion as the focus (beyond the masters they may already possess).[6] The stated emphasis on teaching in inclusive classrooms was consistent with state and national trends for general educational settings in which curriculum and the process of teaching and learning were revised to include *all* students. Professional training opportunities would encourage the participation of all personnel to address the learning needs of students with the *full range* of abilities and disabilities. Teacher preparation would occur, not in isolation, but in a context that affirms a dual focus on cultural and systemic variables in the educational context. Cross-disciplinary teams composed of content teachers and special education teachers could apply to SOEUR as a cadre for professional development or a master's degree. They would collectively produce a multiple-authored master's essay derived from a school-based research project that addressed school-wide inclusive schooling. Their research would inform both the final *Project* evaluation, and inform GCSD's ongoing research and development. It was my hope that this whole-school approach would discourage the typical danger of inclusion initiatives borne off the backs of individual teachers (Ware 2000). Curiously, this particular component raised concerns among SOEUR faculty who argued that a multiple-authored research project would 'water down' their established high standards. Further, because GCSD was underwriting the program, any teacher was eligible to enrol in the program. In effect this incentive for teachers would sully the SOEUR tradition of rigid qualification requirements for admission into their highly selective master's program.

Although professional development was suggested as its centrepiece from the outset I sought assurance from GCSD for their commitment to address the structural barriers that often impede efforts to develop and sustain inclusion (e.g. Falvey 1995; Ferguson 1996, 1997; Fisher *et al.* 1999; Jorgenson 1998; Lipsky and Gartner 1997). The proposal identified eight key principles and practices characteristic of inclusive and restructuring schools from the research of Fisher *et al.* (1999) and Jorgenson (1998):

- Decisions about inclusive education and school reform must originate in administrative vision that is unwavering in the face of uncertainty and the difficulties of putting principles into practice.
- Inclusion of students with disabilities must be solidly based within general education reform efforts.
- Support for teachers and administrators during the change process must be provided through internal structures and through association with an outside critical friend.
- Social justice issues, including disability, must be infused throughout the curriculum.
- Creative use of time through implementation of innovation school schedules is essential.
- General and special education teachers with new job descriptions that reflect shared responsibility for all students must collaborate to design the curriculum, teach, and evaluate students.
- Tracking has been eliminated, and most classes are heterogeneously grouped.
- The curriculum must be thematic, performance-oriented, constructivist, and based on high achievement standards for every student.

In addition, I would introduce the *Project* across the district through a series of school-based meetings rather than in a district-wide outside-expert address. Once schools agreed to participate, interested faculty would be encouraged to shape the initiative informed, but not bound by the proposal outline. In the first year, over twenty presentations were made to school board members, to the community, to administrators in district meetings and to faculty in their own schools. Each presentation drew from the same proposal outline, however, each was shaped to engage the target audience.

That is, when presenting to the school board I invited them to spend a few moments prior to my address in drafting a definition of inclusion. Their responses included both social and education specific interpretations which initiated thinking beyond inclusion as a special education initiative.[7] Their definitions were considered along with several informed by the literature including that offered by Corbett and Slee:

> Inclusive education is a distinctly political 'in-your-face activity' [it] proceeds from larger political, as opposed to technical questions about the nature of society and the status afforded to people in varying forms and structures of social organization. As a political movement in the first instance, inclusion is about establishing access for all people. It is not conditional, nor does it speak about partial inclusion. Its impetus emanates from the recipients of professional services rather than from being orchestrated by professionals themselves.
>
> (Corbett and Slee 1999: 134)

Since GCSD agreed that the *Project* participants would author the district's definition of inclusion it was important to explore a range of possible meanings of inclusion. This activity was then replicated in several classes in the master's program to engage teachers and pre-service teachers in a similar conversation on the politics of this reform. Early on, I hoped to challenge both naïve and romanticised interpretations of inclusion and the stereotypical approaches to understanding disability common to K-12 educational settings. On one occasion, in a presentation to a large group of administrators (n=40), I asked them to recall their first memory of disability and to spend a few minutes writing about this memory. Both personal and professional recollections by the participants served to create the context for my presentations framed by the question: 'When will disability be understood as anything other than misfortune or tragedy?' There was a notable absence of medicalised-diagnosis-driven-cure/care-technical-tropes. The accounts offered were personal and as many related afterwards, this in-service activity was unique in that it invited personal reflection on disability. Thereafter, when I was introduced in GCSD, administrators favourably recalled the presentation, given that our discourse minimised Individual Educational Plans, deficits, medical terms and the implicit burden-to-society analysis. As one high school principal related her excitement about the *Project*:

> It provides a real opportunity for moral growth for all of us. With 28 years in the system and two more years before retirement . . . maybe now I can retire with as much excitement and pride as I had in my early years as a teacher.

Finally, when I presented to teachers, I led with the question, 'Where in the curriculum do we find accounts of living with disability?' This component of the *Project* would later receive additional external funding from the National Endowment for the Humanities and has been considered more thoroughly elsewhere. (Ware 2001, 2002, in press). This approach to disability, from a social, political, and economic perspective, sought to move the conversation beyond disability *in* school, and in special education in particular, to launch a conversation on inclusion that is long 'overdue' and rarely undertaken by schools. Understanding disability not as abnormality, but as another varia- tion on the theme of humanity is rare in schools. The absence of a more humane perspective disrupts status quo assumptions about disability at the level of both structure and culture. By coincidence the summer prior to formally launching the *Project*, GCSD administrators and teachers were invited to attend an international inclusive education conference I organised with funding awarded by the Spencer Foundation.[8] The conference, *Ideology and the Politics of Inclusion*, proved to be a timely introduction to critical knowledge that challenged status quo assumptions about education, special education and inclusion. Rather than hold to the view of inclusion as an education initiative, conference speakers, both nationally and internationally recognised scholars, examined disability in relation to social, political and economic issues traced to K-12 educational contexts. Inclusion concerns moved far afield from the traditional technicist concerns of special educators, past the justification demands of general educators, beyond the 'place and practice' issues raised by inclusionists to address disability as a product of cultural rather than purely biological forces. Teachers, administrators, parents and community members attended this week-long event. Although no SOEUR faculty attended the conference, their absence was noted by one parent, a health care executive and longtime resident who commented, 'This is pretty radical stuff for this community – I'm not sure they're ready for it!'

The *Project* was officially launched in the fall of 1999, less than a year after initial planning began. In the same semester several key administrative changes occurred in SOEUR that ultimately posed significant obstacles to the success of the *Project*. A new department chair was appointed, who, within months, became the interim Dean (and later the Dean), prompting the appointment of a new department chair. Prior to their administrative appointments these individuals did not support the *Project* nor were they able to consider disability in other than clinical terms (discussed below). Equally significant were the departures from the University of both the Associate Dean and the Dean – two key supporters of the *Project*. Readers familiar with institutional politics know that at this point, the plot has not so much thickened as concluded. However, for purposes of this chapter, the SOEUR context continued to inform this research. Plotting the points, in the hopes of making connections between the two settings revealed details that exposed the values of each institution.

SOEUR – a context

The SOEUR programs were described in terms of both a mastery discourse and with an emphasis on 'collaboration and collaborative research, teaching, and consultation'. Public relations documents emphasised the creation of 'world-class leaders' trained in a critical tradition that relied upon 'intensive reflective practice' and an approach to educating teachers to 'lead struggles for social justice'. This rhetoric was, on the surface, consistent with the *Project* goals; however, over time it became apparent that faculty disapproved of the *Project's* focus on disability. The established view of disability as limitation and deficiency placed disability outside the agenda for social justice. More importantly, SOEUR and the university enjoyed a reputation premised on selectivity, where 'some' – not 'all' students were welcome. Faculty held firm to the belief that a selective admissions policy was key to program quality. Students with visible or invisible disabilities experienced tremendous obstacles to enrolment in SOEUR programs despite the posting of the university's diversity statement in their recruitment materials.[9] Simply put, the SOEUR culture assumed and encouraged elitism as a value, as a given. Despite the rhetoric that washed over the SOEUR public transcript[10] as a program invested in social justice, efforts to explore program coherence relative to the meaning of inclusive schooling were consistently dismissed by faculty. Frequent episodes in SOEUR ultimately signalled the obvious, inclusion was incompatible within a community bound by privilege, entitlement, elitism and ablism. In retrospect the signs appear like lights at the end of a runway, but at the time, my awareness of this contradiction surfaced coincident with research on the *Project*. That is, SOEUR faculty presented a cluster of attitudes, beliefs, assumptions and behaviours that might readily be characterised as a 'syndrome' of sorts, uncomplicated by the workings of the institution which sanction selectivity and exclusivity.

Recipes for the retarded

Early in my first semester, SOEUR faculty questioned my interpretation of 'reasonable accommodation' as ordinary rather than 'special' educational practice (so described on my syllabus). I explained that given the centrality of this concept in successful inclusive classrooms, students in my classes were asked to consider reasonable accommodation as something more akin to an act of humanity rather than a federal 'mandate'. That is, over many semesters of teaching I had observed that given life's sometimes unpredictable detour from assumed routines, ample occasions arose to test out, with students, the *practice* of reasonable accommodation. I teased with SOEUR faculty that at a minimum it might prove to be a 'healthy experience' for future educators to practise a request for 'reasonable accommodation'. My rationale was situated in episodes with students. For example, in our first class meeting, students consider what they informally view as their own learning strengths, learning styles and learning motivations. This small-group activity is not intended as a diagnostic self-assessment, but instead signals a key aspect of my teaching in which building community is encouraged at the outset through explicit occasions for collective learning. Near the end of the class I ask the students to speculate about any possible accommodations they might require. Informed by their own familiarity with this concept via special education we create a list that includes transportation, technology, additional time for testing, frequent tardiness, etc. Initially, few identify any need for special 'breaks' until I refer back to previous semesters and the accommodations required by former students. For example, many students work as research technicians in labs at the medical school and as a consequence of data collection that are not always easy to predict or control they are sometimes late to class. Others might have to contend with traffic that, likewise, eludes prediction and control.

Despite the positive response by students in my classes to this seemingly small lesson, SOEUR faculty were unconvinced that such an exercise held merit for the students. Indeed, my example provoked the admonition that as a private institution the university was 'exempt' from policies for the disabled. This misunderstanding was surprising given that the Americans with Disablities Act (ADA) was the most recent civil rights legislation in the United States. In fact, the ADA (1990) applied to all institutions that received federal support, and the university with its well-funded medical school was no exception to the law. This seeming lack of awareness of disability issues prompted my call to the University Disability Resources Office[11] where the program coordinator confirmed the prevalence of this perception of exclusivity from public policy, not only in SOEUR but across the university. Since she had targeted education and outreach as first-year goals for this newly established office she offered to make a brief presentation for SOEUR. I imagined her address would serve as a 'wake-up' call for faculty; however, the call was clearly mine upon hearing the profound intolerance for disability-related issues expressed by SOEUR faculty. One professor wondered why the topic necessitated a ten-minute presentation when none of our students were disabled. Another challenged the 'logic' of 'forcing' individual departments to underwrite the cost of 'supporting' disabled students given that some departments would 'disproportionately' bear the hardship of this expense. This burden-to-society analysis was a central feature in his teaching of educational administration courses. Later this same professor would challenge my scholarship in support of inclusion as 'intellectually irresponsible' given, in his view, my failure to 'consider the problem of just distribution of limited resources' (personal correspondence).

Department meetings in the teaching and curriculum program were equally hostile to disability-related issues. In an early presentation to

SOEUR faculty, I screened two short videos from the California Systems Change Project and the research of Doug Fisher, a colleague in my previous research at the University of New Mexico (Keefe *et al.* 1999; Ware 2000). *What We Learned* (1998) describes the obsolescence of a dual knowledge base for teacher educators in the twenty-first Century. In just under three minutes a series of still images depict collaboration among adults and students as shaping a more humane approach to inclusion in schools and society. The second video, *Christina's Journey* (1998, approx. 5 min.) is the senior high school project of Christina Principel, a participant in Fisher's research. The video opens with images from Christina's first home, an orphanage in Romania, and continues to the present – her arrival in southern California and subsequent enrolment in high school. Christina reads over the images that capture her adventures in classes, with her peers outside class, on the swim and track teams, at the prom and at graduation. Although Christina's speech is somewhat imperfect and includes traces of an accent, she offers a typical account of her final year in high school. A long silence followed the screening of these videos until a faculty member (who would later become the Dean) opened with the question, 'How retarded is she?' 'Excuse me?' I replied. 'The girl, how retarded is she?' Another professor (who later became the department chair) offered, 'We're all aware of the conditions of orphanages in Romania – so the question is really about what kinds of classes was she in – special ed, inclusion, or regular ed?'

Attempting to return to my opening remarks about the film, the soon-to-be-Dean interrupted with the demand, 'What we need from you are recipes, the strategies, or whatever you call it – to prepare teachers for the retarded students that come into their classes. They need to know what to do with those kinds of kids.'

Classify, categorise and control

On the surface, these concerns may appear to parallel those raised by K-12 general educators who ask, 'But what do we do on Monday?' The concern emanates from the scientific tradition in education that relies upon a research-informed knowledge base for classroom practice: the acquisition of discrete and observable skills, and implicit assumptions for social regulation and control. However, SOEUR faculty persistently disavowed this approach and yet, they simultaneously dismissed the videos because they failed to make explicit 'what to do' through the conventional classification and codification of teachers' actions. The question, 'how retarded is she' was, for the future Dean, critical information congruent with her worldview. She firmly believed that if teachers were to be responsive to special education students in inclusive classrooms, they would need problem-solving skills tied to linear relations, taxonomic categories and universal sequences: towards this end, *Christina's Journey* served as little more than an anecdotal scrapbook.

In contrast, when GCSD teachers viewed the videos, no one inquired about Christina's 'labels', nor did they demand placement status inform-ation. Typically, the teachers were excited to share the videos with colleagues in their schools and to learn more about Doug Fisher's work. Those with prior experience attempting inclusion reform in their schools celebrated the video's affirmation of their efforts. One high school special education teacher used *Christina's Journey* in her English classroom comprising both general and special education students as part of a writing assignment to bring more disability-related issues into the curriculum. Like their teacher, the students found confirming evidence to support their beliefs about living in an inclusive society. This alternative[12] secondary school 'broke all the rules for exclusion' as one senior in the class explained it in a class discussion. Later that year the school's valedictorian delivered an address that compared his early school years when he was targeted because of his autism to his high school years when his right to be in the world informed school-wide inclusion as it was practised in his high school.

These GCSD educators supported educational contexts that exceeded the need for recipes: they understood classrooms as far more complex settings. Like many K-12 educators, they were not strangers to the now decades-old calls for inclusion reform. They had long since been pitched into the process of making room for disabled students in the absence of the luxury of time for an attitude adjustment. By their assessment, inclusion had been 'on the table' for more than two decades although many different routes had been taken to negotiating an understanding of its meaning in context. In contrast, SOEUR faculty were sheltered by their reputation as a school for 'some' but not 'all' students: they were entitled to dispense with the realities facing schools because they occupied a safe space outside those concerns. The context was bound by ablist assumptions common to institutions of higher education in which privilege and entitlement underwrite intolerance (Jung 2002; Luna 2002). Further, SOEUR faculty could in fact be selective about what qualified as an issue of social justice, or 'reflective practice'. Since many SOEUR faculty held firm to a model of expert knowledge the *Project* goal of encouraging schools to work as a team, in small study groups led by their own research questions, was incongruent with the SOEUR definition of 'reflective practice'. When the department chair refused to teach courses for the *Project* on site in the district, for fear that her 'institutional identity' would be challenged, other SOEUR faculty concurred. Curiously, her rationale was rooted in an insecurity that positioned schools at the ready to 'attack academics'. Indeed, as Popkowitz (1993) suggested, 'the rhetoric of professionalism legitimates the practices that emerge' (p. 293).

'Over my dead body'

The *Project* was launched coincident with several new state-mandated reforms including the immediate return of special education students to general education classrooms, new K-12 performance standards and an increased use of standardised testing that would severely limit the options for high school graduation. This 'get tough' approach to school reform served as the backdrop for my presentations in GCSD, quite in contrast to my recommendation that inclusion be framed through more humane understanding of disability. The department chair's expressed fear that schools were poised to 'attack academics' might have held in the example of the following episode, when after a high school presentation, the Q & A turned to a 'lively discussion' over the contradiction between higher standards and the large-scale return of special education students to general education classrooms. However, the situation was more a reflection of historic forces outside the control of teachers. That is, with average tenure for GCSD teachers at 22 years, most had experienced years of reform initiatives. Frustration accompanied the deluge of current changes and, not surprisingly, teachers felt they lacked the appropriate skills to help their students, general or special, through these hurdles prior to graduation. After listening to a litany of concerns, I asked for possible solutions, but most agreed it was a bit late for solutions. One teacher rose to his feet and generated an impromptu list of 'changes' he had survived over the years and with one finger jabbing the air, insisted

> I will not be a part of this reform. I never taught special education students and with two years left before retirement, I'm not going to start now. Maybe the superintendent believes this nonsense, but if he were here now, I'd tell him the same thing – 'over my dead body'.

This teacher's response was both warranted and unacceptable, but I had, after all, encouraged input. In response, I attempted to remind him that larger forces were at play: changes originated from the federal government that, in turn, mandated state reform that, in turn, demanded changes at the district level – and yes, the net effect did indeed target him and his students. My pointing out the evolution of special education that dated back to asylums, reformatories and state schools visibly failed to allay his frustration. Later, I realised that his response was an interesting reverse of that of the administrator who months before expressed her enthusiasm to participate in the *Project*. Whereas this teacher felt wholly troubled by spending his last two years being renamed a failure by this version of reform, the administrator, in contrast, felt the potential to reclaim enthusiasm. Such were the perceptions of fear and anticipation that came into play in this research. In the present moment, however, neither a sociological nor a historical analysis would do, so with all due respect, I asked the teacher, 'Tell me this, if other teachers agree to participate in this initiative, will you step out of the way and let us give this a try?' At once the silence seemed to numb the anguish many of us felt during the exchange. Finally, with equal sincerity, the teacher responded, 'Yes m'am, I will.'[13]

Months later, interviews conducted with teachers revealed that this episode verified a genuine interest and willingness on my part to listen to faculty. It also served to demonstrate the impact of social/historic forces, in that prior to mainstreaming it was never the expectation for general education teachers to teach special education students. Like the SOEUR Dean, this teacher was institutionally conditioned to his lack of involvement with special education students. But clearly, unlike the Dean, this teacher reflected on his position, and, in support of the handful of colleagues in his school who began to understand disability differently, he did indeed step aside.

Conclusion

These episodes are not intended to suggest either typical or atypical readings of what one might expect to encounter when attempting to support inclusive education reform in either setting. In fact, I have borrowed from both settings to reveal the complexity and multi-layered realities of these contexts when disrupted by inclusion, particularly when disabled students are part of the equation for reform. Were one to weigh the evidence, GCSD was far more willing to understand disability differently than was SOEUR. Recall that, as Barton (1997) suggests, 'the intentions and values involved are an integral part of a vision of the whole society of which education is a part' (p. 234). Participation is assumed in any such vision for social justice if the goals are to exceed the rhetoric of equity and excellence. Although efforts were made to engage SOEUR faculty in support of inclusion and inclusive practices, they held firm to established structures and frameworks of the past. They felt no urgency to grapple with inclusion in their own context or to examine the selectivity they assumed and that exclusion authored. Simply put, inclusion, in the SOEUR was a 'non-issue' (Anderson 1990).

This chapter raised concerns about teacher educators who assume the authority to support inclusive education in the absence of engaging and sustaining difficult conversations with their peers. The data presented here reveal that if we refuse to examine the workings of privilege, entitlement, elitism and exclusion embedded in teacher education programs then it is doubtful that teacher educators can meaningfully inform the curricula and pedagogies necessary to support inclusion. Undoubtedly, teacher educators possess the tools to re-examine their intentions and values and to probe the limits of existing knowledge in the example of reform for inclusion. As more inclusion proponents attempt the challenge of institutional reform in their own departments and programs, the cluster of attributes that contribute to the locus of exclusion embedded in society will become more readily transparent and, with any luck, more swiftly extinguished.

Notes

1   The distinction between suburban and urban school districts in the United States is important to note given the historic disparity between the two with respect to funding allocations, quality of instruction, student performance and minority representation. In addition, high concentrations of poverty are more often associated with urban school districts.

2   Contributors include: Syracuse University (New York), Providence College (Rhode Island), California State University San Marcos, Utah State University, Saginaw Valley State University (Michigan), the University of Connecticut, the University of Florida, the University of Alabama, the University of Cincinnati (Ohio) and the University of Wisconsin-Milwaukee.

3   Many of the terms used by the contributors are left unproblematised, consistent with the nomenclature of special educators and inclusionists. In the US, much of the inclusion literature lacks a critical perspective and relies on rhetoric. While special education is marked by troublesome terms linked to normative assumptions, the inclusion literature is marked by troublesome terms assumed to have universal meaning. In deference, I have refrained from use of quotation marks on terms I would otherwise flag for their ambiguous meaning.

4   GCSD was found to be in violation of federal and state regulations due to their identification rate of nearly 18%. The state averaged between 11–14%.

5   In brief, urban schools in this area reported 70% of its students qualify for free lunch, an indicator that reflects the concentration of poverty. In contrast, suburban schools reported within the range of 2% to 20% eligibility. This demographic reflects the 'white flight' from Richland's urban areas to its suburbs during the late 1960s and 1970s, a national phenomenon recast by Feagin (1998) as 'urban apartheid'.

6   GCSD agreed to underwrite faculty planning time to develop the inclusive education master's degree; to underwrite all tuition expenses for teachers who enrolled in the master's program, and they supported my research on the *Project* buying out two course releases. This level of support was commonly obtained with large federal grants, but it was the first such award from a school district to an individual faculty member.

7   This meeting was taped for broadcast on a local public television network that enabled its use in courses for the new master's degree. Because the board members could be viewed as a cross-section of the community, their engagement with the ideas was very powerful.

8   Speakers included Julie Allan, Scotland; Keith Ballard, New Zealand; Len Barton, United Kingdom; Tony Booth, United Kingdom; Lous Heshusius, Canada; Kari Nes, Norway; Jude MacArthur, New Zealand; Roger Slee, Australia; Marit Stromstad, Norway; Sally Tomlinson, United Kingdom; and from the United States, Ellen Brantlinger, Tom Skrtic and myself.

9   During my tenure I was contacted by the Office of Civil Rights on two occasions to verify the claims made by disabled and minority students who filed discrimination complaints against the university.

10 Scott (1990) defines the public transcript as the 'self-portrait of dominant elites as they would have themselves seen. Given the usual power of dominant elites to compel performances from others, the discourse of the public transcript is a decidedly lopsided discussion. While it is unlikely to be merely a skein of lies and misrepresentations, it is, on the other hand, a highly partisan and partial narrative. It is designed to be impressive, to affirm and naturalize the power of dominant elites, and to conceal or euphemize the dirty linen of their rule' (p. 18).

11 The university has, for over ten years, successfully stalled a class action suit filed by disabled former students for lack of compliance and physical access. This office was established to demonstrate their commitment to disability concerns despite the unresolved litigation.
12 Alternative schools explore various 'alternative' mechanisms and structures to encourage student completion of the programme (e.g., curriculum, flexible school day, pedagogy, and student-centred practice all might differ from a traditional high school).
13 Unfortunately, a central office administrator who was in the audience at this presentation reported the teacher's behavior to her superiors. In less than 24 hours I was pressed to disclose the name of the teacher who would be cited for 'insubordination.' In a lengthy memo to the district I outlined why such a response was uncalled for, and likely to be detrimental to the Project. I reasoned that the teacher's expression was justified and targeted at no one in particular. It was an honest response, and honesty was central to building trust in the district. Given his very dignified response that he would in fact 'step out of the way', he demonstrated the value of our exchange. Several phone calls later, the issue was dropped.

References

Allan, J. (ed.) (in press) *Inclusion, Participation and Democracy: What is the Purpose?*, The Netherlands: Kluwer.
Anderson, G.L. (1990) 'Toward a critical constructivist approach to school administration: invisibility, legitimization, and the study of non-events', *Educational Administration Quarterly* 26(1), 38–59.
Baker, B. (2002) 'The hunt for disability: The new Eugenics and the normalization of school children', *Teachers College Record* 104(4), 663–703.
Barton, L. (1997) 'Inclusive education: romantic, subversive or realistic?' *International Journal of Inclusive Education* 1(3), 231–42.
Blanton, L.P., Griffin, C.C., Winn, J.A. and Pugach, M.C. (1997) *Teacher Education in Transition: Collaborative Programs to Prepare General and Special Education Educators*, Denver: Love.
Campbell, F. (2000) 'Eugenics in a different key? New technologies and the "conundrum" of "disability"', in Crotty, M., Germov, J. and Rodwell, G. (eds) "*A Race for a Place": Eugenics, Darwinism, and Social Thought and Practice in Australia*, Newcastle, AU: University of Newcastle Press.
Cerf, C. and Durkee, B. (2002). 'Leave No Child Behind', as cited in Schemo (2002).
Corbett, J. and Slee, R. (1999) 'An international conversation on inclusive education', in Armstrong, F., Armstrong, D. and Barton, L. (eds) *Inclusive Education: Policy, Contexts and Comparative Perspectives*, England: David Fulton Publishers. pp. 133–46.
Falvey, M.A. (ed.) (1995) *Inclusive and Heterogeneous Schooling: Assessment, Curriculum, and Instruction*. Baltimore: Paul H. Brookes.
Feagin, J.R. (1998) *The New Urban Paradigm: Critical Perspectives on the City*, Washingotn, DC: Rowman & Littlefield Publishers, Inc.
Ferguson, D. (1996) 'Defining change: one school's five year collaborative effort',

paper presented at the Annual Meeting of the American Educational Research Association, NY, New York, April.

Ferguson, D. (1995) 'Changing tactics: research on embedding inclusion reforms within general education restructuring efforts', paper presented at the Annual Meeting of the American Educational Research Association, Chicago, IL, April.

Fisher, D., Sax, C. and Pumpian, I. (1999) *Inclusive High Schools: Learning from Contemporary Classrooms*, Baltimore: Paul H. Brookes.

Fisher, D. (1998) 'Christina's Story', produced by John Graham, San Diego, CA: San Diego State University.

Gore, J.M. (2001) 'Beyond our differences: a reassembling of what matters', *Journal of Teacher Education*, 124–35.

Jorgenson, C.M. (1998) *Restructuring High Schools for all Students: Taking Inclusion to the Next Level*, Baltimore: Paul H. Brookes.

Jung, K.A. (2002) 'Chronic Illness and Educational Equity: The Politics of Visibility', *National Women's Studies Association Journal* 14(3), Fall.

Keefe, E.B., Ware, L., Howarth, S. and Blalock, G. (1999) 'Pilot study of inclusive education models in New Mexico (1996–98)', a three-year field-initated research project prepared for the New Mexico State Department of Education.

Kirst, M. (1991) 'Improving children's services', *Phi Delta Kappan*, 615–18.

Lipsky, D. and Gartner, D. (eds) (1997) *Beyond Separate Education: Quality Education for All*. Baltimore: Paul Brookes Publishing.

Liston, D.P. and Zeichner K.M. (1991) *Teacher Education and the Social Conditions of Schooling*, New York: Routledge.

Luna, C. (2002) '"But how can these students make it here?" Examining the institutional Discourse about what it means to be "LD" at an Ivy League University', paper presented at the annual meeting of the American Educational Research Association, New Orleans, LA (April).

McNeil, L. (2000) *Contradictions of School Reform: Educational Costs of Standardized Testing*, London: Routledge.

Popkowitz, T. (Ed.) (1993) *Changing Patterns of Power: Social Regulation and Teacher Education Reform*, New York: SUNY Press.

Schemo, D.J. (2002) '"No Child Left Behind", Is a Hit Song to Bush Team', *New York Times*, June 23, A-16.

Scott, J. (1990) *Domination and the Arts of Resistance*, New Haven: Yale University Press.

Tomlinson, S. (1982) *A Sociology of Special Education*, London: Routledge & Keegan Paul.

Tomlinson, S. (1996) 'Conflicts and dilemmas for professionals in special education', in Christensen, C. and Rizvi, F. (eds.) *Disability and the Dilemmas of Education and Justice*, Buckingham and Philadelphia: Open University Press.

Ware, L. (2000) 'Sunflowers, enchantment and empires: reflections on inclusive education in the United States.', in Armstrong, F., Armstrong, D. and Barton, L. (eds) *Inclusive Education: Policy, Contexts and Comparative Perspectives*, London: David Fulton Press, pp. 42–59.

Ware, L. (2001) 'Writing, identity, and the other: Dare we do disability studies?' *Journal of Teacher Education* 52(2), March/April, 107–23.

Ware, L. (2002) 'A moral conversation on disability: risking the personal in educational contexts', *Hypatia: A Journal of Feminist Philosophy* 17(3), 143–71.

Ware, L. (in press) 'Working past pity: what we make of disability in schools', to appear in Allan, Julie (ed.) *Inclusion, Participation and Democracy: What is the Purpose?*, The Netherlands: Kluwer Academic Publishers.

Weiss, L. (1996) in Levinson, B., Foley, D.E. and Holland, D.C. (eds) *The Cultural Production of the Educated Person: Critical Ethnographies of Schooling and Local Practice*, New York: SUNY Press, pp. ix–xii.

Chapter 10

Developing inclusive teacher education

Drawing the book together

Tony Booth, Kari Nes and Marit Strømstad

Introduction

The authors of this book have explored inclusion in teacher education in different ways. They have focused on the cultures, policies and practices of teacher education institutions, on what pre-service and post-graduate students are taught about inclusion as well the role of teacher educators in in-service education and inclusive school development. In this concluding chapter we ask what the chapters in this book tell us about the extent to which teacher education *is* inclusive, barriers to its inclusive development, how these can be overcome, and importantly, how teachers can be enabled to meet the challenge of inclusion in their daily work. We ask what can be learnt from the differences between countries in the attempts to develop inclusive teacher education.

What is inclusion?

How do the authors view inclusion? Not all the chapters present a clear definition. In the opening chapter we emphasised the importance of a broad conception which is about developing the cultures, policies and practices of education and social systems to make them more responsive to diversity. The subsequent chapters, however, had a variety of emphases. Several of the chapters convey an impression that inclusion is about or emerges from a concern with disabled children and young people or those categorised as having special educational needs (Allan, Ware, Haug), others start from a focus on the education of a specific group such as ethnic minority learners (Engen), others with a broader focus on education systems involving school development (Ainscow, Nes and Strømstad) or the development of teacher education institutions (Booth, Nes and Strømstad, Ware, Ballard) or the responsiveness to cultural difference (Ballard). Whether these different focuses signal a disagreement about what inclusion is about or merely different starting positions is open to question. However, it is clear that the overall meaning that is conveyed to the reader is weighted towards some issues rather than others.

Peder Haug's chapter is about 'special needs education' and the way student are prepared to cater for the pupils categorised as having 'special educational needs' in the compulsory school in Norway. In his introduction, however, he explicitly states that inclusion is about recognising and understanding all learners irrespective of their attainment, interest, talent, gender, class and ethnic background. Thus he emphasises a comprehensive understanding of inclusion though he is looking more closely into only one aspect of it.

Linda Ware, in Chapter 9, refers to inclusion as being about establishing access and participation for all. The focus of the project she describes is primarily on disabled people and how schools might develop from this perspective. A major part of Julie Allan's chapter is concerned with the lack of real inclusion in policy documents on disability. Both these and Haug's chapter may signal that inclusion is primarily about disability or 'special needs', even if the authors all advocate a wide understanding of inclusion.

Two chapters are predominantly on inclusion and cultural diversity. In his introduction Keith Ballard states that inclusion is concerned with issues of social justice and the necessity to identify and discuss values. From that starting point he explores the oppression of Mäori culture in New Zealand. Thor Ola Engen's chapter is also on the oppression of minority cultures in a Norwegian context where 'integration' has often been understood and practised to mean assimilation. His concern is that 'integration' by tradition is restricted to adapting teaching to individual attainment levels while the majority culture was taken for granted. Inclusion, on the other hand, must embrace a recognition of, and respect for, cultural diversity.

Ainscow in his chapter defines inclusion as overcoming barriers to the presence, learning, participation and achievement of all learners in neighbourhood schools. He specifically argues that inclusion aims at a transformation of the system itself to reduce the number of students who are marginalised in schools.

The list in Table 10.1, grouped under main headings provides a composite view of inclusion that can be derived from the Chapters in the book. This inevitably glosses over differences of view.

Is initial teacher education inclusive?

Though the concept of teacher education in this book is not restricted to pre-service teacher education this is a concern of several chapters. During their education, students obviously learn from cultures and policies of the institutions in which they study, as well as from what and how they are taught. Is there inconsistency in the messages they recive which may make students doubt the necessity and usefulness of aiming at inclusive cultures, policies and practices in the schools they are to work in?

Table 10.1 A composite view of inclusion

Diversity
- inclusion is not about any specific group of students, but concerns all learners in school
- diversity is valued
- categorisation is minimised

Learning and participation
- inclusion is about removing barriers to learning and participation for staff and carers as well as for students
- inclusion means participation in the academic, social and cultural community of the neighbourhood school
- inclusion implies every student's right to learn

Democracy
- inclusion means that all voices should be heard
- inclusion means that collaboration is essential on all levels

The school as a whole
- barriers to learning and participation are found in all aspects of a school. They should not be seen primarily as existing within individual learners
- inclusion implies that all are learners; students, staff, carers and the surrounding communities
- inclusion is not only about the practices in school, but also about the cultures and policies of educational institutions at all levels of the system
- it is the school as a system that has to change

The society at large
- inclusion and exclusion in education should be related to justice for all in society
- inclusion is political and conflictual
- inclusion is a continuous process, not a state that can be reached

Inclusion in the documents

Although incomplete, the data from the national documents presented in Chapter 1 give an impression of how inclusion/exclusion is interpreted within teacher education. It appears that central documents regulating teacher education have embraced the concept of inclusion. The awareness of the issue is present in all the countries examined, even if variations within countries are great, particularly in the US. England has a particularly large number of documents related to inclusion which present its educational implications in great detail. The visibility of issues linked to inclusion in the laws, national and local policy documents might be seen as a major step forward towards an inclusive development in teacher education and in schools. However, both Allan and Booth suggest that this should be read with caution and in their different ways argue that official inclusion policy may have a rhetorical force which is undermined within the policy documents themselves.

The national documents are less explicit on institutional policy than on what students should be taught during their education. Allan and Nes and Strømstad refer to policy documents affecting their higher education institutions, which may influence students' experience of inclusion during their education. Allan has deconstructed documents concerning access to teacher education and the evaluation of 'fitness to teach'. Allan talks about the 'ghostly presence' of inclusion. Even if the intention of the documents may have been to ensure the rights of vulnerable students and learners, in effect the message is ambivalent or may even discourage efforts to greater inclusion by implying it is there already.

Teaching inclusion

The countries represented in this book differ in the extent of national control over initial teacher education. In the USA there are few national requirements except for the length of studies and a new national reporting system on the quality of teacher preparation. That means that there are great variations as to content and organisation of teacher education between states. Norway is the only country which has a common national curriculum in teacher education, although the statutory National Curriculum in schools in England coupled to standards for 'Qualifying to teach' applies a similar force.

Several of the contributions in this volume (Booth, Haug, Nes and Strømstad, Ware) demonstrate a discrepancy between the inclusive rhetoric of national education policies and guidance for teacher education and the reality described. In Haug's study of Norwegian teacher education, at least some lecturers claimed that they were preparing students for the 'school for all'. He found that other lecturers seemed to be unaware of the implications of inclusion for education. There was a general reservation when speaking of the inclusion of 'all'. For some the term 'all' seemed to mean those who are deemed to profit from the lessons given. Education is still strongly influenced by the psycho-medical approach to special needs education which takes for granted the nature of instruction and the way it is organised and views educational failure as arising from 'deficits' within individual children (Clark *et al.* 1995). From an inclusion perspective, barriers to learning and participation are understood as located within all aspects of a school, not primarily within individual learners.

The outcome for students

There is relatively little comment in the book on teacher education students' impression of inclusion in their courses. But it seems that many students enter teaching with little understanding of inclusive values and what these mean for teaching and learning in schools. Institutions may send a dual message through familiarising students with words about inclusion, without preparing students to tackle the barriers to inclusive development when they start working in schools.

Barriers to inclusive teacher education

What then are the barriers to a more inclusive teacher education? These are seen to occur within cultures, policies and practices within national administrations, teacher education institutions and schools. Booth talks of a move from opposition to compliance to advocacy and ownership of inclusion. Some of the chapters point to barriers to compliance with government requirements when it is barriers to ownership of the ideas that may be the most important to overcome.

Different interpretations of inclusion

Engen and Booth point to the differences in the conceptualisation of inclusion within government policies, and such differences can impede the development of a coherent response in schools, colleges and universities. They discuss the persisting view of inclusion as mainly about children categorised as having special educational needs. Booth refers to a paradigm war in higher education institutions between proponents of this view and others who interpret inclusion as a responsiveness to, and valuing of, diversity. But he also refers to the way different ideas about inclusion can reflect different responsibilities in the institution. Such differences can become a resource, helping to understand the implications of inclusion for all aspects of the workplace. Allan points to the dangers of over-simplifying complex matters and avoiding ambiguities and paradoxes. She points to the need to reflect on the difficulties that teachers have in supporting teacher education students to maximising the achievement *and* inclusivity of learners in schools. As Ballard (1999) had argued previously student teachers have to be prepared to engage with uncertainty in their professional lives.

Barriers in the teacher education curriculum

In Norway the reforms in compulsory education are mirrored to some extent in the policies for teacher education. But as shown, especially by Haug, the presence of inclusion within the teacher education curriculum does not ensure that the knowledge and values described in the text are actually taught. One reason given is that the implications of the curriculum may not be sufficiently clear. Nes and Strømstad report that there is a set book for Norwegian teacher education, about special educational needs, which makes few links to an inclusion agenda. It is also suggested that there are no consequences for non-compliance with inclusion and it is easy for lecturers to reinterpret reforms to fit in with what they are already doing. Any calls for greater accountability in Norway has to take account of the dangers of the accountability culture in England as described by Booth, which dominates the lives of many teachers in schools and staff within higher education institutions.

Barriers in cultures and policies

Is the culture of teacher education institutions a real barrier to inclusion? Teacher education can appear as relatively conservative and resistant to change (Haug, Ware). Changes to policy documents may occur more frequently than deeper and more persistent developments in cultures and practices. There are rarely clear procedures for institutional development let alone ones which make such development inclusive. Booth's case study is a good example of the mix of progress and barriers that arise in the absence of clarity over institutional change. Both Ware and Haug point out that institutions lack inter-disciplinary discussion of the assumptions underlying teaching and learning approaches, and suggest how these can be improved.

Ballard and Booth argue that ethnic, gender and other forms of discrimination in our own institutions need to be challenged. This involves looking at representation in staff, students and in courses and at how people from minority backgrounds can be actively supported.

Ware points to the privilege, entitlement, elitism, ablism and exclusion embedded in institutions. She is concerned about the institutional arguments that have to be won if teacher educators are to have the authority to support inclusive education.

There is an emphasis on human rights in the chapters by Ballard and Ware. They and others emphasise the political nature of inclusion. Education is always deeply political despite the wish of some to pretend that it is not. This latter view generally conceals political support for the status quo. The way in which discussion of inclusion makes explicit the values and politics underlying education represents a challenge to many in teacher education.

How language is used is an important part of reviewing the cultures and content of teacher education. We have seen how the word 'all' in 'the school for all' is often taken to mean less than everyone. The use of other words like 'us' and 'them' have to be scrutinised too. Ballard does this when he questions his own position as 'pakeha' writing about Mäori. Ware describes in her chapter an incident with a colleague asking for 'recipes' for working with the 'retarded' – a case of unconscious use of a devaluing language. In New Zealand, as discussed by Ballard, the terminology of the market has invaded education, not only with its 'inputs' and 'outputs', teachers as 'providers', students as 'consumers' or 'customers' and researchers as 'science providers'. Such ideas were imported from England, which has persisted with the use of business language throughout education.

Barriers in special needs education

In theory, courses about 'special educational needs' in teacher education are offered to student teachers in most countries. Although, in practice the time devoted to it may be very limited. In addition there are optional post-graduate courses in all countries. In the USA one may also qualify to become a special teacher without a general teacher certificate. That model can inhibit the inclusion of learners categorised as 'special', simply because such special teachers may have no experience of mainstream schools and their demands and benefits.

The content of special needs teacher education is ambiguous about inclusion. Although inclusion is highlighted in many courses for teachers about special educational needs, it seems that a deficit model still predominates. The mere existence of well-developed traditions of special needs education undermines the calls for inclusion and the school for all, signalling that some children are 'other' and not the responsibility of the general teacher.

What can be done?

The authors make several suggestions for overcoming barriers to more inclusive teacher education. These include not only changes to teacher education institutions, but ways of working more directly with teachers in schools. There can be no general prescription. Barriers arise within particular national, local and institutional contexts and ways of overcoming them have to be sensitive to these contexts and draw on available resources.

Reducing curricular barriers

Within Norway, with its fixed curriculum and texts in teacher education, it is suggested that inclusion will be limited without a change in these texts to make them less ambiguous, and with a clearer analysis of the implications for practice (Haug). But the way lecturers and students respond to the texts is important, for actions cannot be related to values unless student teachers are taught in a way that encourages critical reflection. For example, students should be helped to explore the assumptions which 'frame their windows' in order to unveil deficit-oriented or other exclusionary ways of thinking. Ballard points out the necessity for teachers to overcome the variety of ways in which cultural differences can be seen as deficiencies, a position that privileges the dominant culture. Student teachers must acquire the necessary theoretical tools for analysing prevailing discourses, including, Ballard suggests, the historical and philosophical roots of racism.

Everyone has a culture, not only those from ethnic minorities: cultures are far more diverse that is often supposed. There are no strictly uniform majority or minority cultures. An understanding of cultural diversity has to become an important area of study within teacher education, and this has to be part of all subject areas.

Student teachers need to be prepared through a critical analysis of the language they and others use to confront linguistic barriers to inclusion. For minority students in schools and perhaps in teacher education institutions, support for learning an additional language may be an essential part of their inclusion. Engen discusses the issue of bilingual education which he regards as important to the creation of identity, but for many children who speak a language for which classroom support is not available, other ways of ensuring cultural respect and cultural transitions must be found.

Reducing barriers in cultures and policies

Dialogues around inclusion are a way themselves of challenging dominant attitudes and cultures in teacher education as we argued earlier. But when excluding pressures are exerted by a major structural and cultural shift within educational institutions such as those associated with managerialism and the accountability culture described by Booth, then any counter movements requires similarly powerful forces. Ware argues that, unchallenged, the prevailing discourses will continue, as part of the 'historic tensions, contradictions and silences'. She suggests that the absence of debate about 'discursive tensions' in teacher preparation programmes is a major barrier to the development of inclusion and a culture for managing conflicts. Discursive arenas have to be established in teacher education, inviting all stakeholders to take part – the lecturers, the students, the practice supervisors and other staff. Ainscow, Ware and Haug refer to the development of collaborative cultures, and participatory work in and with schools, in which all members of the school community are drawn into dialogue.

Excluding pressures exist at all levels of the system. Although authors of the chapters in this book contribute to national policy formation through membership of advisory committees and, for example, with the national endorsement of the *Index for Inclusion* in England, there are considerable constraints on the possibilities for influencing the national policy context. Where governments produce conflicting policies, an exemplary inclusion document may have limited influence where it conflicts with more pressing concerns. In England Booth and his colleagues are initiating work with users and national policy makers by setting up a forum entitled Putting Initiatives Together, to explore the compatibilities and conflicts between the strands of inclusion policies.

Allan and Nes and Strømstad indicate the way documents and practices concerning teacher fitness might be scrutinised for exclusionary implications. It seems that Norway has avoided some of the pitfalls revealed in the Scottish fitness documents by not listing categories of causes for possible non-fitness. Support policies have to be in place to support students, such as disabled or ethnic minority students, who may experience exclusionary pressures within the institution. And the institution has a responsibility to ensure that no student is disadvantaged in seeking work either through discriminatory rules about recruitment as described by Allan or because of racism or gender stereotypes as described within Booth's and Ballard's chapters.

The development of cultures and policies in the institution would be helped if diversity among students and teacher educators expanded, for example, by including more disabled staff and students and more members of ethnic minorities. Nevertheless there can be something of a vicious circle if the absence of diversity restricts the opportunities for staff to learn how to overcome discriminatory pressures.

As indicated within Ainscow's chapter and to some extent within Nes and Strømstad, considerable possibilities exist for working with schools on their own inclusive development. The creation of partnerships within schools where inclusion is explicitly on the agenda, as implied by Booth, may be a way of bridging the school and institutional development.

Reducing barriers concerned with special needs education

In principle, as argued by Haug, in the inclusive school there should be no need for special needs education. This does not mean that the impairments of disabled children and young people should be ignored, or that teachers do not need to know about and have experience of working with disabled learners. But we should avoid the expansion of disability into a wider group of 'children with special educational needs' and the explanation of educational difficulties solely in terms of either impairments or deficits within the learner. Individual support should always be provided with the purpose of minimising the dependence of students on that support and assisting classroom and subject teachers in including students within their ordinary teaching plans. Through their work with the Index for Inclusion schools have shown that they are able to replace the notion of 'special educational needs' with 'barriers to learning and participation' (Booth and Ainscow 2002).

The editors of *From Them to Us* (Booth and Ainscow 1998) suggest that special needs education should be redefined and incorporated within a field concerned with inclusionary and exclusionary processes affecting all learners, a view supported within Ballard 1999. The present book has clearly taken a step in this direction, but many challenges remain. There needs to be more open discussion on the interactions between a discourse of special needs education and other educational discourses (see Ware's chapter). Existing specialities in special needs education should be challenged. Since we argue that a paradigm war persists between a special needs approach and a valuing diversity approach to inclusion, change will be resisted. Barriers may be most evident where there is the possibility of separate special initial teacher education as in the USA. Booth discusses the beginnings of a coming together of different approaches in his institution and Ware reports on the progress made within several institutions in the USA to draw together specialist and mainstream courses and approaches to the education of student teachers.

Improving accountability and control?

Haug suggests that greater accountability should be established within teacher education in Norway to avoid it being a collection of individual projects and to assist the implementation of significant and agreed policies. Other countries do have accrediting organisations for teacher education, together with well-defined standards or 'outcome statements' for teachers. Some forms of accountability may be helpful in improving teaching quality, but the experience of England, New Zealand and the USA which have gone furthest in creating an accountability culture is that this can be a deeply alienating experience for teachers in schools and in higher education. Although top-down approaches to implementation can appear attractive, by definition they cannot be inclusive. The inclusive development of schools and teacher education institutions requires a supportive and participative approach which involves colleagues rather than external inspectors. All assessments, whether of children or of institutions, should be formative.

Collaborative approach to school development

The chapters by Ainscow, Ware and Nes and Strømstad provide evidence of the benefits of teachers learning about inclusive development within their schools. Such 'continuing professional development' including induction programmes for newly qualified teachers forms an important part of teacher education in many countries. (Norway is the only one of the five countries discussed here without a programme for new teachers in schools.). In Chapter 2, Ainscow discusses how teacher education staff can help by presenting strategies whereby teacher education staff help schools to move inclusion forward, by assisting staff in schools in their own action research inquiries, by supporting the development of a language of practice, and through offering alternative approaches. Ainscow works from the conviction that much of the knowledge that teachers need in order to change their practice is accessible to them, often within their own work place. But existing knowledge may not be explicit and even when it is, it may not be shared. This can happen through partnerships between teachers observing each other's classrooms or videos of each other's practice. Exchange of knowledge and experiences between schools can extend knowledge communities.

Future research

Research is important in supporting the development of more inclusive teacher education institutions and schools and in the analysis of policies, their production and implementation. Descriptive studies of the development process and of attempts to change the content and approach to teaching can play an important role as can action-oriented research within teacher education institutions and by teachers in their schools, with support as necessary. Ainscow has attempted to develop an approach to school and classroom research that allows the perspectives of all stakeholders to be revealed, and for them to collaborate in bringing about improvements. Such a process encourages the voices to be heard of the least powerful participants, such as students, parents and non-teaching staff. Booth has given examples of 'researching the institution' and has also suggested how the research process can be used to promote inclusion in the institution through wide involvement.

Ware has argued that there should be research into how teacher education institutions respond to educational reforms in addition to those on primary and secondary schools. According to Haug, research is needed which helps to put policies into practice and is carried out in close collaboration with schools and teachers. More knowledge is also required about the teaching philosophies, values and conceptualisations of teachers, at all levels of education. This may be best approached in ways that show how teacher actions are linked to the assumptions and theoretical positions behind them. Ballard refers to Alton-Lee and colleagues who have provided case studies of how discussion of the actions of teachers, the reasons underlying their practice, and its effects, has led to proposals for alternative ways of working (Alton-Lee *et al.* 2000).

In Ware's chapter we see how formal post-graduate qualification programmes started from an inclusive school development initiative. Documentation and evaluation of such examples are useful for others irrespective of whether or not they are sustained. It is as important to become aware of barriers to implementation as examples of relatively smooth innovation. People cannot integrate research into their practice in any mechanical way but learn from instructive examples about how their values might inform their practice.

An interesting project might be to compile an index for inclusion in teacher education (Booth, Nes and Strømstad). The starting point for the development of such an Index would be the experience of developing and working with the Index for schools, but it would draw on existing knowledge about the barriers to, and resources for, the development of inclusive teacher education within texts written about each country, including those within this volume. Participants in the gathering of information for and trialling such a project would include the full diversity of teacher education students, teacher educators, and national and local administrations. Such a project across two or more countries might be used to systematically investigate the similarities and differences in the cultures, policies and practices in teacher education and the differences in possible approaches to its development in each country.

Concluding remarks

In this final chapter, we have attempted to draw out some of the main issues arising in the earlier chapters in this book. We argue that much can be learnt from reflecting on the differences between accounts about the implications of inclusion for the development of teacher education in the countries represented in this book. We are aware of the limitations of our own efforts to influence practice within the context of more powerful forces in societies in which strong excluding pressures persist in creating vulnerability and disadvantage. We are also aware of the pressures for education to be approached in similar ways internationally and in particular, the current vogue for attending to simple measurable outcomes and for attempting to drive up educational standards through competition and inspection. Where such reforms have taken root, the development of inclusion is considerably impeded, even where it also appears to be a major element of government policy. Inclusion offers an alternative approach to educational development motivated by a wish to see values of equity, entitlement, community, participation and respect for diversity put into practice within teacher education institutions and schools. Because it involves commitment to an explicit set of values it makes us accountable for our own actions to ourselves as well as to others, and thereby increases responsibility and accountability. It also nourishes the idea and practice of public service, on which must depend the future of equitable systems of teacher education and education more generally.

References

Alton-Lee, A., Rietveld, C., Klenner, L., Dalton, N., Diggins, C. and Town, S. (2000) 'Inclusive practice within the lived cultures of school communities: research case studies in teaching, learning and inclusion', *International Journal of Inclusive Education*, 4(3), 179–210.

Ballard, K. (1999) 'Concluding Thoughts', in Ballard, K. (Ed.) (1999) *Inclusive Education: International Voices on Disability and Justice*, London: Falmer Press.

Booth, T. and Ainscow, M. (1998) 'Making comparisons: Drawing conclusions', in Booth, T. and Ainscow, M. (Eds) (1998) *From Them to Us: An International Study of Inclusion in Education*, London: Routledge.

Booth, T. and Ainscow, M. (2002) *Index for Inclusion. Developing learning and participation in schools* (2nd Edition), Bristol: Centre for Studies in Inclusive Education.

Clark, K., Dyson, A., Millward, A. and Skidmore, D. (1995) 'Dialectical analysis, special needs and schools as organisations', in Clark, C., Dyson, A. and Millward, A. *Towards Inclusive Schools?*, London: David Fulton Publishers, pp.78–95.

Eisner, E.W. (1991) *The Enlightened Eye: Qualitative Inquiry and the Enhancement of Educational Practice*, New York: Macmillan.

Index

ablism 149–50, 156, 159
accountability 2, 11, 37, 69, 175
action research 16, 53
adaptation 117–18, 119–20, 123–4
Ainscow, Mel 11, 29, 39, 59, 117–18, 166, 167, 173, 174, 175, 176
Allan, Julie 12, 143, 166, 168, 169, 173, 174
alternative schools 159, 163n12
Alton-Lee, Adrienne 72, 176
Americans with Disabilities Act 157
anti-racism 72
assimilationism 39, 81, 84, 85
asylum seekers 35, 50–1
autism 159

Baker, C. 81, 88
Ballard, Keith 11, 15, 166, 167, 170, 171, 172, 174, 176
Balshaw, M. 23
Barton, L. 151, 161
Basic Interpersonal Communication Skills 87, 88
behavioural problems 34, 41
Bergent, T. 103
biculturalism 91
bilingualism 85, 91, 92, 121, 173
Bishop, R. 65, 72
Bjørkavåg, L. I. 87
Black-Hawkins, Kristine 53
Blaiklock, A. 68
Blanton, L. P. 148, 149, 150
Blunkett, David 35, 50
Bøggild Mortensen, L. 88
Booth, Tony 11, 39, 59, 97, 117–18, 166, 168, 169, 170, 171, 173, 174, 176
Boston, Jonathon 62
Brantlinger, Ellen 68
bullying 127
Bush, George W. 147

California Systems Change Project 158
Cantillon, B. 63
carers 118, 127
Centre for Studies on Inclusive Education 51
child-to-child cooperation 19, 27
Christ Church College 41–2
Christina's Journey video 158, 159
citizenship 38
civil rights 157, 162n9
Clark, Helen 60
classrooms: collaboration 19; observation 19–20, 28; participation 27
The Code of Practice for Students with Disabilities (QAA) 130, 131–2
collaboration 17, 53, 148–9; classroom 19; school development 175; teacher education 148–9, 150–1; teachers–students 158; teacher-training institutions 123
colonialism 61, 81
colonisation 64–7
commercialisation of education 61, 62–3, 106–7
Commission for Racial Equality 34
commodification 70
community education 35–6
competences 137, 142–3
competition 2, 66–7
comprehensive education 35–6
confidentiality 18
connoisseurship 79, 82
continuing professional development 6, 8, 10
Cook, James 65
Corbett, J. 154
core content, teacher education 148–9
co-teaching 117–18
Count Us In. Achieving Inclusion in Scottish Schools 8

Cuban, L. 102
culture 61; collective 109; colonialism
    81; diversity 41–2, 125, 172–3;
    dominance 65, 68–9; education
    117–18; ethnic minority children 91,
    167; homogeneity 81, 86; language
    69–70; leadership 28–30; New Right
    ideology 73

deconstruction 131–2, 138
democratisation 98, 118, 127, 168
Denmark 80–1, 88
Derrida, Jacques 131–2, 136–7, 138,
    141, 142, 143
Dewey, J. 74, 110
direct action 143
disability: access 122, 167; burden to
    society approach 157–8; clinical
    approach 155; inclusion 1, 33, 153;
    personal tragedy approach 154;
    reasonable accommodation 156–7;
    social justice 59; social
    understanding 121; student teachers
    130, 132–5; teacher education 51–2,
    130; teacher-training institutions 121
discrimination 11, 34, 59, 61, 167, 171
diversity 119, 168; cultural 41–2, 125,
    172–3; equality 51–2, 55; learning
    19, 25, 53–4, 157; religious 41–2;
    thinking styles 123
documentation 121–2, 168–70, 173
Dooley, K. 65
Durie, Mason 70
dyslexia 122, 125
Dyson, A. 100

Easton, Brian 61, 69
education: achievement 70, 147;
    adaptation 117–18, 119–20, 123–4;
    changing society 78;
    commodification 70; culture
    117–18; Mäori people 60; market
    model 60, 62, 171; New Right
    ideology 59, 61–2, 67–8; religion 46,
    92; social class 79–80
Education Act, Norway 80
educational policies: changes 112–13;
    England 11, 15, 33–7; inclusion
    33–4, 168–70; Norway 78; practice
    132, 169
educational theory 111
Eisner, E. W. 79
Engen, Thor Ola 11, 91, 166, 167, 170
England: accountability 175;
    educational policies 11, 15, 33–7;

National Curriculum 5, 7, 34;
    teacher education 4–6, 9–10, 168
equality: citizenship 38; diversity 51–2,
    55; gender 121, 122; Norway 78, 80,
    81, 85
Erstad, K. 89–90
ethnic minority children 166; culture
    91, 167; inclusion 34; language 84,
    85, 86–7; literacy skills 88, 89–90;
    Norway 81, 167; racism 45
ethnicity 130, 147, 171
Evans, J. 101
exclusion 15, 118; ablism 149–50;
    fitness to teach 137–8; gender 118,
    130; inclusion 40–1; Norway 98;
    social 34; SOEUR 156

falsifiying of scores 147
Finnish language 81
Fisher, D. 153, 158, 159
fitness to teach 12, 120, 130, 135–8,
    173–4
formative assessment 26–7
Freiberg, H. J. 103
From Them to Us (Booth and Ainscow)
    174

Galbraith, J. K. 68
Garner, P. 52
gender: discrimination 59, 171; equality
    121, 122; exclusion 118, 130;
    primary teaching 54; promotion 54,
    122; stereotyping 174
General Teacher Education, Norway
    119
General Teaching Council of Scotland
    130; Standards 131–2, 135, 139
global aspect 15, 41
Glynn, T. 65, 72
Gore, J. M. 150
governmental guidelines 84–5
Grace, Gerald 69
Graceland Central School District
    151–2, 154–5, 159, 160
grammar schools 35–6, 45

Handbook for Inclusion 117–18, 124,
    126, 127–8
Handbook for the Award of Qualified
    Teacher Status 5
Hargreaves, A. 107
Hargreaves, D. H. 28–9
Harker, R. 66
Hart, Susan 43
Haug, Peder 11–12, 82, 83, 84, 122,

166, 167, 169, 171, 172, 173, 174, 175, 176
Higgins, Nancy 71
higher education 36–7, 47, 169
Higher Education Funding Council 47
home language competence 86–7, 90
homophobia 71
Howe, K. R. 97
human rights 40, 151

immigrant children 11
Improving Teaching project 20–6
inclusion 1–2; composite view 168; developing practices 18–20, 79–82; disability 1, 33, 153; educational policies 33–4, 168–70; ethnic minorities 34; exclusion 40–1; key principles 153; political factors 151, 154; social 34, 168; special educational needs 1, 4, 39, 55, 99, 106, 174–5; student teachers 169–70; teacher development 126–7; teacher education 10–11, 12, 34–5, 38–9, 50, 98–9, 119–26, 141–3, 166, 167–8; teacher-training institutions 120–1, 130–1, 169–70; transformative 2, 29–30; whole school approach 152–3
Inclusive Elementary and Special Education Program, Syracuse University 149
incorporation 83, 85
The Index for Inclusion 117, 173, 174, 176
Initial Teacher Education 52
in-service education 10, 12, 126–7
insitutional development 48–9, 50; see also teacher education institutions
integration 11, 82–3, 84–6, 124–5

Jesson, Bruce 69
Jewish children 73–4
Jordell, K. Ø. 91
Jorgenson, C. M. 153
Juell, N. 86

Kelsey, J. 63, 69
Kissen, R. M. 71
Klarsfeld, Serge 73–4
Kuhn, T. S. 92
Kulbrandstad, L. A. 90
Kvalbein, I. A. 103

L97 (Norwegian National Curriculum) 116, 118–19, 124–6
Lagemann, E. C. 110
language: BICS 87, 88; culture 69–70;

ethnic minority children 84, 85, 86–7; Finnish 81; home language 86–7, 90; Sami people 82; textbooks 81; see also bilingualism
leadership 28–30, 37
learning diversity 19, 25, 53–4, 157
Learning for All 34
learning support 19, 27
lesbian pupils 71
Lewis, P. 54
Lewisham local education authority 20–8
Liberal Party Teachers 80–1
Liston, D. P. 150
literacy skills 87–8, 89–90
Lunt, I. 101

McCarthy, M. 87
McCrone Committee 131, 138, 141
Mackay, Alexander 66
Malin, Merridy 61, 72
managerialism 36–7
Mäori people: achievement 70; colonisation 64–5; discrimination 11, 167; education 60; New Right ideology 61; and Pakeha 171; poverty 63, 66
marginalisation 15, 25–6
market model 60, 62, 171
Meeting the High Quality Teachers Challenge 9
Mills, C. Wright 133
multiculturalism 78, 92, 121

nation-building 81, 83
National Curriculum 49; England 5, 7, 34; Norway 84, 91, 104–6, 107, 119
National Endowment for the Humanities 155
national examination results 15
national inspectorate of schools 43–4
Native Land Acts 70
Nes, Kari 12, 166, 169, 170–1, 173, 174, 175
New Right ideology: commodification 70; culture 73; education 59, 61–2, 67–8; Mäori people 61; Pakeha 61, 68–9; welfare 69
New York Times 147
New Zealand 167, 171; accountability 175; commercialisation 61, 62–3; Labour Party 60; New Right ideology 59, 61–2, 67–9, 70, 73; poverty 60, 63; racism 70–4; teacher education 6–7, 9–10; see also Mäori people; Pakeha

newly qualified teachers 97, 100–1,
138–9
No Child Left Behind 9, 147
Norway: accountability 175;
commercialisation 106–7; dual
school system 79–80; Education Act
80; education policy 78; ethnic
minority children 81, 167; exclusion
98; Faculties of Education 100;
General Teacher Education 119;
integration 11; legislation for
inclusion 116–19; L97 116, 118–19,
124–6; men as primary teachers 54;
National Curriculum 84, 91, 104–6,
107, 119; RME 116; Sami 11, 81,
82, 84; special educational needs 7,
80, 109–10, 167; teacher education 7,
9–10, 169, 170–1, 172; Teacher
Education Act 110; unitary school
80–1, 83

Office for Standards in Education 36,
38, 47
O'Neill, Onora 37

Paige, Rod 147
Pakeha 61, 63, 65–7, 68–9, 70, 171
parents 2, 118, 127
participation 27, 85, 98, 168
participatory research 18
participatory rural appraisal 17
pedagogy 27, 42, 122
Persson, B. 97
Pinar, W. F. 107
planning-in-action 27
police checks 120
Popkowitz, T. 147, 148, 159
Poplin, M. 16–17, 18
post-graduate qualifications 176
poverty 34, 59, 60, 63, 66, 69, 162n5
practice: development 18–20, 79–82;
documentation 173; ideology 97;
policies 132, 169; research 18, 110,
176; situated 79, 82
prejudice 44
pre-service training 124–6
professionalism 5, 78–9, 148; *see also*
continuing professional development
Project (Understanding Disability and
Transforming Schools) 146; social-
cultural approach 152–5; SOEUR
151–2, 155; special educational needs
159–60
promotion 54, 122
Providence College 149
Putting Initiatives Together forum 173

Qualifications and Curriculum
Authority 49
Quality Assurance Agency for Higher
Education: *The Code of Practice*
130, 131–2; disabled student teachers
132–5
questioning 24–6

racism 34, 44–5, 59, 61, 70–4, 174
reading lesson 20–2
reading skills 87–8
Regular Education Initiative 149
religion 36, 41–2, 46, 92
research: action research 16, 53;
commodification 70; practice 18,
110, 176; special educational needs
111–12; teacher education 109–10
Research Assessment Exercise 36, 52–3
retardation 158, 171
Reyes-Manzo, Carlos 51
risk-taking 20, 26, 136
Rizvi, F. 72
Robertson, C. 52
Robinson, V. M. J. 18
Rosenholtz, Susan 29
Rowntree Foundation 68
Royal Ministry of Education, Research
and Church Affairs (RME) 116

Sami people 11, 81, 82, 84
Sarason, S. B. 110
Schein, E. 28–9
Schmitt, N. 87
school cultures 29
school development 166, 175
Scotland: *The Code of Practice* 130,
131–2; fitness to teach 12, 130,
135–8; General Teaching Council
130, 131–2, 135, 139; Quality
Assurance Agency 130; teacher
education 8, 9–10, 131
Scottish Executive 139
Scottish Parliament 140
secondary education 45–6, 66
segregation 50–1, 86, 117–18
selection 45–6, 153, 156, 159
Senge, P. M. 29, 124
Siraj-Blatchford, Iram 55
situated practice 79, 82
Skrtic, T. M. 59
Skutnabb-Kangas, T. 81, 84
Slee, R. 154
Smith, Linda Tuhiwai 61, 71
Smyth, J. 72–3
social class 79–80, 118, 130
social justice 39–40, 59, 153, 159

socialisation 91, 97–8, 109
SOEUR (School of Education at the
    University of Richland) 146;
    exclusion 156; inclusion 161; *Project*
    151–2, 155; selection 153, 156, 159
special educational needs, children with:
    desegregation 83; inclusion 1, 4, 39,
    55, 99, 106, 174–5; newly qualified
    teachers 97, 100–1; Norway 7, 80,
    109–10, 167; *Project* 159–60; pull-
    out programmes 126; research
    111–12; teacher education 51–2, 125,
    158, 172; teachers 160–1
Spencer Foundation, *Ideology and the
    Politics of Inclusion* 155
stakeholders 18, 176
standards agenda 2, 11, 36, 43, 175
Stangvik, G. 84
Stenhouse, L. 52–3
stereotypes 44, 174
Stirling University 139–41
Strømstad, Marit 12, 166, 169, 170–1,
    173, 174, 175
Stronach, I. 137
student teachers: competences 142–3;
    disability 130, 132–5; inclusion
    169–70
support policies 173–4
Swainson, Sir William 65
Sylvia, C. 65
Syracuse University, Inclusive
    Elementary and Special Education
    Program 149

Tasman, Abel 65
teacher development 11, 15, 26, 126–7
teacher education 3–4, 9–10; anti-
    racism 72; autonomy 107–8;
    collaboration 148–9, 150–1;
    collective culture 109; core content
    148–9; disability 130; England 4–6,
    9–10, 168; inclusion 10–11, 12, 34–5,
    38–9, 50, 98–9, 119–26, 141–3,
    149–50, 166, 167–8; multiculturalism
    92; New Zealand 6–7, 9–10; Norway
    7, 9–10, 169, 170–1, 172;
    reform/change 102–4; research
    109–10; Scotland 8, 9–10, 131;
    special educational needs 51–2, 125,
    158, 172; tradition 103, 108–9, 113,
    124, 126; USA 8–10, 146–8, 169,
    174–5
Teacher Education Act, Norway 110
teacher-education institutions:
    bilingualism 92; collaboration 123;
    disability 121; inclusion 120–1,
    130–1, 169–70; staff participation
    123
Teacher Training Agency 34–5, 36
teachers: bilingualism 91; context for
    work 67; gender 54; integration
    85–6; newly qualified 97, 100–1,
    138–9; police checks 120;
    professional knowledge 78–9; special
    educational needs 160–1; and
    students 158; support 153, 173–4;
    see also student teachers
teachers' union 139
teaching assistants 22–4
team work 27, 117–18
textbooks/language 81
thinking styles 123
Thrupp, Martin 66–7
Tomlinson, Sally 150
tradition 103, 108–9, 113, 124, 126

Understanding Disability and
    Transforming Schools 151
unemployment 62–3, 64
United States of America:
    accountability 175; inclusion
    initiative 12; poverty 162n5; teacher
    education 8–10, 146–8, 169, 174–5;
    see also Project; SOEUR

Valadez, C. 88
video recordings 24–6
Vygotsky, L. 88

Waitangi, Treaty of 65–6
Waldegrave, C. 63, 68
Ware, Linda 12, 152, 166, 167, 169, 171,
    173, 175, 176
Waxman, H. C. 103
Weeres, J. 16–17, 18
Weisman, E. M. 65
Weiss, Lois 146
welfare 69
Weston, C. 54
What We Learned video 158
wheel-chair access 122
White, B. C. 65
whole school approach 152–3, 168
Will, Madeline 149
Wong Fillmore, L. 88
Wyatt-Smith, C. 65

Zeichner, K. 110, 150